To

Genevieve Watston

I
find
hope
in
friends
like
You!

[signature]

365
POSITIVE
THOUGHTS
for
TODAY
AND
OW

This is an authentic

D1112499

INTRODUCTION

In preparing this book my dream is to help you enjoy the beautiful possibilities God has available for you.

A very important scripture in my life is Jeremiah 29:11: *"For I know the plans I have for you... to give you a future and a hope"* (The Living Bible).

My prayer is that these 365 Positive Thoughts will encourage you to discover and enjoy all of the good and wonderful plans prepared for each of your todays.

As you read 365 Positive Thoughts, be sure to put your reactions in writing on the response pages. I have found them to be most helpful to many people.

God loves you! Believe it and live in His love daily.

Let God reconstruct, remodel, restyle and recreate you as you let go, dare, open up, and move empowered into the 21st century.

[signature: Robert A. Schuller]

ROBERT H. SCHULLER
Garden Grove, California

(All Bible verses are from the Possibility Thinkers Bible unless indicated otherwise.)
©1998 Crystal Cathedral Ministries

ONTENTS

JANUARY
  Think Possibilities
  Live Possibilities
  Commit Yourself!
  Be Confident!

FEBRUARY
  Persevere!
  Have Courage!
  Peace Be Yours
  Lovingly Forgive

MARCH
  Hope!
  New Life
  Expect Growth!
  Follow The Leader
  Jesus Is Lord

APRIL
  Come-Alive-Power
  Unlock The Gate
  God's Presence
  God's Peace

MAY
  Peace Of Mind
  More Than Conquerors
  God's Prosperity
  Prayer Is The Key
  Abundant Living

JUNE
  Forgiveness
  God Is Able!
  God Cares!
  God Saves!

JULY
God Will!
Talking With God
Self-Love
Peak To Peek

AUGUST
Discover Yourself
It's Possible
The Future
God-Power Within
Enthusiasm For Today And Tomorrow

SEPTEMBER
Never Be Afraid
Tranquilize Tension
Liberate Your Imagination
Winning Is Beginning

OCTOBER
Listen And Glisten
Exalt Courage
Scars Become Stars
Know Where You're Going

NOVEMBER
Grow Faith
Power Steering Living
Change!
Gratitude
Welcome The Unexpected

DECEMBER
Expect More
Expect Love
The Star Of Joy
Expect Miracles

THINK POSSIBILITIES

"For with God, nothing is impossible." -MATTHEW 17:20

This New Year can be filled with happiness, thrilling excitement and youthful enthusiasm, if you will learn to *think possibilities.* Most unhappiness and despair come from problem thinking. When you focus on problems, you are defeated. But when your attention is on the possibilities that accompany any problem, you're on the road to success!

How do you think possibilities? Begin by deciding upon some big beautiful dream that seems impossible. Write down a description of your dream:

_____

_____

_____

Now let your imagination run wild. Only your moral and ethical principles will limit you. Legal questions and money problems will not constrict the flow of your creative ideas, as you think of 10 ways to solve this problem or to bring your impossible dream into the realm of probability. Do it now!

1. _____   6. _____
2. _____   7. _____
3. _____   8. _____
4. _____   9. _____
5. _____   10. _____

I enter this New Year with high expectations and a happy heart, for with God nothing is impossible!

THINK POSSIBILITIES

Ten Commandments for Handling God's Ideas

1. I will vote "yes" to an idea even if "it's impossible."

2. I will never block a helpful thought because it entails problems, or wait to begin until I find solutions.

3. I will welcome a possibility even if I've never done it before or can't imagine how it could be done.

4. I will design my plan to lesson the risk of failure.

5. I will cooperate in supporting a potentially good idea even if I can see something wrong with it.

6. I will never squelch a creative idea because no one else has ever succeeded in perfecting it.

7. I will declare any constructive concept to be possible even though I lack the time, money, brains, energy, talent, or skill to achieve it.

8. I will never discard a plan or project just because it's not perfect.

9. I will never resist a proposal because I didn't think of it, won't get the credit for it, won't personally benefit from it, or may not live to see and enjoy it.

10. I will never quit because I've reached the end of the rope, I will thank God for the knot at the end of the rope and hang on!

Success is God's idea, so
He manages all of my life!

Think Possibilities

"All things are possible to you who believe!"
-MARK 9:23 *(New American Standard Bible)*

When my wife and I came to California to build a great church, we were met on our arrival with the information that there was no available place to begin services. Nothing available! What impossible, negative advice!

While driving to California, my wife and I made a list of 10 possible places to meet. Now we were faced with a problem, and our list of 10 possible solutions became very valuable. My only assets were a mortgaged organ and five hundred dollars.

I took the list and started checking out the possibilities. Number one on the list was a school. I quickly found out that the school boards in the area felt the law did not allow them to rent facilities to churches. So I went to my next option—a Seventh-Day Adventist church. Since they meet on Saturdays, why not rent their facilities on Sundays? But someone else had already thought of that and possibility number 2 was scratched off my list. Down the list I went—3, 4, 5, 6, 7, 8. Option number nine was a drive-in theater. Three miles east of our home, I found the Orange Drive-In-Theater. The manager listened curiously, but politely, to my peculiar request. A week later he phoned and said, "It's yours to use on Sunday."

From that modest beginning, God has worked miracle after miracle. Make a list of the possible ways to make your dream come true, then use your list. God still works miracles for you too!

*All things work together for good,
because God works and I work!*

THINK POSSIBILITIES

"The things which are impossible with you are possible with God."
-LUKE 18:27 KJV

This joy-producing, energy-generating, success-stimulating process, will work miracles in your life if certain principles are followed. One of these basic principles is that your creative energies must be directed at a serious objective. There must be some deep inner concern which gets the creative energy started and keeps it going.

Only when your subconscious mind deeply believes the mind-bending project to be very, very important will the hidden powers slumbering deep in the dark regions of the unconscious rise up and awaken your creative conscious.

Some years ago I experienced an example of this potential principle. A group of us were sitting around discussing the serious illness of a mutual friend. Our friend was in serious trouble because the arteries to his heart were almost completely blocked. There was no known surgical technique to help him at that time. But, God specializes in impossible problems, and today many of us are the recipients of by-pass surgery, heart valve replacement and even heart transplants. All impossible a generation ago.

Turn your impossible problem over to God and trust that He has a solution, somehow, someway, someday. If you care enough and "tune in" to God's ideas, your problem can be solved. Your dream can come true!

Believe in God's miracle working power to make all things possible!

$\mathcal{T}$HINK POSSIBILITIES

"Lord, you will guide me all my life with your wisdom and counsel."
-PSALM 73:24

Once you have spotted what appears to be an opportunity, don't plunge recklessly ahead without asking sensible questions. Success-test your opportunities. Challenge all positive ideas by asking success-spotting questions. Let me give you my four success-spotting, possibility-measuring, opportunity-testing questions:

1. Will my dream fill a vital human need? Is it practical? Will it help people who are hurting? How does my dream measure up? _____

2. Will my dream inspire people? People are attracted to the individual or the dream that inspires and uplifts the heart and the human spirit. My dream may help me most, but will my success inspire and uplift others?

3. Can I do my dream in an outstanding way? Excellence is a vital key to success. Can my dream be both monumental and instrumental? _____

4. Is my dream pace-setting? Almost anything that is being done can be done differently and better. And when God is involved in my dream, it deserves to be pace-setting! Has it been done before? _____

God is opening new paths to me.
My future is bright!

THINK POSSIBILITIES

"In this place I will give prosperity, says the Lord of hosts."
-*HAGGAI 2:9 Revised Standard Version*

When you commit yourself to a dream—you must assume that you will find solutions as you move along. To a degree there is a tinge of confident recklessness in being a possibility thinker. Confidently you assume that no one is a failure if he has tried to do something wonderful.

I have a close friend who practiced possibility thinking in his business. If faced with a legal problem, then nothing short of changing the law will do. If a law is blocking progress, then that law must be changed.

My friend decided to build a shopping center over a ten acre parcel of land through which a flood control channel flowed. One law prohibited construction over flood control channels. That law blocked the fulfillment of his dream of an elaborate and functional shopping center in an area that needed such a facility.

So there was only one thing to do. That law should be updated in accordance with modern construction possibilities. The result? He tried. He believed. He kept on pressing. He crusaded. And the law was changed! Today, the Brashears Center has a flood control channel flowing harmlessly inside a reinforced concrete tunnel underneath a twelve story building! Nothing is impossible to those who believe in God!

I abide in a constant flow of God's abundance, circulating in and through my life and my plans! This is God's will for me!

$\mathscr{T}$HINK POSSIBILITIES

"If you can believe, all things are possible to him who believes."
-MARK 9:23

Speaking at the University of the Pacific in Stockton, California, I was impressed by the magnificent tower which guards the entrance to this beautiful campus. The tall Neo-Gothic structure rises stately and tall from a spacious green-lawned island immediately within the gates.

The university president told me how the tower was built. Some years before, a water shortage developed, and engineers were called in to study the problem. They said that the only solution was a new water tower, and the only place it could go was immediately inside the entrance of the campus.

The thought of an ugly, monstrous water tank marring the front entrance of the university was a nauseating suggestion to the president. But on further thought, this possibility-thinking man thought, "Perhaps this ugly structure could be made into a sublime monument."

The result? The water tower was erected. Around it, a 30 foot square cement tower was built rising 150 feet into the sky. Stained-glass windows were placed on the top 50 feet to hide the water tank. The lower two-thirds of the tower were divided into nine floors and today houses modern administration offices, a board room, and a radio station. Few universities in the world have a more inspiring architectural landmark to greet incoming students and visitors. Proof-positive that every adversity hides a possibility!

I have the faith to believe that every adversity hides a beautiful possibility!

LIVE POSSIBILITIES

"Oh God, I will keep on expecting You to help me.
I praise You more and more." -PSALM 71:14 (Living Bible)

Possibility thinkers are resourceful people. They follow the old maxim: "Where there's a will, there's a way." One of my first experiences in Garden Grove was a meeting with six Protestant ministers. "How many homes are there in the city?" I asked. "Fourteen thousand," one minister answered. "Have you taken a census of the religious affiliation of these people?" I asked. Amused silence and negative nods gave me my answer.

"Let's get all the churches together and canvass all fourteen thousand homes," I enthused. "Then we'll find out who belongs to a church and we invite those who don't."

Their response was not overly enthusiastic. "That's impossible," they countered. "Do you realize how long that would take?" And with that positive-idea-squelching question, they killed the idea.

I mentioned my disappointment to a businessman friend in my church, who was a real possibility thinker.

"Fourteen thousand? That's easy!" he exclaimed. "All we need is forty people who will agree to make three hundred fifty calls. My wife and I will make up sheets with thirty-five addresses on them. Then each person will take ten sheets and the job will be done!"

Great idea! He made up the sheets. We got the forty volunteers who came to a dinner on a Friday and picked up their ten sheets. Two Saturdays later, fourteen thousand doorbells had been rung. Forty possibility thinkers did what six professionals insisted was impossible! There's a solution to every problem!

God gives me a solution
to every problem!

LIVE POSSIBILITIES

"I will sing to the Lord because He has dealt bountifully with me."
-PSALM 13:6

You must mentally picture success. You throw your mind into the future. See your problem resolved. Imagine your dream a reality! Listen to the sounds of success—laughter, applause, congratulations! Enjoy mentally, the rich fruits of your accomplishment.

As you use your powers of imagination to propel you into the high feeling of proud achievement, enthusiasm begins to bubble deep within you. Excitement enthralls you. Energy surges within you as your desire mounts. With God's help, you have reached your objective! What a great moment!

Picture again the problem or opportunity you wrote down last week. Now picture what you will feel and what the situation will be like when your objective is accomplished. Write down your imagined description or draw a picture of the scene.

*I am a beloved child of God. He sees
my needs and my opportunities and
He is at work with me in my task!*

LIVE POSSIBILITIES

"This is the day the Lord has made. We will rejoice and be glad in it."
-PSALM 118:24

Fred Hostrop was not only a confirmed possibility thinker, he lived and acted on his possibilities. He once wrote to me, describing his condition:

"For years I have suffered from acromegaly, which is caused by a tumor on my pituitary gland. This makes my gland over-active, which in turn causes me to grow abnormally large. I'm 73 years old and still growing!

"My skeleton is four times larger than normal. As a result, I have severe backaches and headaches, almost constantly. I can't pick up anything on the floor or ground because I cannot bend over that far. Since my equilibrium is poor, I can't stand in any one place very long, and I need two canes to help me walk. I can't walk more than 200 feet without collapsing.

"Dr. Schuller, the above description may sound like negative thinking. But instead of saying, 'I can't do this or that,' I think of the possibilities and say to myself, 'What can I do about this situation?'

"Here's an example of one thing I'm doing. I used to love to play golf, but I can't play on the golf course anymore. But I can enjoy playing in my own backyard." And with the letter he showed me a picture of one of his "Hostrop-inventions"—it picks up the golf ball and sets it on the tee. He adds, "Hurrah! I can even use this to pick up litter in our yard every day!"

God is my help in every need!

LIVE POSSIBILITIES

"Do not fear. For it is your Father's good pleasure to give you the Kingdom." -LUKE 12:32

The great violinist Paganini was once performing before a most distinguished audience. Suddenly, one of the strings on his violin snapped. The audience gasped, but the master musician continued, unruffled, to play on the three remaining strings.

Snap!—a second string broke. Still Paganini played on without hesitation. Then, with a sharp crack, a third string broke! The audience now became awestruck. For a brief moment, the artist stopped, raised his famous Stradivarius violin high with one hand and announced, "One string—and Paganini."

With furious skill and the matchless discipline of a gifted craftsman, he finished the selection on a single string. The performance was done with such matchless perfection that the audience rose as one to give him a tumultuous ovation.

There will be times in your life that one string after another will snap. You will go through circumstances that would make quitters out of lesser men or women. You need to insure yourself against "drop-out-itis." You do this by connecting yourself with an unfailing spiritual power source.

You will not quit. You will keep up your brave performance because the very power of the Eternal God surges deep within your being!

I let the power of God flow through me. He strengthens me and gives me the desire to get started and keep going!

LIVE POSSIBILITIES

"Do not be afraid; only believe." -MARK 5:36

No force or emotion is more paralyzing than fear. One of two emotions will dominate and drive you—either faith or fear. Like oil and water, the two do not mix. The only antidote to fear is faith!

Live your possibilities! What fears can stop you? Fear of failure? Fear of embarrassment? Identify the negative fears that threaten to paralyze you:

1. _____

2. _____

3. _____

Now put your faith to work and give God these fears. Affirm your faith in His power at work in your life:

Dear God, _____

_____

_____

_____ Amen!

My fears are gone!
My faith is growing stronger!

LIVE POSSIBILITIES

"For God alone my soul waits in silence, for my hope is from Him."
-PSALM 61:5 *Revised Standard Version*

Modern chemistry is able to turn almost any cast-off product into a useful and profitable enterprise. Can you find something that is being discarded as worthless material?

A swampy area in Southern California was considered worthless until an enterprising developer imagined channels dug to turn the swamp into a beautiful lake, with canals leading off from the lake like spokes from the hub of a wheel. He imagined houses built on the canals with a private dock for each owner. He has made millions of dollars from this idea.

There was a gypsum mine near Grand Rapids, Michigan, which opened in 1907. It was a multi-million dollar plant until 1943, when it was considered "finished." An imaginative opportunity-spotting possibility thinker saw potential in that mine. The underground tunnels had a constant temperature of fifty degrees. That old gypsum mine is today a very profitable storage company. Turkeys, eggs, nuts, potatoes, and beef are just a few of the many foodstuffs stored underground.

There is a story in the Bible of a man named Simon who was a vacillating fisherman with good intentions, but no backbone. Jesus saw within him the possibilities of leadership. He gave Simon a new name—Peter—and a new responsibility as a leader in the first church.

When God looks at you, what great possibilities does He see?

I will meet all of my challenges today with confidence!

*L*IVE POSSIBILITIES

Turn, O Lord, my fears around.
Let them become a positive force
for good in my life until I—
Fear not that I might fail.
  But fear rather that I might
never dare to discover my potential.
Fear not that I might be hurt.
  But fear rather that I might never
experience growing pains.
Fear not that I might love and lose.
  But fear rather that I might
never love at all.
Fear not that people may laugh at
my mistakes.
  But fear rather that God will say
to me, "O you of little faith."
Fear not that I might fail if I try again.
  But fear rather that I might miss my
great chance for happiness if I failed to
give hope another opportunity.

Amen.

COMMIT YOURSELF!

"Be glad in the Lord and rejoice, you righteous and shout for joy."
-PSALM 32:11

Many years ago, Arvella and I joined with over a thousand friends—including many of Hollywood's great stars—to salute Ethel Waters. It was a beautiful evening! But the greatest part of the event was when Ethel Waters herself, in her own inimitable, open, honest and transparent style, told the people gathered how happy she was because Jesus was in her heart.

We all sat enthralled as Ethel performed again, and as we had the privilege of seeing film playbacks of her great life, and as she sang and talked as only Ethel Waters can, I thought again of the tremendous odds she had overcome.

She was born an illegitimate child and raised in poverty in a ghetto. By every standard of modern psychology, Ethel should have been an emotionally scarred person with a limited range of emotional development.

But when we saw and heard her, we found one of the greatest, and most beautiful souls that walked on planet earth! And there is no way to explain her life except that something gave her a great big, loving, bubbling, beautiful heart. She said that something was a Somebody—His name is Jesus!

I am enriched and filled to bubbling over ~ flowing joy, by the power of my Lord!

COMMIT YOURSELF!

*"There are three things that remain—faith, hope and love—
and the greatest of these is love." -1 CORINTHIANS 13:13*

Over the years I have been working on a list of what I call the <u>seven</u> positive human values. My list started while I was attending a World Psychiatric Congress. The subject for the last session was "Human Values in Psychotherapy." The program did not say what these values were, so in anticipation of that seminar, I made my own list.

When the final event of the Congress finally arrived, I was ready. The first speaker, an American, delivered a lecture on the importance of <u>faith</u> in the human life. He was followed by a West German, who dramatically portrayed the dynamic value of <u>hope</u>. He described the sudden change that occurs when something ignites the spark of hope within a person—healing takes place and life returns.

The final lecturer, from Peru, presented a paper on the importance of <u>love</u>. As I left the lecture hall, I was amazed at how the conclusions of these three psychiatrists were the same as the Bible, the words of St. Paul's.

What dynamic human values would you add to this list? Think a moment and then write down any additional values which you feel are important:

_____

_____

_____

*My heart is tuned to the spirit of God.
I can feel His values becoming
my values!*

Commit Yourself!

"Commit your way to the Lord. Trust also in Him, and He shall bring it to pass." -PSALM 37:5

The first value on my list is COMMITMENT—that is my word for faith. I've deliberately chosen not to use the word faith, because for too many people, this word is a "cop-out." It is simply too easy to say—"Oh, I believe," or "Yes, I think God can do it." Anyone can say those words. That's faith, on a shallow level. And a shallow faith does not help when the going gets rough!

So I use the word COMMITMENT. That is FAITH IN ACTION! Commitment is putting your faith on the line. It is coming clean; being honest and forthright; taking action!

As a human being, you have three powers which animals do not have. You have the power to choose—to make a vocal choice. You have the power to react in an intelligent, rational and logical way. And third, you have the power to make commitments!

Oscar Wilde once said, "An idea that isn't risky is hardly worth calling an idea." Make your commitments! Strength will come to provide you with support and energy. Enormous spiritual forces will be unleashed as you commit yourself in action to Jesus Christ.

I rejoice in the vibrant, God ~ given power within me as I commit myself to action!

COMMIT YOURSELF!

"Commit your works to the Lord, and your thoughts will be established."
-*PROVERBS 16:3*

A major source of personal fatigue and lack of energy, excitement and enthusiasm is caused by lack of commitment.

But when you make that COMMITMENT, guess what happens? Enormous power flows into your mind—brilliant flashes of insight explode within you! The energy to say "no" to what is wrong and "yes" to what is right surges within. It is amazing what you will be able to do. All because you make a commitment.

Where is your faith indecisive? What commitments are you attempting to ignore? Make your commitments to action now! Then write them down!

MY COMMITMENT

_____

_____

_____

_____

_____

_____

*Yes! I decide today
to do something with
the one life I have!
And to a plan of action!*

COMMIT YOURSELF!

"If you wait for perfect conditions, you will never get anything done."
-ECCLESIASTES 11:4 (LB)

The New American Standard Bible translates our verse this way,"He who watches the wind will not sow and he who looks at the clouds will not reap."

Now, being born on an Iowa farm, I know what that means. If the farmer thinks a wind is going to come up, he puts off sowing his seeds. For if you try to sow in the wind, the gusts will only blow the seed away before it can penetrate the ground and be fertilized. But you might never plant your crop if you are too cautious.

On the other hand, when the wheat or oats become ripe, if the farmer thinks it might rain, he will put off cutting because if the grain gets soggy with rain right after it is cut, it is ruined. The soggy grain gets moldy and never dries out. But if you never reap your harvest, the grain will rot anyway!

If you feel a breeze coming up, you'll never sow your seed. Or if you see some clouds, you'll never reap. And you'll never get started! Now that's the word of God! <u>COMMITMENT is making an all-out plunge of faith before you can be sure how anything is going to turn out</u>. The most important commitment you can make is to Jesus Christ. That is where you need to begin! Do it now!

Today, Lord, I am not going to look at conditions. Instead, I am looking to You to draw from You the power to begin!

COMMIT YOURSELF!

"Surely the Lord God will help me!" -ISAIAH 50:9

Before we built the Arboretum on the Crystal Cathedral campus, this area was nothing but orange groves with some walnut trees. One day I parked my car at the edge of the field to pray. Suddenly I heard the snap of a twig. I looked up and saw a man coming at me with a shotgun. I was startled, but he smiled and said, "I'm sorry, I didn't mean to frighten you."

With a heavy accent, he continued, "I just came to America from Europe. We are very poor, so I hunt rabbits for our food, but I haven't seen any today."

"Look," I enthused, "over there. There are some rabbits."

"Oh," he responded dejectedly, "they are too far away. I could never get them."

"Why don't you sneak up on them?" I suggested.

Then he went into an explanation about the way a rabbit feels vibrations through the bottom of his feet. He was a real impossibility thinker! But I guess his empty stomach helped me convince him to try and sneak up on them. "Maybe I'll try," he finally agreed.

Ever so slowly he started sneaking up on the rabbits. I kept thinking he was close enough, but still he crept along. Finally he raised his gun and fired! He took off running into the grove and a minute later reappeared with his rabbit—dinner for his family.

"Maybe I'll try," he said. And that commitment meant his family had dinner that night!

Lord, I am going to try beginning today!

COMMIT YOURSELF!

"For the Lord God will help me; therefore, I will not be disgraced, therefore, I have set my face like a flint and I know that I will not be ashamed."
-ISAIAH 50:7

Two of the greatest people I've ever known were Dorothy and Henry Poppen. They served over 40 years in China, preaching, teaching, and building schools, hospitals and churches.

Those were dangerous years. Besides the risk of disease, bandits, plague and accidents at sea or in the mountains, they were driven out of China by the Communists, barely escaping with their lives.

One day I asked Dorothy, "What drove you onward all those years?"

"We thrive on adventure!" she answered with fire in her eyes.

That dynamic adventure-tension in both Henry and Dorothy was baptized by the Spirit of Jesus Christ and grew out of a commitment they made early in life. What a way to live!

How are you doing on your dream? If you find yourself wavering or doubting, simply reaffirm your commitment. And then live expectantly the life full of adventure.

COMMITMENT—The first of seven life-changing human values—is where living really begins!

With every breath I breathe, I recommit myself to all of God's great possibilities for me today!

 Be Confident!

O God,

I come to you to find power
 to be really strong.
Save me from the make-believe strengths
 that leave me weak.
Help me be the kind of person
 nothing can upset,
 for I am confident within!
I expose myself to Your strength.

I believe you are taking away from me
 all negative thinking,
 all inclination to shun responsibility,
 all fearful attitudes.
You are inspiring me now to face life
 with confidence
 and with a song!
            Thank you, Lord!
            Amen

*I'll make my mountain a molehill,
      with God's strength.*

$\mathscr{B}$E CONFIDENT!

"Expect God to act! For I know that I shall again have plenty of reasons to praise Him for all that He will do. He is my help! He is my God!"
-PSALM 42:11 (LB)

COMMITMENT—faith in action—is the first human value on my list. If you make a commitment, then you must have CONFIDENCE (second on my value list). You must believe that with God's help, you can accomplish the task to which you have committed yourself.

Now self-confidence doesn't last very long unless you are constantly working at renewing it.

What will you do this week to help you feel more confident?

_____

_____

What other things do you enjoy that help you feel good about yourself?

_____

_____

Continue, now, to think of other ways in which you can build a positive, self-affirming, growth-producing feeling of self-confidence.

Thank you, God, for all the good reasons You give me for feeling good about myself. Thanks for loving me!

$\mathcal{B}$E CONFIDENT!

"So God created man in His own image, male and female he created them."
-GENESIS 1:27

Nothing is more important than your own self-confidence and your own affirmative self-image. That's why the second dynamic human value on my list is CONFIDENCE.

I heard the story of a minister who was very depressed and had a very negative self-image. He was the senior minister and things obviously were not going right.

Feeling very low, he entered the sanctuary, knelt at the altar and prayed a very negative prayer. "O God, I am nothing. I am nothing," he repeated over and over again.

Just at that point, the assistant minister walked by and was very impressed by the senior minister's humility. So he joined him in praying, "O Lord, I am nothing, I, too, am nothing."

At that moment the janitor happened to enter the auditorium and was awestruck by the humility of the leaders of the church. Not to be outdone, he joined them at the altar and said, "O Lord, I, too, am nothing, nothing, nothing."

The assistant minister stopped, looked at the janitor, then turned to the senior pastor and said, "Now look who thinks he's nothing,"

I chuckle every time I think of that story, but I also feel like crying because so many Christians believe in that kind of humility. That concept is not Christian humility! God wants you to be confident for you are made in His image!

O God, I am great! I am great because You made me in Your image! Wow! I am made in God's image!

$\mathscr{B}$E CONFIDENT!

"We are confident that we have a good conscience, in all things desiring to live honorably." -HEBREWS 13:18

The story of Zacchaeus found in Luke 19:1-10 is a remarkable one. Jesus was passing through Jericho one day surrounded by people trying to get a glimpse of the Miracle Worker! One man who was too short to see over the crowds ran ahead and climbed into a sycamore tree beside the road. He clung to the strong branches of that enormous tree and watched for Jesus.

Zacchaeus was one of the most influential Jews in the Roman tax-collecting business. But he was a traitor to his own people—a Jew who surrendered his patriotism by selling out to the Romans!

The small man forfeited his patriotism to get money. He thought money would give him power, and power would give him self-confidence!

Now why would Zacchaeus want to see Jesus? To collect money? No! Zacchaeus was searching for self-confidence, which is really a hunger for God. Only God can satisfy. Money, power, following the crowd—none of these provide the deep satisfaction that comes when we place ourselves in a position to find God. That's why Zacchaeus climbed the tree! He put himself in a place where he and God could meet!

I shall look to today for my confidence.

 Be Confident!

"Therefore, do not cast away your confidence, which has great rewards."
-Hebrews 10:35

Imagine that you and a friend are walking along a dusty road outside of Jerusalem, around the year 31 A.D. As you walk, someone approaches from the other direction—a man. Your friend knows that man, and stops to introduce you to him. He says, "Jesus, I want you to meet (your name)."

What would you like our friend to tell Jesus about you?

Write out your introduction and then read it over several times during the next few days:

_____

_____

_____

_____

_____

_____

_____

I feel more confident today because
I am a child of God.

BE CONFIDENT!

"O' Lord, You have searched and known me...You are acquainted with all my ways...such knowledge is too wonderful for me...I will praise you for I am wonderfully made" -SELECTED VERSES FROM PSALM 139

Imagine how Zacchaeus must have felt when Jesus called him by name. Jesus knew Zacchaeus even before they met! There was Zacchaeus, inwardly all torn up by guilt. He probably expected a sermon, a tirade, a scolding or a slap on the wrist from Jesus. Instead, Jesus looked at him and said, "Zacchaeus, I am going to be a guest in your home today!"

Go back to the scene you imagined yesterday. Your friend has just introduced Jesus to you, and told Him several things about you. Now Jesus speaks and says, "It's good to meet you, but I already know you. I know that you...

Now write down what Jesus would say about you:

_____

_____

_____

_____

_____

*Jesus loves me and accepts me as I am,
so I love and accept myself today!*

$\mathcal{B}$E CONFIDENT!

"Fear not, for I have redeemed you. I have called you by your name. You are mine!" -*ISAIAH 43:1*

I have confidence because God is my Father! Jesus Christ is my personal Savior, the Holy Spirit lives in me!

God has reached down and of all these billions of human beings, He has spotted me, called me by name, lifted me up and embraced me. He has forgiven me of my sins, put His arms around me and said, "Look, we're going to walk through life together, you and I!" Wow!

There is nothing greater than that. It's called salvation. You can have this same experience, and then you discover the source of confidence!

Once there was a Rabbi who was asked, "When should a man repent?" And the wise old Rabbi answered, "On the last day of his life."

"But," they said, "none of us can be sure which day is the last day of our life."

The rabbi smiled and said, "Then repent now." Repentance is not a negative self-condemnation. Repentance is "turning around" to walk God's way!

Have you experienced salvation? Someday you will stand before God, and He wants to compliment and praise you. Decide, today, to invite Jesus Christ to live within you. Discover the source of real self-confidence! After all, if God is on your side everybody else might as well be also.

I invite You into my life, Lord Jesus.
Thank You for seeing the possibilities
within me, for not condemning me,
and for being for me!

ERSEVERE!

"I have prayed for you that your faith may not fail."
-LUKE 22:31 *Revised Standard Version*

What's the best thing that has happened to you in this past month? Already, nearly the first month of this new year is complete.

_____

_____

_____

If you had a difficult time thinking of any "best" thing, it's probably your fault. Because, you see, God has given you great possibilities! And the secret of dynamic and effective living is really up to you.

Making confident commitments unlocks the door, which means that you establish a long-range goal and objective. Too many people have only a vague idea of what they want to accomplish in their own lifetime. Therefore nothing of any significance ever happens.

To live an exciting, growing life, you first establish a firm objective to which you can confidently commit yourself. Then translate this objective into immediate steps, intermediate steps, long-range steps and ultimate steps.

Once you have done this, all you need is our third dynamic human value—PERSEVERANCE! PERSEVERANCE makes it possible for you to live in such a spirit that good things will happen to you!

I am filled with the triumphant,
Spirit of Jesus Christ!

PERSEVERE!

"Let patience have its perfect work, that you may be perfect and complete, lacking nothing." -JAMES 1:4

Let's try working on a goal. Describe one important objective to which you would like to be confidently committed:

_____

_____

Now describe two or more long-range steps that would have to be taken in order for you to reach your objective:

1. _____

2. _____

Good! Now take one of the above steps, and outline all of the immediate and intermediate measures that you will need to accomplish in order to reach your long-range step in the direction of your goal. (You will probably want to expand all of this on a separate sheet of paper.)

1. _____

2. _____

3. _____

You will find it helpful to estimate the amount of time it will take to meet your immediate and intermediate objectives, but do not be afraid to change the dates if you find it is taking longer than you planned.

I am strong in the Lord. I can keep on keeping on until my goals are reached. Thank you, Lord!

ERSEVERE!

"The Lord will work out His plans for my life—for Your loving kindness, Lord, continues forever." -PSALM 138:8

A Sunday School class was discussing the story of Jonah. The teacher explained how the Lord punished Jonah for running away from Him, by arranging for a huge fish to swallow the frightened man. For three days Jonah cried out to the Lord praising and thanking Him from the belly of that great fish. On the third day God ordered the fish to spit Jonah onto the beach.

In closing, the teacher asked her students, "What does this story teach us?"

One little boy quickly answered, "Well, I think the story teaches us that you can't keep a good man down!"

He was right you know! And that's why perseverance is on my list of dynamic, life-changing values. But we all have experiences at times in our life when we are really down. Perhaps there is something happening to you this week that threatens to hold you back or knock you down. Describe the situation:

_____

_____

_____

Now, confidently commit this situation to God in prayer. When Jonah had lost all hope, he turned his thoughts once more to the Lord. His reason? "For my deliverance comes from the Lord alone."

What has appeared to me to be an impossible situation is fast becoming a possibility!

PERSEVERE!

"Today salvation has come to this house ..." -LUKE 19:9

I read the other day about a professional athlete who, the newspaper says, is still holding out. They do not think he will sign this contract until he gets everything he wants. But, the article continued, he is in danger of holding out too long. He may not only end up without what he wants, he may also end up without a contract.

Some people hold out on life. They hold out until they can be sure they will succeed. They hold out until there are no uncertain ties or until they can see a solution to every problem. They wait until there are no risks. They forget that holding out on life can be the biggest risk of all.

> "THE SADDEST WORDS OF
> TONGUE OR PEN ARE THESE:
>
> 'IT MIGHT HAVE BEEN!'"

"Will it work out?" "Can I be sure?" "Can I wait until the risk is gone?" These negative thoughts come like birds snapping up the seed of positive, life-renewing, growth-producing, risk-taking thoughts that are intended to inspire us to live happier, more joy-filled lives. Determine today to stop holding out. Sign the contract. Take the risk.

*Today I will let God's
positive ideas control my thinking.*

ERSEVERE!

"Pray without ceasing." -I THESSALONIANS 5:17

When life is severe — and it often is ... what will you do?

Yes, the work is not finished. Pressures mount. Tensions threaten you.

All of life is pressure. We all live with it. That means you are alive! Professional pressures. What career do I choose? How do I advance? What decisions are smart for my professional development? Do I need to go back to school again? Should I shift to a new profession?

Property pressures. The car, house and garden all produce pressure. Have you had something break down this week? The more things you own, the more things are going to break down. That's life.

On top of these pressures you add a little thing called personal pressure. You look in the mirror and say, *"Ah, I'm getting gray. Is my tummy showing? I think my skin is sagging a little."* Personal pressures.

All of these are the **pressures of living!**

Stop! Hold on! Suddenly, under all of these pressures, you don't feel connected to God anymore.

I once asked Mother Teresa, *"When God is so beautiful, and Jesus is so wonderful, why isn't everybody a believer?"*

"Oh," she answered, *"distractions."*

What do you do when you are distracted by all of life's pressures?

Time to exercise the fine art of persevering through **prayer and meditations.** Take a deep breath.

Blow away the pressures, fears, anxieties, discouragements, resentments — blow them all out.

Breathe deep again! Take in the fresh air of new hope!

*Teach me how to pray, O Lord,
with every breath I take.*

PERSEVERE!

POSSIBILITY THINKERS CREED

When faced
With a mountain
I WILL NOT QUIT!
I will keep on striving until
I climb over, find a pass through,
tunnel underneath—or simply
stay and turn the mountain
into a miracle
with God's help!

ERSEVERE!

"When a person falls, he jumps up again!" -JEREMIAH 8:4 (LB)

Some years ago, a stockbroker I knew went through a very difficult time in his business. He lost almost everything he owned. During this time he decided to practice possibility thinking and believed that God could help him.

The first thing he decided was that he had to find a way to feed his family. He had no money, but he took his station wagon out at four o'clock in the morning and drove down the alleys of his neighborhood picking up all the old newspapers he could find in people's trash. This was before the city recycling campaigns began. In the evening when no one could recognize him, he did the same thing. That first week he earned almost $70.00 collecting old papers and selling them.

Then he got his boys into the act. They went to apartment houses and offered to collect old newspapers. The managers of the apartment house thought it was a great way to be rid of some trash. When he told me this story, he was making over $1000 a month collecting old newspapers, while still working at his brokerage office.

His associates couldn't understand why he was so happy. He told them, "I practice possibility thinking and I have faith in God." And I could add to that the fact that he had developed the dynamic human value of PERSEVERANCE!

I rejoice in developing my ability to persevere, God and I are up to doing some great things today!

Have Courage!

"Be strong! And of good courage! Do not be afraid...For the Lord your God goes with you. He will not leave you nor forsake you." -DEUTERONOMY 31:6

I told you last month about Dr. Henry Poppen, one of the first missionaries to go to China, and who spent over forty years there. He once told me about the time he went to a remote village where presumably missionaries had never before visited.

Dr. Poppen told them about Jesus—how Jesus was gentle, kind, loving and able to forgive easily. When he finished talking about Jesus, one of the village men came to him and said, "Oh, we know Jesus! He has been here!"

"No, no," the missionary protested, "Jesus lived and died in a country far from here long ago."

"Oh no," the people replied. "He died here. Come, we'll show you his grave."

The villagers led Dr. Poppen outside the city to a Chinese cemetery where an American was buried. There on the tombstone was the name of a Christian medical doctor who, all on his own, felt called by God to go and live in this village, and to die there. When the villagers heard what Jesus was like, they remembered the doctor.

COURAGE—the fourth dynamic human value on my list. And how courageous that doctor must have been. He knew what St. Paul meant when he wrote, "We, too, are weak in our bodies...but how we live and are strong...and have all of God's power to use!" (2 Corinthians 13:4).

*By the power of Christ in me,
I am courageous!*

Have Courage!

"In quietness and confidence is your strength." -ISAIAH 30:15

A missionary in India told how he was kneeling at his bed praying one night when a giant python snake uncoiled itself from the rafters and wrapped itself around his body.

The python, which is not uncommon in India, kills its victim by squeezing it to death. The missionary told how a Bible verse immediately came to mind as the meandering serpent enveloped his body. *"In quietness and confidence is your strength."* (Isaiah 30:15). And suddenly he was filled with the calm assurance that God was in control! He remained perfectly still, praying and meditating like he never had before!

Had he struggled, hesitated or tensed up, the coils of the mighty creature would have constricted and crushed him! Instead he waited, prayed, stayed calm and didn't move a muscle. Slowly, the snake uncoiled itself and retreated back to the rafters.

Most of us admire that kind of quiet COURAGE. I don't believe there is a value that is more recognizable and admirable in a human life than courage. Claim the courage that is yours as a child of God. God wants you to be courageous!

I am made for confident, courageous living. Today I can feel my fears slipping away as God fills me with courage!

Have Courage!

"Be strong, be brave, and do not be afraid...for we have the Lord our God to help us!" -2 CHRONICLES 32:7,8

This week we have seen two examples of COURAGE, both different. One person lived boldly and courageously. The other had the courage to be still, and therefore lived. Perhaps you feel a strong desire for more courage in your own life. Take a moment and reflect on your circumstances. Where do you need to be more courageous in your life?

_____

_____

_____

What would you do if you had more courage:

_____

_____

_____

I want to challenge you to live today, believing that what you have just written is true! And if you believe it, you will discover that it is true!

This remarkable spirit of courage is overpowering me. What a relief!

Have Courage!

"The Lord is my helper and I am not afraid of anything that any human can do to me." -HEBREWS 13:6

Years ago a person went to an orphanage and asked, "Is there any orphan here that nobody wants?" The matron answered, "Indeed there is. She's ten years old, ugly to look at and has a very horrible hunchback. In fact, the only decent thing about her is her name—Mercy Goodfaith."

The inquirer said, "That's exactly the child I want." And together they left.

Thirty-five years later, the head of the orphanage Inspection Department in the state of Iowa turned in a report about another orphanage that said, "This home is outstanding. It is clean, the food is good, and the matron of the place has a soul that oozes love.

"All of the children are well cared for and show the effects of the matron's love. As they gathered at the piano following dinner, I observed an atmosphere unlike any I have seen in my work. Never have I seen such beautiful eyes as in that matron. They were so stunning that I almost forgot how homely her face was and how unattractive was the hunchback. Her name is Mercy Goodfaith."

Because some nameless person had the courage to care for an unwanted orphan, Mercy Goodfaith learned how to love and has multiplied that love a hundred times over. My prayer for you today is that God will give you the COURAGE to care!

I dare to believe that God is giving me the courage to care enough to do something wonderful today!

Have Courage!

"Share each other's troubles and problems, and so obey our Lord's command." -GALATIANS 6:2 (LB)

Sometimes God sends into our lives people who are unlovely and very difficult to care for. All too often these people give us plenty of reasons for not caring, when in reality they need to be cared for.

What unlovely, uncaring person has God sent into your life recently? Describe why it is hard for you to be caring to this person:

1. _____

2. _____

3. _____

4. _____

5. _____

6. _____

7. _____

Inch by inch, I can feel my love for _____ growing! I have the courage to care!

HAVE COURAGE!

"Out of His glorious, unlimited resources He will give you the mighty inner strengthening of His Holy Spirit." -EPHESIANS 3:16 (LB)

For over fifteen years, Lois had battled cancer. Yet all of those years she served as my personal secretary. I never in my life expect to meet anyone more courageous than she was.

Often she had days when she was so ill that getting out of bed took all the strength she had! Lois would deliberately fall out of bed, walk on her hands and knees to the bathroom, reach for the sink and pull herself up. Finally standing on her feet, she would pull a brush through her hair, wash, and then force herself to get dressed.

Then she would stumble into the kitchen, drink some water, eat a dry piece of toast, search for her purse and walk to the door. Perspiration pouring off her forehead, she would stand up straight, look at her husband and say, "Well, Ralph, I think I can make it now."

And she would walk out the door, get into her car and drive to the church. She was always there before me, and when I came in with my usual greeting: "Good morning, how are you?" She would smile and say, "Great!" Her commitment to the ministry gave her the courage to stay alive many more years than her prognosis. Only God can give you that kind of COURAGE.

Come, Lord, and transform my melancholy spirit until my heart erupts with joy and courageous happiness!

PEACE BE YOURS

Let the words of my mouth and the meditation of my heart be acceptable in Your sight, O Lord, my strength and my redeemer." -PSALM 19:14

As I watched my youngest daughter struggle over her spelling one night, I remembered how I had to write the spelling words over ten times, and then if I missed one on the test, the teacher made me write it over twenty-five times! Then I thought, "What if I wrote an affirmation ten times?" And I tried it. It was amazing! By the third time, the words began to take on a new clarity. By the tenth writing, the affirmation really impacted me.

Try it yourself. Slowly and thoughtfully write out your affirmation for today ten times.

1. _____

2. _____

3. _____

4. _____

5. _____

6. _____

7. _____

8. _____

9. _____

10. _____

As I meditate, I find confidence to do my work today with strength and enthusiasm.

Peace Be Yours

"My peace I give to you; not as the world gives do I give to you."
-JOHN 14:27

There was a Jewish lad who, as a young boy, decided to make a list of the great values he would pursue in his lifetime. He wrote down "fame." Then he thought awhile, and added "fortune" to his list. Sometime later he added "good health" to the other two values he had chosen. When he was satisfied that his list was complete, he presented his list to his rabbi, who scanned it quickly.

The rabbi shook his head and said, "No, no. You have missed one of the most important values of life, and that is *Peace of mind*. What good is money, what good is fame, what good is a fortune or good health if you do not have PEACE at the core of your life?"

The Jewish people today still have the greeting. "Shalom"—meaning PEACE. It was customary in the time Jesus lived to greet each other with that wonderful word.

It was very natural then for Jesus to utter these words just hours before He died on the cross:

"I am leaving you with a gift—peace of mind and heart! And the peace I give you isn't fragile like the peace the world gives. So don't be troubled or afraid." (John 14:27).

These words are for you today! And that is why PEACE is on my list of dynamic human values.

Shalom ~ Peace to you.

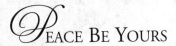EACE BE YOURS

"These things I have spoken to you, that in Me you may have peace...
Be of good cheer. I have overcome the world." -JOHN 16:33

How would you define the word PEACE? Yes, a definition surely would include "the absence of war and conflict." Another definition might simply say, "no hassle" or "no stress." Yet, when I read Jesus' words about peace in the midst of trials and sorrows, I have experienced a peace that is beyond comparison or understanding.

How about your definition—how would you describe the meaning of PEACE? Write out a definition or simply list the qualities or characteristics of peace:

_____

_____

_____

_____

_____

_____

_____

At the center of the great storm of
activity that surrounds my life, I feel
peace deep within my being!

PEACE BE YOURS

"God will keep you in perfect peace, whose mind is stayed on Him, because you trust in the Lord forever." -ISAIAH 26:3

I discovered the secret to peace of mind years ago as I was returning from a special mission in Korea. On the way home, I stopped in Hawaii and there I saw a beautiful sculptured statue of Jesus Christ returning to the sheepfold carrying the lamb that had been lost.

Jesus' weary expression confirmed my belief that He had spent long hours walking up and down the steep slopes, through crevices and canyons, until He finally found the lost sheep.

What struck me particularly about the statue was the peaceful appearance of the lamb as it seemed to curl itself around the neck of the Good Shepherd. The two front feet were folded gently, the one relaxed across the other. You could almost sense the feeling that perhaps the baby lamb was still trembling a little and his tiny body was still damp and cold. But as he relaxed on the shoulder of Jesus, he was warming up and a sense of calmness and security swept over him.

He was safe on the shoulder of the Good Shepherd. He was lost, but now he'd been found. What peace flooded his being. He had been saved!

The secret of real peace of mind is to be found in Jesus; born anew through His Spirit, and trusting your future to Him! Jesus Christ is my source of true PEACE.

As I turn my attention to Jesus my Savior, I can feel tension and anxiety slipping away and a strong awareness of peace flood my being!

PEACE BE YOURS

"Let the peace of God rule in your hearts. And be thankful." -COLOSSIANS 3:15

Peace of heart and mind—your privilege and responsibility! Take a moment now to meditate and pray. Ask God to make you aware of the areas in your life where you are not experiencing peace. What is spoiling your peace of mind? After praying and meditating, write down the areas that God brings to your attention:

_____

_____

_____

When you finish your list, take each item and turn the source of lack of peace back to God. He has promised you that peace of heart and mind is your privilege. Trust Him to keep His promise to you!

Now write out an affirming prayer of thankfulness for the sense of PEACE that God is giving you:

_____

_____

_____

God's peace is mine today. I will allow nothing to rob me of God's gift of peace of heart and mind!

PEACE BE YOURS

"May peace and blessing be yours from God the Father and from the Lord Jesus Christ." -GALATIANS 1:3

A man lived in the mountains with his daughter. They raised sheep. One day they went out looking for a missing lamb and found the small animal caught in a thorny thicket. Carefully, and ever so gently, they lifted the lamb out, but it was still scratched and bleeding in places. The little girl was crying as she said, "Father, that's a bad bush. Let's cut it down."

The next day they returned with an ax to cut the bush down. As they approached the thorny branches, the little girl saw a small bird flutter down to a branch, open its beak and grab a mouthful of wool that had been left on a thorn as the little lamb had struggled the day before. The tiny bird tugged and tugged and tugged until he had a mouthful of wool and then he flew away.

The little girl looked up at her father and said, "I think God has a good reason for this thorny bush. I don't think we should cut it down for the thorns are helping that bird get soft wool for its baby's nest."

Don't allow the thorns of life to mar your perspective. The thorns may hurt and cut and seem to have no purpose. But in God's great plan and purpose for you, every thorn can be an opportunity for increasing your vision of God's great possibility in your life. When your path is thorny, be at PEACE, for God is walking with you!

*I am resting in God's peace today.
His peace is more overwhelming than
any of life's circumstances.*

$\mathcal{P}$EACE BE YOURS

"When God gives quietness, who then can make trouble? -JOB 34:29

"I will lie down in peace and sleep,
for though I am alone,
O Lord, You will keep me safe."
-PSALM 4:8

"He will give His people strength.
He will bless them with peace."
-PSALM 29:11

"...heaven's dawn is about to break upon us,
to give light to those who sit in darkness
and death's shadow, and to guide us
to the path of peace."
-LUKE 1:78,79

"May the Lord of peace Himself give
you His peace no matter what happens.
The Lord be with you all."
-2 THESSALONIANS 3:16

*The peace of God rules my heart
today ~ nothing will disturb the calm
peace of my soul.*

PEACE BE YOURS

"May they prosper who love You. Peace be within your walls."
-PSALM 122:6,7

Henry Drummonds tells the story of two artists who were commissioned to paint a picture that would depict genuine peace.

One painted a landscape with a mountain lake—calm, quiet, tranquil, serene, unperturbed. The background setting was one of beautiful green hills, ringed by tall slender pine trees reflected in the mirror-like surface of the lake.

The second artist painted a very turbulent scene with a violent waterfall crashing down on jagged chunks of a birch tree, with its fragile branches reaching just above the crashing foam. And in the fork of one of the branches was a bird's nest. In the nest lying very calmly and serenely, glistening from the spray of the waterfall, was a small bird fast asleep.

The second artist captured the feeling of peace that can be ours in the kind of world and life in which we have to live. God does not promise us there will be no problems. There will always be difficulties and problems, but God has promised that it is really possible for us to experience PEACE—real PEACE—in the midst of life!

Lord, I take my eyes off my problems and difficulties and turn them to You. As I do I can feel Your peace within me, a calmness in the midst of the storms of life!

Lovingly Forgive

"Be kind to each other, tenderhearted, forgiving one another, just as God in Christ has forgiven you." -EPHESIANS 4:32

Number six on my list of seven dynamic human values is FORGIVENESS. Someone looking at my list asked, "Why haven't you included 'love'?" My answer is that the word love at its depth, really means FORGIVENESS.

The Greeks had three words for love. The richest word was *agape*, which is unlike any other word used for love. *Agape* means to love somebody even when they do not deserve to be loved. And that's the kind of love that God has for you and me. The interesting thing is *agape* can also be translated, "to forgive!"

God loved us even when He had no reason to. That's what *agape* means. And that's what *forgiveness* means. It is God's love in action for people who do not deserve it!

I was taught that only God can truly forgive. Nature does not forgive. If, in a fit of anger I cut off a hand, it isn't going to grow back. Educators do not forgive. If I do not study for an exam, I will flunk. Society does not forgive. If I commit a crime, I must pay for it and my record will follow me every place I go. Forgiveness is a miracle only God can perform! And the cause of His forgiveness is His great love—*agape* love. I can be lovingly forgiven!

I live today without fear or guilt for God has lovingly forgiven me!

LOVINGLY FORGIVE

"As far as the east is from the west, so far has God removed our transgressions from us." -PSALM 103:12

When God forgives, God forgets! Someone once said that when you bury the hatchet, don't leave the handle above the ground. You can always find the hatchet again that way, and dig it up again. God never digs up our past when He forgives! Isn't that beautiful! I am set free by God's loving forgiveness.

Reflect a moment on what that tremendous thought can mean for you. Finish the following sentence many times.

BECAUSE GOD FORGIVES ME, I CAN

_____

_____

_____

_____

_____

_____

_____

*Today I will live
in the joy of my forgiveness!*

LOVINGLY FORGIVE

"O' Lord, there is forgiveness with You." -PSALM 130:4

Forgiveness is non-judgmental love. That's the only real love. Most people love judgmentally: I'll love you if you agree with me politically. I'll love you if you'll start living a cleaner life. If you don't meet my expectations, I will not love you.

Even though we do not believe in God, He still loves us non-judgmentally. There are no "ifs" in God's love for you and me!

In the Sermon on the Mount, Jesus said that if we love only the people that agree with us, what is so great about that? Even scoundrels and crooks love their fellow crooks. Jesus went on to say that genuine love is shown when God allows the sun to shine on the just and the unjust, and His rain falls on the good as well as the evil.

That may seem unjust to you, but let me assure you this concept is filled with mercy. And there will always be a tension between justice and mercy! If you are having difficulty forgiving someone because "what they did is just not right," let me encourage you to forgive as you have been forgiven.

I can sense my anger and bitterness slipping away as I thank God for His forgiveness. I am forgiven. Therefore I shall forgive!

Lovingly Forgive

WHY FORGIVE? BECAUSE...

> "Whatever you sow, that you will also reap."
> -GALATIANS 6:7 RSV

> "The measure you give will be the measure
> you get, and still more will be given to you."
> -MARK 4:24 RSV

> "Your heavenly Father will forgive you if you
> forgive those who sin against you; but if you
> refuse to forgive them, He will not forgive you."
> -MATTHEW 6:15

> "Give generously, for your gifts will return
> to you later." -ECCLESIASTES 11:1

*Positive, wholesome ideas penetrate my mind
when I listen to the quiet voice of God.*

LOVINGLY FORGIVE

"Be gentle and ready to forgive; never hold grudges. Remember, the Lord forgave you, so you must forgive others." -COLOSSIANS 3:13 (LB)

I submit that FORGIVENESS, as a human value, is the most powerful healing force there is. Some of you are carrying a grudge against someone, and you need to forgive. Some of you may need to forgive yourself. And that is the only way you will find healing for your sorrow, the removal of jealousy, or the erasure of bitter memories.

Where in your life do you need the miraculous power of forgiveness? In a few words, identify the area of your life where you need to experience forgiveness:

_____

_____

Now, in your mind imagine that you are approaching the one whom you need to forgive. You explain the feelings you have had and the need you now have to be forgiving. In love, you ask forgiveness for not having been forgiving of them. Then imagine that you experience the warmth of reconciliation. Enjoy that feeling, and then begin plans to work out the above scene in real life.

God, in my own strength I cannot forgive. But I am willing to be made willing. Already, I am able to feel Your power at work in me. Help me to forgive.

LOVINGLY FORGIVE

"I am persuaded that neither death nor life,...nor things present nor things to come...shall be able to separate us from the love of God in Christ Jesus, our Lord." -ROMANS 8:38, 39

Back in the 14th century, a monk announced to the people of his village that he was going to preach the greatest sermon ever preached on the Love of God. He urged everyone to attend.

At the appropriate hour, the cathedral filled with the old and the young. Throughout the service, everyone anticipated the great discourse. At the proper time, though, the monk did not enter the pulpit, but instead went to the candelabra, drew a long burning candle and then walked high in the altar to the sculptured form of Christ nailed to the cross.

He silently lifted the candle until the glow was directly underneath one of the pierced hands. He held the candle there with his back to the congregation.

Then he shifted and he held the candle below the other pierced hand of Jesus. Slowly he moved the candle to the side of our Lord where the spear had pierced Him. And then he dropped to his knees in prayer, now holding the glimmering light so that the glow fell on the nail-pierced feet.

After a moment, the monk stood and turned, holding the candle before him so that the people could see the gentle tears on his face as he said, "My beloved people, that is my sermon on the love of God for you." And he dismissed them with a benediction!

My heart is filled with love~ God's love. I cannot help but be a forgiving person today!

Lovingly Forgive

"Love does not hold grudges." -1 Corinthians 13:5 (LB)

As a boy, I loved the winter snows. But what I didn't appreciate were the blizzards, because they would come in with driving winds of 50 to 60 miles an hour and close the roads. We would be isolated on our farm. The only good thing about the blizzard was that I didn't have to go to school.

But soon we would look out down the road and see the snowplow coming, cutting through the drifts, slicing through the snow, chopping it up and blowing it into a huge spewing stream in the ditch. And as the plow would pass, we were free to go to the store, and I could return to school.

Resentments are like snowdrifts and forgiveness like the snowplow. You see, in the eyes of many people, forgiveness is simply a matter of passive acquittal. But in the Christian context, forgiveness is a snowplow—opening the road, removing barriers, permitting communication to be restored.

There are a lot of resentments that can build up in our lives in the course of a day. And the only way to put joy on your face and in your heart is to find an overwhelming love that can remove resentments and fill you with FORGIVENESS.

"I forgive you" is the language of love!

Today I speak the language of love.
I am immune to resentments and
grudges because I can lovingly forgive!

HOPE

"Why be discouraged and sad? Hope in God! -Psalm 42:5 (LB)

HOPE is the seventh human value on my list for dynamic living. I recall the words of a prominent psychiatrist as he described the power in HOPE. He said, "All of us have had patients who sat in our offices, week after week, month after month, depressed, lifeless, dull, emotionally sick with skin sagging, eyes drooping, glassy and dull.

"Then came that moment in one of our counseling sessions when everything changed. We can't recall saying anything profound, and probably didn't, but we will never forget when the change took place.

"Suddenly the lifeless eyes come alive. The drooping eyelids open wide and the sparkle of life returns. The grey color of the skin changes as the whole person is suddenly alive and alert to life! Why? Because hope has returned.

"And what is hope? How can we as doctors define this emotion, where it comes from and what it does to a person? We can only call it a human phenomenon."

I know what that doctor was talking about and I know how to define the powerful spirit of hope that can change a person so dramatically. Call this spirit of hope by the right name—call it GOD! Hope is God's Spirit coming into a human being to change their life and perspective!

I am certain you have heard the sentence, "Where there is life, there is hope." I want you to permanently change that sentence to, *"Where there is hope, there is life!"*

I know that God is planning something good for me today!

HOPE

"Be joyful in hope." -ROMANS 12:12 (NIV)

When I was in Calcutta, India, many years ago, I had my first visit to Mother Teresa's "Home for the Dying." The whole world knows of the life-saving ministry of Mother Teresa and the Sisters of Mercy performed for many years in India, and still continues today after her death.

When Mother Teresa saw people dying in the streets of Calcutta, she was so moved that on her own, she dragged their dying bodies into a deserted temple which she had cleaned up. There she provided loving care. "Every human being at least deserves to have somebody loving them while they are dying," she said.

When I arrived at the home, the place was filled. There were narrow, low ceilings and dim lights, but everything smelled clean and sweet. One of the nurses told me: "Dr. Schuller, an interesting thing is happening. We accept only those people who are dying of some terminal disease. But, the amazing thing is that when they come here and feel the love of Christ, they are filled with hope and many of them stop dying. In fact, we're thinking of changing our name to the "Home for the Living!"

An incredible place, and a perfect example of hope—Where there's hope, there's life! There is tremendous power in HOPE!

I am filled with joyful hope.
Life is exciting!

Hope

"All things work together for good to those who love God..." -ROMANS 8:28

Everywhere I go, I meet people who tell me, "My life has been changed!" And it is because there is change that there can be hope! Whatever your circumstances are today, they will change. Tomorrow will be different. And the amazing thing is that you can choose how your tomorrow will be different.

Think about that for a moment, and then write down how you would like tomorrow to be different:

_____

_____

_____

_____

_____

_____

Now choose to believe that through God's power at work within you, the tomorrow you have described will be yours.

Today I begin anew!

OPE

"Let everything that has breath praise the Lord! Praise the Lord!
-PSALM 150:6

What do you do when all hope seems gone? Especially when you feel hopeless? I find the Psalms a great source of help at these times.

Right now, try reading Psalm 146 through 150. They are short enough to read in one sitting. Then, after you have read these five short Psalms, add your own thoughts:

Praise the Lord, all you _____

_____ !

Praise Him for _____

_____

I will praise Him with _____

_____

_____

_____ !

Congratulations, you've just written Psalm 151. Now, when feelings of hopelessness start to come, shut them off by re-reading your Psalm of praise!

I am praising God. As I am filled with praise, I am also filled with hope!

$\mathcal{H}$OPE

"My soul claims the Lord is my inheritance; therefore, I will hope in Him."
-*LAMENTATIONS 3:24 (LB)*

Do you know what the alternative is to HOPE? Despair! I am amazed at how often famous men have expressed the feelings of hopelessness—despair.

In 1801, Wilberforce said that he dared not marry because the future was too unsettled.

In 1806, William Penn said, *"There is scarcely anything around us but ruin and despair."*

In 1848, Lord Shaftsbury said, *"Nothing can save the British Empire from shipwreck."*

In 1849 Benjamin Disraeli said, *"In industry, commerce, and agriculture there is no hope."*

In 1852, the dying Duke of Wellington said, *"I thank God that I shall be spared from seeing the consummation of ruin that is settling in around us."*

And in 1914, Lord Grey said, *"The lamps are going out all over Europe; we shall not see the light again in our lifetime."*

Prominent experts of international repute have an amazing inclination to spread despair. Apparently they have never discovered the secret shared by the prophet Jeremiah: *"My soul claims the Lord as my inheritance; therefore I will hope in Him"* (*LAMENTATIONS 3:24*).

I choose to hope in God and I feel surrounded with His presence!

Hope

"Blessed is the one who trusts in the Lord and whose hope is in the Lord."
-*JEREMIAH 17:7*

You are filled with HOPE! But as you look around, you see friends who are filled with despair and hopelessness. Stop a moment and consider which friend might need your encouragement today. Write down their first name:

_____

From your perspective, why are they filled with despair?

_____

Write down some words of encouragement and hope that you can share with this person today, either in person or in writing. Remember, hope is nourished by affirming the possibilities available. Keep your encouragements on a positive note:

_____

_____

_____

_____

Because I have hope, I can be a messenger of hope to someone else today. That gives me a greater awareness of hope in my own life!

HOPE

"And now, Lord, what do I wait for? My hope is in YOU." -PSALM 39:7

Robert Louis Stevenson was a sickly child who never forgot his childhood experience of watching the old lamplighter coming down his street in Edinburgh, Scotland. Every night, the faithful man would come, lighting the oil lamps one-by-one as darkness began to approach.

In his later years, Stevenson remarked, "What I remember most about the lamplighter each night was that he always left a light behind him! And the light was a guide to those that followed afterwards."

What's the most beautiful sight in the world? A sunset? A snowcapped mountain peak? Confucius, the Chinese philosopher, is quoted as saying, "The most beautiful sight in the world is a little child going confidently down the road after you have shown him the way." The greatest joy in the world is to point someone who is lost in the right direction! You and I can do that!

When people ask me why I have hope in this life, I take them by the hand, point them to Christ and say, "There's the reason. Jesus gave me pardon, a purpose and hope!" "And the Lord will guide you continually, and satisfy your soul, and strengthen your bones; and you shall be like a watered garden." (Isaiah 58:11).

I believe that whatever happens to me today will prove to be a beautiful blessing!

New Life

"If anyone is in Christ, he is a new creation; old things are passed away. Behold, all things are new." -II Corinthians 5:17

Four weeks after our first televised church service a motorcycle pulled into the parking lot; the driver was a young army officer. On the back of the motorcycle was a box. He came into my office. He said, *"I have never in my life heard anything as crazy as what you said, 'Go to your window and say, 'I believe, I believe!' But I was in the hospital, hopeless and helpless.*

"Assured that no one was around, I got out of bed and I went to the window. I said it softly, 'I believe! I believe! I believe!' I didn't realize what I was doing, but now I know why it works. I was opening the door of my heart. It was closed until then."

He continued, *"I believe in Jesus Christ today. And I have to give you a gift. It's a very precious gift. I bought it when I was in military service in Italy."* He handed me a most precious porcelain figurine. It was a shoe cobbler. Standing by the cobbler is a pitiful little waif of a girl. She is poor, simple, trusting. One foot has no shoe. She has given her shoe to the cobbler. He's looking at it. It looks like an absolutely helpless case of impossible repair.

My new friend said to me, *"Dr. Schuller. Four weeks ago my life was that old shoe. Then I came to Jesus and He took a look at me. He just shook his head. But he didn't throw me away. He patched me up and made me like new."*

My friend died a year later and is in Heaven today. Someday you'll be there because today you, too, can decide to become a believer in the Great Believer — Jesus Christ.

I believe! I believe! I believe!

I am living today controlled by my God ~ inspired positive ideas!

EW LIFE

"I shall not die, but live, and declare the works of the Lord." -PSALM 118:17

I love the story of the poor man who lived in the heat of the Depression. He was a German immigrant. He was in desperate need of finances, so he figured out a way that he could make some money to feed his family.

His wife had a recipe for terrific knockwurst, so he decided to sell knockwurst. The problem was that he couldn't afford to buy the utensils for the knockwurst.

His wife came through for him. She suggested that she make some rolls, which he could fill with knockwurst. It worked; it was a tremendous success and the hot dog was born.

Everyone faces problems and circumstances in his or her life. It's not the problems, but how we deal with them, that makes the difference.

Forecast your way to fulfillment. I believe every problem is really an opportunity for God to work miracles. Describe a pressing problem and then write down all the potential opportunities for God to work a miracle.

My problem is _____

_____

God's opportunities for miracles are _____

_____

_____

I am praising God for my problems which are opportunities hiding God's great possibilities!

EW LIFE

"Light dawns for the righteous, and joy for the upright in heart."
-Psalm 97:11 RSV

Early one morning I went for a long run. I came to an intersection where I could keep on going east, turn to the south, or head north. If I turned south I would have a view of the breaking of the dawn reflecting on the ocean. If I headed north I would catch a view of the mountains in the breaking sunlight. Both options were tempting.

If I kept running east, I would be running up a slight hill. But I would be running toward what was a growing golden glow. I knew I would catch the daybreak, and I would feel the first long shafts of golden sunlight falling on my chilled face.

I started running toward the ocean, but I found I was running with my back to the daybreak, and that was disappointing. I felt I would be missing out on something beautiful.

So I had an easy decision. I turned to the east and *I ran to the sunrise!* And I was not disappointed. When I reached the top of the hill, the sun broke over the horizon and the bursting light was like being born anew.

How do you run to the light? You run to the light of God's Word!

Lord, I am running towards Your sunrise.
I am thinking about You.
I am being warmly blessed right now!

New Life

"Choose to love the Lord your God and to obey Him and to cling to Him, for He is your life...!" -DEUTERONOMY 30:20

All of the great people in the Bible were possibility thinkers. Oh, they were realists—they knew what it was to be discouraged, depressed or on the verge of defeat. But they were great because even in the midst of their troubles, they chose to turn their attention to God's beautiful possibilities for their todays.

Even Jeremiah, the weeping prophet, in the depths of great depression, finally chose to focus on God's great love. When he did, his depression left him (Read Lamentations 3:1-24). He chose to look at God's possibilities rather than pay attention to the negative forces surrounding him.

Are you troubled today? Do you feel that life is closing in on you and there is no way to escape? Don't let your mind dwell on negative thoughts. Choose life! Believe in God's ability to overcome the troubles and give you a great and exciting today and tomorrow. God's message to you is, "I know the plans I have for you...plans for good and not for evil, to give you a future and a hope." (Jeremiah 29:11).

I am choosing life ~ God's life. Therefore, I have nothing to fear.

NEW LIFE

"The steadfast love of the Lord never ceases, His mercies never come to an end; they are new every morning; great is God's faithfulness."
-LAMENTATIONS 3:22,23 *Revised Standard Version*

Psalm 148 encourages *everything* to praise the Lord—even the mountains and the trees. Today, make your own praise list. If you need more space, start a praise notebook. When negative thoughts attack you, read over your praise list. Praise the Lord!

Begin by listing no less than 8 blessings for which you are grateful.

I praise the Lord for:

1. _____

2. _____

3. _____

4. _____

5. _____

6. _____

7. _____

8. _____

Now, keep adding to your list.

Today, Lord, I am praising You.
You are my ray of hope!

New Life

"With you this is impossible, but with God all things are possible."
-MATTHEW 19:26

This story is told about one of America's favorite entertainers—Dick Van Dyke. One night in his Arizona home, he and a number of guests were playing the game: "Who-I'd-Like-Most-To-Be." One person wanted to be Beethoven. Someone else said they would like to be Rockefeller. And so it went. When it came around to Dick Van Dyke, he hesitated, and sincerely, but shyly explained, "I don't want to sound silly," he admitted, "but I'd like most to be Christ."

That excites me because I agree with his choice! For Jesus Christ is the greatest possibility thinker who has ever lived! He really should have been an impossibility thinker—He had every reason.

Yet He knew a secret. Looking at His disciples, He shared with them the secret when He said, "With you this is impossible, but with God all things are possible." (Matthew 19:26). Sharing God's new life makes you one of God's possibility people!

Christ lives within me now!
I am one of His possibility people!

EW LIFE

"I can do all things through Christ who strengthens me." -PHILIPPIANS 4:13

Over a week ago you started with a choice and the encouragement to choose life! Now let's evaluate. Think back over these past few days and write down situations where you made life-generating, life-revitalizing decisions:

_____

_____

_____

Now commit the next week to do a new thing. Something you have never dared try before. Write down your commitment and refer to it during the coming week:

_____

_____

_____

_____

_____

*Thank you, Lord, for Your
strength and power enabling me to do
anything You ask me to do.*

*E*XPECT GROWTH

"If you sow sparingly, you will also reap sparingly. You who sow bountifully will also reap bountifully." -2 CORINTHIANS 9:6

I believe in God! And I rejoice every time I meet someone who has made the decision to take that first small step of faith. Because I believe there are infinite possibilities in little beginnings if God is in it.

I can understand this because of my experience as a boy on our Iowa farm. My dad saw the possibilities within a single kernel of corn. He saw a 9-foot cornstalk growing strong with a crop of multiple ears of corn. I think it was my father's example that inspired me many years later to write: *"Any person can count the seeds in an apple, but only God can count the apples in a seed."*

When we needed more food for the cattle and more grain to sell in the market, my father would simply plow more ground and plant more seed.

I learned that fundamental principle from those early experiences—if you need more, you have to give more! If you want a bigger harvest, you have to plant more seeds. For the laws of nature and growth are consistent: You reap according to what you sow.

I am sowing seeds of faith today.
God is giving me an over ~ flowing
harvest of His goodness and love!

Expect Growth

"In the morning sow your seed, and in the evening do not withhold your hand; for you do not know which will prosper." -ECCLESIASTES 11:6

The miracle of the apple seed is an example of what God can do in any person's life. God wants you and me to enjoy a healthy, prosperous and abundant life.

God is constantly scattering positive seeds into your life. Is it a new dream? An idea you never shared with anyone? If you plant your seed by faith, it will lead to new health, new strength, new abundance and prosperity. Read the Parable of the Sower today that Jesus taught in Matthew 13:1-8. Some seed fell by the wayside and was devoured by birds, other seed fell on stony ground and could not grow. Some seed fell among thorns and were choked, but other seed fell on good ground and yielded a great crop.

What negative circumstances are you and I allowing to delay or stop the growth of positive seeds of faith God has planted in our minds today? God has built into the system of nature, enormous potential and possibility for growth. He wants to do the same with you and me!

Today think about that dream or that idea that may be so small, but has tremendous possibilities. Write it down. It may be one of God's seeds within you.

1. _____

2. _____

3. _____

4. _____

5. _____

My mind is open to the possibilities God has for me. I am cultivating the seeds He is planting!

Expect Growth

"Plant the good seeds of righteousness and you will reap a crop of my love."
-Hosea 10:12 (LB)

We received a call at our Institute for Successful Church Leadership from a desperate pastor. He was ready to quit the ministry. He wanted to attend the Institute, even though reservations were full.

We have a policy that people come first, so we allowed this pastor to come. The five days turned him around completely. He went back to his church enthused and excited about the ministry. In his suitcase was a book he bought while here, the book *Tara* — the story of the daughter of one of our producers of the Hour of Power. Tara had suffered a terrible fall and was in a coma because of a brain injury and was experiencing a number of miraculous comebacks.

Soon after this pastor returned to his hometown, a little girl was struck by a car and rushed to the hospital hovering on the brink of death. This pastor took a copy of the book, *Tara*, to the parents of this critically injured little girl and spent a great deal of time with them offering encouragement and faith.

The parents did not attend church or express any kind of faith. As they read the book, it gave them great faith in God. They prayed and a miracle happened - their little girl recovered. Recently the entire family flew to California to worship with us. What a thrill it was to meet them. It all started with a little phone call.

Lord, I will pay attention today to each little opportunity You place before me and I shall expect a miracle to happen ~ It may be so small I might call it by another name.

EXPECT GROWTH

"May Christ dwell in your hearts through faith that you, being rooted and grounded in love, may be filled with all the fullness of God." -EPHESIANS 3:17-19

One of the most inspiring men I've met was ninety years old. He lived in Ohio. He was a super, twinkly, happy, cheerful, positive person. He wasn't rich in this world's goods. He lived in a simple little house. I asked him, *"What makes you happy in life?"*

He said, *"My garden."*

"Oh! What do you raise?"

"Vegetables and fruit."

I said, *"You live alone, you're a widower. You can't possibly eat all of your harvest by yourself. What do you do with all your produce?"*

"Oh," he replied, *"When the harvest comes in, I put a table by the road with all the fruit and vegetables along with a sign that reads '*__FREE__.' *The cars come and the tourists come and they take the fruit. They can't believe it's free, but when they realize that I really don't want anything in return for it, they are always grateful and happy to receive the gift. Many times people said it was an answer to prayer, that they didn't know where they would get the money for food. It makes me feel so happy to give the fruit and vegetables away."*

Then I asked him, *"What do you do in the wintertime?*

"I think about what I will plant in my garden in the spring and I feed the birds," was his reply.

Only positive people dare to believe and trust that God can do great things through them, no matter how poor or how old they are. They are the people who experience *"All the fullness of God because they are rooted and grounded in love."*

I will expect growth today as I keep my eye on God's creative and constructive plan for me.

Expect Growth

"Thanks be to God, who gives us the victory through our Lord Jesus Christ." -1 CORINTHIANS 15:57

There's a purely mythological story that I heard as a child that helps to make the point about discouragement. According to the story, Satan gathered together all of his devils to discuss how they could attack, undermine and defuse the power of a certain influential believer on earth. Several suggestions were given. One little devil said, *"I suggest we attack him at the point of lust."*

All the other little devils laughed and said, *"You don't know him very well; he's not vulnerable there. In fact, he's very strong."*

Others rose with their suggestions. At each point, the idea was protested, *"He's too strong, he is too shielded, he's too protected."*

Finally one devil spoke up and said, *"Maybe we can go to work on him and get him discouraged."*

Everybody applauded and said, *"That might work! Go for it!"* Discouragement is still the enemy's most effective weapon against God's people.

Some of you live such a powerful, strong, joyous, positive Christian life through the week, and you try to share your faith with others where you work, as well as with members of your families. When they jeer or simply give you the silent treatment, you're bound to be disappointed. Just don't let the disappointment turn into discouragement.

Through Christ, I am victorious!
Nothing will destroy the sense of joy
that comes with victory!

EXPECT GROWTH

"You shall be like a tree planted by the rivers of water, that brings forth its fruit in its season, whose leaf shall not wither, and whatever you do shall prosper. -PSALM 1:3

Sometime ago I became very enthusiastic about olive trees. I was planting them on our church grounds at the time. Olive trees are found in Southern California, having been transplanted here from the Mediterranean region of the Middle East.

In my enthusiasm, I excitedly offered to send a young tree to anyone watching the Hour of Power program. We mailed out thousands of them and many of them arrived dried out. I received an interesting letter from a man who said, *"I was so excited and happy when my package arrived. I gently opened the carton and to my surprise found a plastic bag with a tiny box and a dried out twig! What a letdown! I could have cried!*

But he told me how he soaked the twig and placed it on a table where it received the sunlight. And soon the leaves had lifted and the tiny branch had turned itself to the sun. *"I am excited again,"* he wrote, *"and will let you know how it grows."*

As I read his letter, I wondered how many olive trees were thrown away because people did not have the faith to believe they would live. Who can count the olives on a twig that looks so lifeless? Use the faith God gives you to believe and grow!

The faith that comes from God is flowing through me giving new life to my dreams and ideas!

EXPECT GROWTH

At the beginning of a new day,
Lord, I sit in a choice seat.
I wait expectantly
for the curtain to go up
and for the drama to begin.

Lord, at the end of this day,
I will have been deeply changed,
for I will have grown
as I open myself more and more
to the reality of the love of God
at work within me!

Thank you Lord!

*I am living today controlled by my
God ~ inspired positive ideas!*

FOLLOW THE LEADER

"Be strong and of good courage; do not be afraid...for the Lord your God is with you wherever you go." -JOSHUA 1:9

Years ago, Olympic champion Charley Paddock was speaking to the young men at East Tech High School. "If you think you can, you can!" he challenged the youths. "If you believe a thing strongly enough, it can come to pass in your life!"

Afterward, a spindly-legged boy said to Mr. Paddock, "Gee, Sir, I'd give anything if I could be an Olympic champion just like you!" It was that lad's moment of inspiration. His life changed. In 1936 that young man went to Berlin, Germany, to compete in the Olympics. He came home with four gold medals! His name—Jesse Owens.

Back home he was driven through the streets of Cleveland to the cheers of the crowd. The car stopped and he signed some autographs. A skinny little boy pressed against the car and said, "Gee, Mr. Owens, I'd give anything to be an Olympic champ like you!" Jesse reached out and put his hand on the boy's arm as he said, "You know, young fellow, I was about your age when I said the same thing. If you'll work and train and believe, you can be an Olympic champion!"

In 1948 at Wembly Stadium in London, England, that same little boy was a young man. He crouched waiting for the starter's gun to go off for the finals of the 100-meter dash. Harrison "Bones" Dillard won the race and tied Jesse Owen's Olympic record!

Everyday, people are being inspired to greatness by the example of someone else. Who's your inspiring leader?

I am enthusiastic! I am alert!
I am ready to follow God's leadership!

Follow the Leader

"Without counsel, plans go awry, but in the multitude of counselors, plans are established." -PROVERBS 15:22

All of us have been inspired to do something through someone else's example. Sometimes it is only a word or two that catches our attention and changes the direction of our lives. Other times, it is the example of someone over a period of time that provides inspiration for our thinking.

When my missionary uncle returned from China on furlough, he visited our Iowa farm. I was only four years old, but I still remember his words to me at the gate: "Bob," he said, "you're going to be a preacher!" That moment changed the direction of my life.

As you think back over your life, who have been the people that have influenced you? Whether by a chance encounter or a long-term relationship, who has influenced your decisions? Stop and think a moment and then write down their names:

_____   _____

_____   _____

_____   _____

_____   _____

Now thank God for the life and example of each of these people. Maybe you could drop one of them a note thanking them for the example they provided for your life.

I am thankful for the people God is sending into my life. They are His messengers to me!

$\mathcal{F}$OLLOW THE LEADER

"If the Lord is God, then follow Him!" -1 KINGS 18:21

What makes a person a leader? What qualities make one person a leader and another person a follower? What qualities do you look for in a boss, a president, or any other person who, at one time or another, is a leader in your life?

Make a list of what you consider to be leadership qualities:

QUALITIES OF A LEADER ARE:

1. _____

2. _____

3. _____

4. _____

NOW LIST THE CHARACTERISTICS OF A FOLLOWER:

1. _____

2. _____

3. _____

4. _____

Are you a leader or a follower?

Name the great leaders of the Bible who were dedicated followers of God!

*I choose to follow God today
as I lead someone along the way.*

FOLLOW THE LEADER

"If you follow Me, you shall not walk in darkness, but have the light of life." -JOHN 8:12

Today, Jesus Christ literally lives in millions of human beings around the world. He lives in my life. He has been, and continues to be, the most influential leader in the history of the human race. Yet He had every reason to be an impossibility thinker.

For example, He was a member of a minority race, who at that time were an oppressed people. His native countrymen were under the rule of the Romans. Taxes were oppressive. They had no political freedom. Yet He seemingly did nothing about those conditions.

He was uneducated. He had no academic degrees or diplomas. Moreover, poverty was His lot all His life. He never owned a home of His own. He Himself said, "Foxes have holes, birds of the air have nests. I have nothing."

He came from the low-class, uncultured people. His father was a common laborer. High-brow critics said of His origin, "Can anything good come out of Nazareth?"

He never married, and was isolated from men of power and influence. He had no powerful connections in the local government. His own band of followers were ragged, rugged, unpolished losers.

He served other people all His life and received little thanks for what He did. In the end, He became the innocent victim of a massive injustice. His friends let Him down and one of them even betrayed Him.

In the end, He even felt forsaken by God. He had every reason to give up, but instead, He changed the whole course of history!

I am a follower of Christ.

FOLLOW THE LEADER

"Let this mind be in you which was also in Christ Jesus." -PHILIPPIANS 2:5

To Jesus, problems were possibilities in disguise. Sick people were an opportunity to perform miracles and show God's love. Even on the cross, He took the opportunity to take care of His mother and the dying thief next to Him.

Jesus purposely sought out the problem people. Those whom the world would blackball, He courted and converted! He believed in the hidden possibilities within each person. A rough-and-tough Peter, a prostitute named Mary, a crooked tax collector named Zacchaeus—all had goodness waiting to be brought out!

Jesus believed in the dignity of the individual. So He never called a person a "sinner." He always saw the individual as a saint. But He also believed in ultimate justice in eternity. So He had as much to say about hell as He did about heaven.

The immeasurable mercy of God was still another great possibility that He proclaimed. Jesus promised that any sin could be forgiven if we would repent.

Christ is changing my attitudes.
I am becoming more positive every day
in every area of my life!

$\mathcal{F}$OLLOW THE LEADER

"Jesus Christ is the same yesterday, today, and forever." -HEBREWS 13:8

Jesus said:

"I am the good shepherd. The good shepherd gives His life for the sheep." -JOHN 10:11

"I am the door. If anyone enters by Me, he will be saved, and will go in and out and find pasture." -JOHN 10:9

"I am the bread of life. He who comes to me shall never hunger, and he who believes in Me shall never thirst." -JOHN 6:35

"I am the vine; you are the branches. He who abides in me, and I in him, bears much fruit." -JOHN 15:5

"I am the resurrection and the life. He who believes in Me, though he may die, he shall live." -JOHN 11:25

"I have come as a light into the world, that whoever believes in Me should not abide in darkness." -JOHN 12:46

*Thank you, Jesus, for revealing
Yourself in a way we all understand.*

FOLLOW THE LEADER

"If you can believe, all things are possible to the one who believes." -MARK 9:23

The most important question of your life is—"What do you think of Jesus Christ?" The Roman commander in charge of Jesus' execution turned away and was heard saying, "Truly this man was the Son of God!"

What do you think? Is He alive at the center of your life? Have you ever invited Jesus Christ into your life as your Savior? If not, I encourage you to choose Him as your leader. Turn over the control of your life to the only One Who can give you a fresh new beginning. Pray this prayer:

"Lord Jesus Christ, I am discovering that many things are possible that I never before believed were possible. I am becoming aware of the fact that you want to live within me, guiding and helping me as I live each day. I believe that you were sent by your Father into this world to become my Savior. I ask you to forgive me and change me. I accept you now. Thank you, Lord. Amen."

Now that you have discovered the power of Jesus Christ in your life, you will want to tell someone else the good news! What special person in your life would be interested in knowing about God's good news? Call them, or write them a letter sharing what you discovered this week about Jesus Christ.

The joy of Jesus Christ is mine. He is my leader. I am becoming a better, more positive person because Jesus Christ lives within me!

*J*ESUS IS LORD

"Heaven and Earth will pass away, but my words will by no means pass away." -LUKE 21:33

Do you dare to trust God? Jesus did. As He made His triumphant entry into the city of Jerusalem, Jesus was saying to all the people, "I dare to trust My Father Who is in heaven." He dared to trust God even when He knew how costly that decision would be.

Roll back the centuries and watch the Roman emperors as they enter their cities, riding in golden chariots drawn by six or eight stallions. As they enter the city, the streets are cleared for two miles. What pomp! What excitement!

Then there was Caesar. He had to be different, so his chariot was drawn by six tawny lions. Pompey used elephants to pull his chariot, and when kings of Portugal, England, Austria, and Prussia entered their cities, they rode in magnificent, splendid carriages carved out of fascinating woods. The fenders were adorned with carved cupids, then entirely overlaid with gold! The kings rode into their cities in these gold-plated, cupid-carved chariots.

And then there was Jesus—King of Israel and Lord of all creation! He entered His capital city riding on a donkey! No pomp, no show, no lofty pride, just love in His face!

Jesus, Your love draws me closer to You this day!

$\mathcal{J}$ESUS IS LORD

"I am the resurrection and the life. He who believes in Me, though he may die, he shall live." -JOHN 11:25

JESUS preached these grand possibilities:

*You **can** be born again!*
*Character **can** be changed!*
*You **can** become a new person!*
*Life **can** be beautiful!*
There is a solution to every problem!
There is a light behind every shadow!

Yes.

JESUS had an unshakable faith in these ultimate possibilities:

God exists!

Life goes on beyond death!

Heaven is for real!

He was prepared to prove it: by dying — and rising again!

He saw the possibility of ultimate justice!

So

He had as much to say about hell as

He did about heaven.

JESUS

Was impressed by what the world could become —

Never depressed by what the world was.

He truly believed in the possibility of transformed lives.

He truly believed that common people can become

Uncommonly powerful.

I believe it's possible ~ that Christ
is alive this moment and trying to penetrate
my life through my brain as I read these words!

$\mathcal{J}$ESUS IS LORD

"For He shall give His angels charge over you, to keep you in all your ways." -PSALM 91:11

I have had many very real experiences with Jesus Christ. Each of them, in their own way, unique. Yet, each of them, in their own way, alike. I cannot share them all with you. But I want to tell you about an experience that my daughter, Carol, shared with me just yesterday.

As many of you know, Carol was thirteen years old when her left leg was amputated at the knee due to a motorcycle accident. The accident nearly took her life. There were a lot of complications regarding Carol's healing and, consequently, she was hospitalized for nearly seven months in Children's Hospital of Orange County. Seven months is a long time to be in a hospital!

Yesterday, Carol relayed to my wife and I something we'd never known. She said to me, *"Dad, you know Jesus is alive. He really is."* Then she explained, *"There were times in the hospital when I remember being all alone. The time came when Mom could no longer spend every night at the hospital with me. Gretchen needed a mother too."* (Gretchen is our youngest daughter, and two years younger than Carol.)

Carol continued, *"So Mom would leave. Then the nurses would finish their routine with me, and they would leave. And I remember the first night that this happened. I was alone in that isolation room. It was dark. It was lonely. I prayed, 'O Jesus, You are alive, aren't You? Will You be with me tonight? Will You stay with me? Will You sleep with me?'"* And then with tears in her eyes as she shared this with Mrs. Schuller and I, Carol said, *"And He did! I can still recall it, Dad. I turned on my side, hugging my favorite stuffed dog. And He came. I could feel **Him.** I felt so suddenly peaceful. So safe. Then I fell asleep."*

$\mathcal{D}$o you believe that $\mathcal{J}$esus is real?

$\mathcal{J}$ESUS IS LORD

"God so loved the world that He gave His only begotten Son that whoever believes in Him should not perish, but have everlasting life." -JOHN 3:16

When you allow Jesus Christ to come into sharp focus in the core of your mind, a fire ignites—the fire of the Holy Spirit of the living God. You are turned from negative to positive, and that's exciting!

The positive idea that Jesus expressed as He sat to eat with His disciples is so simple that we often are inclined to ignore it. It's as revolutionary as tomorrow! The idea is the powerful, positive idea of love, love, LOVE!

What gets me so excited is that until the coming of Jesus Christ, there was no form of worship or religion that really was centered in love. The Old Covenant in the Old Testament was centered on the law. The emphasis was on obedience and regular blood sacrifices for the atonement of sin. It was not love, even though it was very loving.

But Jesus said He marked the beginning of the New Covenant. And the New Covenant of Love answers the two most important questions any person can ask:

What can I expect from God?

What does God expect from me?

And the answer to both questions is the same - LOVE! God's grace is so great that He loves me even when I don't deserve it. And everything leading up to the cross and the crucifixion is the evidence of God's unfailing, unlimited and sacrificial love for you and me! That's the message of the New Covenant!

I invite the transforming love of God to do its work in me!

JESUS IS LORD

"Even when walking through the dark valley of death I will not be afraid, for You are close beside me, guarding, guiding all the way." -PSALM 23:4

By all the laws of known psychological development, Jesus Christ should have become the world's greatest impossibility thinker. He was a member of a despised minority, a citizen of an occupied country, a Jew, and the world hated the Jews.

With the racial prejudice He experienced as a child, He should have grown up to be oversensitive, touchy and defensive. Taxes were oppressive. Freedom was limited. Survival was uncertain. Religion was in the minor key—restrictive, negative and joyless.

Yet Jesus never grew up to make an inflammatory speech, never organized a guerrilla force in the mountains, and never led a march on Rome.

He was uneducated, untraveled and without honor. He did not know the politicians, or the other "important" people of His day. In fact, it was said of Him, "Look how He attracts the losers, not the influential."

He lived and died in poverty. He had no home of His own, no insurance or retirement plan, and no wife to comfort Him. But the miracle of miracles, He grew up to be the World's Greatest Possibility Thinker!

He believed in, and proved, the ultimate possibilities, such as: "I am the resurrection and the life. He who lives and believes in Me shall never die!" And when He died, He rose again! And through His death, He lives to give life and meaning to each of us!

I live because Jesus lives!

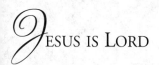ESUS IS LORD

"Greater love has no one than this, than to lay down one's life for his friend" -JOHN 15:13

What does the cross mean in your life? We wear gold or silver crosses around our neck as symbols of our faith. We place crosses on steeples of churches and in the front of our sanctuaries. But for Jesus, the cross was an instrument of suffering, pain and death.

The tremendous possibilities of our faith is the way God can take a cruel instrument of death and turn it into a symbol of hope and life.

Think for a moment about the possibilities available to you today because of the cross of Jesus Christ. Describe the meaning of the cross in your life today.

THE CROSS OF JESUS CHRIST MEANS _____

_____

_____

_____

_____

_____

_____ TO ME.

God's love turned the minus into a plus
at the cross. A symbol of "at~one~ment"
where God reached down so we could be
"at~one" with Him.

JESUS IS LORD

"God did not send His Son into the world to condemn the world, but that the world, through Him, might be saved." -JOHN 3:17

Towering high above the converging freeways in Orange County is the 100 foot tall cross sitting on top of the Tower of Hope. Rising over 250 feet above the ground, it is a light that shines continuously—symbolizing the hope promised by Jesus Christ.

Pilots landing at Orange County Airport tell me they use our cross as a reference point, making certain they are in the right landing path. People lying on hospital beds in the U.C.I Medical Center look out their window at the lighted cross. Many lives have been changed by its silent witness.

One night, just after midnight, a security guard making his rounds found a young woman lying unconscious in our parking lot. He called one of our NEW HOPE counselors, asking for someone to come and check on her.

The counselor came downstairs just as she was starting to babble. They carried her upstairs and gave her some coffee and wrapped her in a warm blanket. For four hours, the counselor stayed with this girl until she was coherent. As she was leaving to receive medical attention, she said to the counselor, "I knew that if I could just get to the cross, I would find help!"

My friend, the cross is where each of us must come to find the answer to our deepest needs. At the cross, help is always available!

I come to the cross and I meet Jesus.
He fills my soul with courage
and strength.

COME-ALIVE-POWER

"Blessed are these who have not seen, and yet believed." -JOHN 20:29

Even to a possibility thinker, there are some things that are impossible. For someone to stand at the beginning of a day and say to the sun, "Today you shall not make your sweeping sail through the sky." Or for someone to go to the seashore and draw a line in the sand at low tide and say to the sea, "Today you shall not rise above this line." These will not produce the possibility.

For the Roman soldiers to put a stone in front of the tomb where Jesus lay and say, "You shall never rise again!" was not a possibility! In the same way, it is impossible for you to invite Christ into your life and not receive His Come-Alive-Power! The sun will shine, the tide will rise, CHRIST IS ALIVE AND WHEN He comes into your life, you will receive power.

Christ gives *Come-Alive-Power!* Perhaps some of you have never experienced this dynamic power. It can happen! You can know this power in your life!

This week we will look at four words that describe the Come-Alive-Power that Jesus Christ gives when He transforms you. They are four simple words that you can easily remember.

First of all, *courage.* Second, you receive *confidence.* Third, you find *companionship.* And fourth, you discover the capacity for *communication!* When these four words are a reality in your life, then you have discovered *Come-Alive-Power!*

It is possible for me to know Christ's come~alive~power in my life today!

Come-Alive-Power

"Be strong and of good courage; do not be afraid for the Lord your God is with you." -JOSHUA 1:9

Everyone needs courage! I need it; you need it. Stop a moment and look at your life. Where could you use courage today? What situation are you faced with that stirs up feelings of fear within you? Describe the situation briefly:

_____

_____

_____

Christ's Come-Alive-Power gives you courage. Imagine in your mind how you would act in that situation, exercising the power of Jesus Christ to give you courage. Now describe how you will act with courage in that instance:

_____

_____

_____

_____

_____

I am courageous! I can feel Christ's power in my life giving me courage. I am no longer afraid.

$\mathscr{C}$OME-ALIVE-POWER

"Oh death, where is your sting? O grave, where is your victory? Thanks be to God who gives us victory through our Lord Jesus Christ." -1 COR. 15:55-57

Christ gives courage! Real dynamic courage. And He can do this because everyone knows Christ is risen, and we no longer need to be afraid of dying. When you have eliminated the fear of death, you have eliminated the source of all fears.

Some time ago I was reading in the British annals when I came across an interesting anecdote. There was a time in the West Indies when there were five ships anchored in the harbor. One was a British ship.

Suddenly an unexpected storm came up and the waves rolled fiercely into the harbor. The British officer raised the anchor and set his ship at sea directly into the mounting, rolling waves. He sailed out of the harbor into the face of the storm.

Two days later, battered and bruised, but still afloat and intact, he came back to the harbor. In the calm that hovered over the now still waters, he surveyed the scene and found that the other four ships that had not weighed anchor for fear of the storm had been driven onto the shore had been destroyed!

There is only one way to conquer a fear and that is to face it! If Christ is your Lord and God, you can face any fear, even death, without being afraid! *Come-Alive-Power gives courage*!

Because Jesus Christ lives all fear is gone.

COME-ALIVE-POWER

"I have set before you today life and death...therefore choose life that you and your descendants may live." -DEUTERONOMY 30:19

The second thing that Christ gives is confidence! Confidence eliminates the anxiety that comes from irresponsible liberty. Do you realize that today our country is one of the most anxiety-plagued societies in history? And this rise in anxiety comes in a period of time when we have, supposedly, more freedom and liberty than ever before.

Psychologists have studied this. One test was made on a playground. The researchers felt that fences around playgrounds led to feelings of oppression, so for one group of students, they took down the fences—total freedom!

Guess what happened? The children became anxiety prone. They huddled together and played in the center of the playground. They didn't dare to run for fear that they might run into danger. But when the fences were put up again, they would race across the playground and run with their hands outstretched into the fence. Fences mean security! Especially when the fences are positive!

When Christ comes into your life, you have a new moral consciousness. You have positive fences. You say, "I will be true to Christ, to God and to those around me." And this gives confidence! You can face anyone unashamed. You have no dark secrets. And that produces confidence at the deepest possible level!

I have confidence that God is going to see me through this day, and each new day, because He lives within me!

COME-ALIVE-POWER

"As the Father loved Me, I also have loved you; abide in my love." -JOHN 15:9

We are plagued by loneliness today. Companionship is something we treasure. But some of us no longer know the beauty of a companion. We lack enthusiasm, happiness and joy because we suffer from loneliness. Inwardly we feel lonely and we dare not share it with anyone.

Some of us suffer from the loneliness of failure. We think we have failed at something and we dare not talk to anyone else about it. Others are successful and still suffer from loneliness. These people do not share their success because of the fear that others would think they are boasting. I don't know which is worse—the loneliness of failure or the loneliness of success.

Some suffer from the loneliness of sorrow. Alone in your grief you mourn for someone who is gone. Others suffer the loneliness of sickness and pain and may not even tell their spouse or their children how much it hurts. They simply suffer in the loneliness of silence.

There is only one cure for loneliness. And that is the realization that there is One companion who understands, truly understands you. Only Christ can come and save you from loneliness—that isolation of the spirit. He alone is the cure for that negative emotion. Our hearts are homesick for companionship with our Creator. The Come-Alive-Power of Jesus Christ brings companionship!

I am not alone.
Jesus Christ is my constant companion!

COME-ALIVE-POWER

"In response to all He has done for us, let us outdo each other in being helpful and kind to each other and in doing good." -HEBREWS 10:24

When do you ever feel lonely? Describe what "lonely" means to you:

_____

_____

_____

Who are the lonely people around you? Think of several people who might be lonely. What could you do to ease their loneliness?

NAME   WHAT I COULD DO

_____   _____

_____   _____

_____   _____

_____   _____

_____   _____

*Because Christ gives me come~alive~
power, I am His instrument in easing
loneliness in those around me.*

COME-ALIVE-POWER

"All your children shall be taught by the Lord... and great shall be the peace of your children." -ISAIAH 54:13

Years ago I had to discipline my youngest child, Gretchen. She was a darling girl, but she misbehaved and I had to punish her. She ran off to her room and closed the door behind her.

After a few minutes, I walked down the hall and listened at her door. Everything was so quiet so I turned the doorknob ever so slowly and peeked my head through the opening. There was her small figure hidden beneath the blankets.

As I walked over to the bed I noticed her treasured toys were scattered across the bed and cuddled next to her was her dolly. I stroked her hair and held her tear-stained face in my hands as I whispered, "Gretchen, are you awake?" She turned her head as she popped open her eyes. Still hugging her dolly, I knew she wanted to hug her daddy.

"Gretchen," I explained, "I disciplined you because I love you." Her hands came out from under the covers, let go of the dolly, and reached up around my neck. A dolly is never a substitute for a daddy. As she put her slippery wet cheek next to mine, I prayed, "Dear God, thank you for Gretchen!" That tender moment was a time of special communication between us.

God wants to love you, but you have to let go of your substitute. Let Jesus Christ love you today!

I come to You, Lord, because You understand me. Your love gives me come~alive power!

Unlock the Gate

"A dream comes through much activity." -ECCLESIASTES 5:3

What's holding you back? By now you know there is:

a goal you should be pursuing

a dream you should be launching

a plan you should be executing

a project you should be starting

a possibility you should be exploring

an opportunity you should be grabbing

an idea you should be working

a problem you should be tackling

a decision you should be making!

I say it's time to unlock the starting gate! NOW is the time to take action and STOP postponing. But what's holding you back? What are your favorite excuses for not beginning? Write them down:

I can't begin today because _____

_____

and because _____

_____

and also because _____

_____

I am enthusiastic and confident!
I am ready for all that God
has planned for me!

Unlock the Gate

"I have set before you an open door and no one can shut it..You have kept my word and have not denied my name." -REVELATION 3:8

Frieda Schulze was 87 when I heard her story. At 77 years of age she took the plunge toward a new life. "I still shudder a bit when I think about it," Frau Schulze said, "but it was worth it...I couldn't stand their politics," she added, shaking a gnarled finger for emphasis.

When the East Germans built the wall in Berlin, Frau Schulze lived on the ground floor of an apartment house smack on the border. The sidewalk was West Berlin, but the apartment house was in East Berlin. The windows on the ground floor were bricked up after a number of people had escaped through them. The remaining residents were moved to the upper floor apartments.

"They moved me up, too, and when I got to the new place I sat there as if I were paralyzed," she remarked. She had no lights, but plenty of light from the searchlights outside. Her sleep was interrupted constantly with shots, sirens, the voices of West Berliners urging someone to escape and the vulgarities of the East German guards.

Finally, Frau Schulze had enough. She climbed out on her window sill and was immediately spotted by West Berlin police. They called out the fire brigade with the nets and urged her to jump. Then she heard the door of her apartment kicked open and two East German guards grabbed her. Finally, she struggled free and jumped—to freedom. She opened the gate! It's never too late to begin!

Jesus sets me free.
I begin, today, with a clean slate!

Unlock the Gate

"My grace is sufficient for you, for my power is made perfect in weakness."
-2 Cor. 12:9 RSV

Thomas Carlyle had finished his tremendous manuscript on the French Revolution. He gave it to his neighbor, John Stuart Mill, to read. Several days later, Mill came to Carlyle's home pale and nervous. His maid had used the manuscript to start a fire!

Carlyle was in a frenzy for days. Two years of labor lost. He could never muster the energy to write again. A task that was largely overwhelming the first time. The thought of having to write the manuscript over was almost paralyzing.

One day, as Carlyle was walking the streets, he saw a stone mason building a long, high wall. He stood watching for a long time before he was suddenly impressed with the fact that the wall was being built *one brick at a time!* He took inspiration from that experience and decided, "I'll just write one page today, and then one page tomorrow. One page at a time—that's all I'll think about."

He started small and slow. The task was tedious, but he stayed with it and went on to finish the work. The end result was better than the first time!

Don't let bad memories or unfortunate incidents move in and dominate you. You can't get far looking in the rear-view mirror, you must look ahead!

God is mighty in the midst of me as I open myself to Him. I can do all things!

Unlock the Gate

Deep within myself
I have a powerful awareness that
I have made the right decision
and am moving in the right direction.

I will let nothing and no one
deter, detour, distract, depress, or defeat me.
"No man having put his hand to the plow and
looking back is fit for the kingdom of God."

God's spirit is rising within me
now,
making me very determined
to faithfully keep the beautiful promises
I've made.
I will be faithful.
I am reliable.
Thank you, God.
Amen

*Today brings me a glorious
new possibility to survive
and to thrive.
It is a time to move ahead!*

Unlock the Gate

"Forgetting these things we are behind...I press toward the goal for the prize of the upward call of God." -PHILIPPIANS 3:13,14

Have you had so many victories, successes and accomplishments that you're tired and you've decided to back off? Do you look at the trophies, the awards and the prizes of yesterday and lean on these laurels? A salesman told me, "I've gone downhill ever since I won the highest award my company can give in sales. I guess I was trying to prove something to someone and now I don't seem to care anymore."

How do you overcome feelings like that? Perhaps you feel that way even though you haven't been to the top—the struggle has been too difficult. Either way, I suggest you try letting God restimulate you. Read the verse above several times. Let its meaning sink into your mind. Now rewrite the verse in your own words, relating it to your own situation:

_____

_____

_____

_____

Then remind yourself that ease will always lead to disease. As soon as you stop struggling, you lose your power. Press on!

There is a way! I am filled with power as I press forward!

Unlock the Gate

"If you wait for perfect conditions, you will never get anything done."
-*Ecclesiastes 11:4 (LB)*

Several years ago I disciplined myself to jog several miles each day. Then I fell off a ladder, was hospitalized for a short time and then restricted in any physical activity for several months. Of course, I got out of the rigorous self-disciplined habit of jogging. To get myself going again, I mentally told myself that if I started by walking, I would keep my heart healthy, stay thinner, even look younger and maintain a good posture. But still I put off all exercise.

Then one day my barber told me to wash my hair every day for a week and take a walk to dry it. That did it! I had the extra prod to get started. Prior to that time I had good reasons to begin, but it took someone else to push me out the door and get started. My barber unlocked my starting gate!

Have you started yet? If you are at the beginning, build a sense of urgency into your thinking and get going. Just do a little bit—just enough to begin. Decide only to take that first step. Then decide to take the second step. And then the third. Now tell yourself, "I've got a great thing going—I must not stop!"

Remember, the hardest part of any job is getting started. So what are you going to do today to get started?

_____

_____

Beginning is half done! Already I can feel energy flowing into me as I begin the creative task God has given me!

Unlock the Gate

"Beloved, what manner of love the Father has bestowed on us that we should be called children of God!" -1 JOHN 3:1

The human brain is made up of the cortex and the thalamus. The brain is like a walnut—the outside bark is the cortex. In fact, the word cortex means "bark." The inner part of the brain is the thalamus. Now the thalamus is the center of feeling and emotion, while the cortex is the intelligent, thinking part of you.

If your cortex—the thinking you—says, "It's a good idea," while your thalamus—the emotional you—objects saying, "I can't get in the mood," then in these situations, use your head! Use your cortex!

DON'T LET YOUR THALAMUS MANIPULATE YOUR CORTEX!

The thalamus is the inner nerve center and is the active part of the brain in a newborn child. It is the selfish, grasping brain that says, "I want what I want when I want it." If you are not doing what you know you should do, then your thalamus is running your cortex. The baby is running the adult. The emotions have the upper hand over your common sense.

This is true, not only about tasks you set for yourself, it also works in your relationship to God. There will be days when you do not feel like a child of God. Don't listen to your feelings. Listen to the facts—YOU ARE A CHILD OF GOD! Don't let your thalamus rule your cortex!

I keep my thoughts tuned to God.
My attention is on His power.

God's Presence

"If anyone is in Christ, he is a new creation; old things are passed away, behold all things become new." -2 CORINTHIANS 5:17

God's presence—behind you, in front of you and around you. You can feel it, know it, believe it, have it and hold on to it; you can face anything, anytime, anywhere, and win—really win!

I really believe that God is before me, behind me and around me. One thing I know—I never asked to be born. I did not choose my father or mother. I did not choose my race, the color of my skin, or the language that I learned as a child in my family home. I did not choose the community in which I was born and raised. I did not choose the school I attended from the first grade through high school. It was not until I graduated from high school that there were forces around me which caused me to select my college, and which influenced me to move in certain directions.

One thing I believe. There is a sense of destiny in my life. There is also a sense of destiny about your life. Everything I've said about myself, you could say about yourself. You are God's idea. You are God's dream!

A poet once said that he wished there was a wonderful place called the Land of Beginning Again, where all our cares, heartaches and griefs could be dropped like a shabby old coat at the door and never put on again. Well, there is such a place—the Land of Beginning Again. It is called NOW. In His mercy, God has granted each of us a new beginning at the dawn of each new day. When God is present within us, all things become new!

New beginnings are always open to me for God is with me!

God's Presence

"The Lord will go ahead of you, and He, the God of Israel, will protect you from behind." -ISAIAH 52:12

God is with you! He goes before you. He stands behind you! He walks alongside of you. So often, we take His presence with us for granted. Only when difficulties hit and we feel that God has forsaken us, are we conscious of our desire for God to be with us.

Today, I want you to think back over the past several weeks or months. Identify an experience in your life where God's presence was clearly seen, if not during the experience, at least in hindsight. Describe that experience:

_____

_____

_____

_____

_____

Now based on that experience, write out an affirmation that will help remind you in the future that God IS present with you, in spite of what the circumstances might appear to say.

_____

_____

I am living today controlled by my God~inspired positive ideas!

God's Presence

"Be confident of this very thing, that god who has begun a good work in you will complete it..." -PHILIPPIANS 1:6

Isaiah says that the Lord will protect you from behind. God is your rear guard. This comes from a scene of battle. In the Israelite campaigns, in the wilderness and across the promised land, the soldiers always had a vanguard and a rear guard. The vanguard was the scouts that went on ahead to explore the unexplored territory and to suggest a plan to move forward. The rear guard always stayed behind to pick up the pieces and make sure they didn't leave anything valuable behind.

God is our rear guard. I really believe that God is the rear guard in my life. I keep moving along, as you do, sometimes living at too fast a pace, doing things incompletely. But God follows up and finishes what I have done in a half-way measure. I can be confident that God, Who has begin a good work in you and me, will complete it.

If you were to take the time to look back, how many tasks would you find incomplete because of the urgency of some new task which called you away before the first task was finished? If you have done your best, God will do the rest! I've talked to parents about their teen-agers. They say, "If only we had..." And I gently remind them they did their best. Now they must trust the rear guard action of God, Who finishes the job and picks up the broken pieces, mending them into something wonderful and beautiful. God is that kind of a God!

*Thank you, God, for finishing the task
I have not completed.*

God's Presence

"I will never, never fail you nor forsake you." -HEBREWS 13:5

Edith, a very dear old friend, was like a mother to me when I was first in California. She was old, and lived in a rest home. As often as I could, I dropped in to see her. She would hug me and we kissed each other. I always said to her, "Mom, I will never forget you."

Her eyes would brighten as she held me and said, "Do you mean that, Bob?" And I assured her, "Yes, Mom, I mean it!"

Edith's only son was killed in World War II, so she used me as a substitute for him. I was able to fill a portion of that vacuum in her life, and our family adopted her as our first California grandmother. We cared for her until the day she died. We did not want her to be forgotten and forsaken.

Where are you feeling forsaken today? Briefly describe the situation:

_____

_____

Now think of that situation and read again the verse from Hebrews 13:5. If God is with you in that situation where you feel forsaken, what confidence can you have? Describe how God's presence in that situation changes both the situation and you:

_____

_____

_____

In spite of the circumstances and in spite of my feelings I believe God is with me. I can begin to feel His presence! I can feel my attitude beginning to change!

GOD'S PRESENCE

"May the Lord bless and keep you; the Lord make his face shine upon you; and be gracious to you, and give you His peace." -NUMBERS 6:24-26

When Napoleon retreated from Russia, he left the rear guard action in the hands of Marshal Ray. Months passed; the army had all arrived safely in Paris. The battle was over. In the officer's club one night, some were wondering what had happened to the rear guard. One said they were probably wiped out completely. At that moment the door opened and into the room stepped a gaunt, haggard man. Staring blankly from sunken eyes and wearing the tattered uniform of a French general, he just stood there.

"Who are you?" one of the officers finally asked. "I am Marshal Ray." The officers gasped, stood at once and saluted. Then one man ventured the question, "Marshal, where is the rear guard?"

The Marshal dropped his head as he answered, "I am the rear guard. There are no others."

As Christians we look at the cross and see Jesus Christ. He is our rear guard—there are no others! And in that action He is picking up the pieces, rehabilitating, restoring, filling the voids we left vacant.

If you're carrying an old box full of unnecessary clutter, leave it behind and let God handle it. If you have hurt someone, pray for them, talk with them, and let God heal the hurt. God goes before you, stands behind you and walks with you!

Peace fills my heart and mind for I know that God is with me!

God's Presence

"Let me see your kindness to me in the morning, for I am trusting you. Show me where to walk, for my prayer is sincere." -PSALM 143:8 (LB)

Arthur Gordon is a favorite writer of mine. Once he came to New York to interview Dr. Blanton, a co-founder of the American Foundation for Religion and Psychiatry. Mr. Gordon sat in a restaurant waiting for the esteemed psychiatrist to arrive. As he waited, his mind went back over his life. By the time Mr. Blanton arrived, Mr. Gordon was sitting there with a frown and a very sad look on his face.

"What's the matter, Arthur?" "Oh," the writer replied, "I've just been sitting here thinking about all the 'ifs' in my life." Dr. Blanton suggested, "Let's drive over to my office after lunch; I want you to hear something."

Later in his office, Dr. Blanton put on a tape and said, "I'm going to let you listen to three different people; they're all patients of mine and they are mentally ill. Listen carefully."

For one hour the great author listened. When the tape was finished, Dr. Blanton asked, "Tell me what single trait all these people had in common." Arthur Gordon thought a moment and then answered, "I can't think of anything."

"Then I'll tell you," the psychiatrist said. "All of them kept repeating the phrase, 'If only...if only...if only.' These words cause mental sickness. They are like poison. These people must learn to say, 'Next time...next time...next time.' These words point to the future, to a new day, to healing and health!"

I trust my past to God.
My eyes are on the future!

God's Presence

"Behold, I will do a new thing...I will even make a road in the wilderness and rivers in the desert." -Isaiah 43:19

God is not only the rear guard, but remember, He is the vanguard also—going on ahead of us. As you look into the future you try to imagine what it will be like. Well, I have news for you. God sees problems of which you are totally unaware coming your way. But He will always lead you through those problems, smoothing and straightening out the road ahead of you.

What is a leader? A leader is the one at the head of a business, a company, a corporation, an institution or a family. The leader is the one who sees problems that no one else sees and then finds solutions for those problems.

God is our leader. He takes action, quietly, subtly, but strongly; He directs and molds and shapes events so that the right solutions become available to you at the right time. He is prepared even before you are aware of the problem. That is the kind of God you and I have—the vanguard moving on ahead.

Some of you look ahead and see little hope as you imagine your future. Don't ever lose sight of God. He is there constantly ahead of you. Give your life completely to Him. His plan for you is to guide you and lead you. Is there some sin hidden inside of you blocking that vision? Drop it. Do you have a dream? Hold on to it. Is there some goal? Reach for it. God is with you. NOW is the time to move out—today!

God is giving me the courage to move ahead. I can make right decisions because God goes before and guides me!

God's Peace

"Then Jesus arose and rebuked the wind and said to the sea, Peace. Be still! and the wind ceased and there was a great calm." -MARK 4:39

A few years ago, Mrs. Schuller and I boarded a huge 747 in Singapore. From the airport, it looked like a pretty nice day. As we took off, and before the plane was at its full elevation, in the stage of flight when there was nothing the plane could do but climb, we suddenly ran into a terrible squall. It was a fierce storm. The 747 seemed to stall as it tried to plunge its way against a rainstorm. Tons of water slapped against the mammoth machine as it coughed and clawed its way through the tropical storm.

Suddenly the seat belt lights went on and the captain said in a calm voice, "Everybody please be seated." Everyone complied, and as I looked around I saw total anxiety on the faces of all the people in the cabin. We made it safely over the China Sea via Thailand, and skirting over Vietnam, back home to Los Angeles.

I realized later what gave me confidence during that whole experience was the voice of the captain. He spoke calmly, firmly, and reassuringly. It reminded me that you and I need that same commanding voice as we head into the private storms of life. We can have that confidence when we have faith that God is in control.

I am serene, calm, undismayed because Jesus Christ gives me His peace!

GOD'S PRESENCE

"God will keep in perfect peace the one whose mind is stayed on Him. For in the Lord is everlasting strength." -ISAIAH 26:3,4

Jesus talks about peace of heart and mind in the midst of trials and sorrows. How can you reconcile those two thoughts in His statement? Suppose someone had just written you a letter. In that letter, it says," I thought as a Christian I was supposed to experience peace of mind. But all I experience is chaos, turmoil and anything but peace of mind. Help me!"

What would you write to them in your return letter?

Write your response here: *I can understand how you feel, but here are some thoughts which may help you:*

_____

_____

_____

_____

_____

_____

_____

*I am centered in God's perfect plan for me.
Nothing can disturb my sense of peace!*

God's Peace

"These words which I commend you today shall be in your heart...you shall love the Lord your God with all your heart, with all your soul and with all your might." -Deuteronomy 6:5,6

I have discovered several principles which, if you apply them to your daily life, will bring you peace of mind. First, enjoy that moment called "Now."

A famous author was raised in the Caucasus Mountains. An old hermit lived up in the hills. It was the custom for parents to take their children to visit the old man.

The author's parents took him, along with a gift for the old recluse. In return the hermit would impart some of his wisdom. When they arrived, there were other families waiting. They stayed until it was their turn. Then the young boy walked timidly up to the stern-faced man with the long beard. Reaching out a wrinkled old hand, the gentle man lifted the young boy to his lap, put his arm around him and then waved the other people away.

The young boy handed the sage the little gift he had brought. Taking it, the wise man smiled and asked, "Son, what do you want to do? Where do you want to go? What do you want to be in life?"

The lad answered as best he could, and then listened to some wondrous tales of the places the old man had been and what wonderful things he had done in his long, long lifetime. Suddenly he looked the boy straight in the eye and said, "My boy, I want to give you something that will be wonderful while you are young as well as when you are old. Something you can use when you're sad and when you're happy. Here it is; never forget it! This moment! Each moment in life is part of eternity. Enjoy it!"

Now is the most important moment in my life. I shall enjoy it!

God's Peace

"Do not worry about tomorrow. God will take care of your tomorrow too. Live one day at a time." -MATTHEW 6:34

Jesus was always intense about the moment. It is amazing to realize how often we fail to live in the reality of the present moment. We either project ourselves into tomorrow, or fill our thoughts with regret about yesterday.

But think about it. The only thing you can be positive about in life is this present moment. Tomorrow may never come and yesterday is gone forever.

How do you enjoy the moment called "Now"? It's a habit developed through practice. It's a matter of self-discipline in order to enjoy a bird feeding in your backyard, to watch the trees bend in the wind, or to linger over the rose growing along the neighbor's fence.

How much time do you spend in the "Now"? Think back over yesterday. How much time did you spend worrying about the future? How much time thinking about the past? How much time enjoying the present moment?

Today I will spend _____ of my time planning my future.

Today I will spend _____ of my time remembering the past.

Today I will spend _____ of my time enjoying the present!

Determine now to live today enjoying the present moments as they unfold. If something about the future comes to mind, make a note. If you remember something of the past, commit it to prayer. Then enjoy to the fullest each moment God gives you!

I will live today as if that is all I have.
God is in the Now!

OD'S PEACE

Sunshine after rain,
dewdrops on a rose,
a baby sleeping sweetly in the crib,
a bird drinking from a fountain,
a leaf floating on quiet water, and
a mind focused on God.

Such is the peace I feel
deep within my being
now
as
I close my eyes and think about Jesus Christ!

Thank you, God.
Amen.

Jesus, help me to explore all the wonderful facets of life!.

God's Peace

"Now acquaint yourself with God, and be at peace; thereby good will come to you." -Job 22:21

To have peace of mind it is necessary to eliminate polyphasic thinking. Now that's a fancy word that simply means the practice of thinking about many things at one time. Many of us have this habit. I got a ticket on the freeway not too long ago due to polyphasic thinking. My mind was occupied with several things. I paid the penalty!

A leading cardiologist pointed out that polyphasic people are more susceptible to heart disease. His remedy—eliminate the distractions and concentrate on one thing at a time!

The computer is patterned after the mind. Like our brain, it has many channels. We can feed our minds through the eye, the ear, the sense of touch or smell. And each of these channels has many variations. Now if you try to feed information into a computer on more than one channel, you're going to clog up the system.

A computer expert told me that the most glorified, sophisticated, exacting computer made cannot be working on two problems at the same time. It goes crazy.

We can't work on two or more problems at the same time, either. Jesus taught the principle that no man can serve two masters. Singleness of mind is the key to peace of mind.

Eliminate polyphasic thinking today! Discipline yourself to think about one thing at a time!

My mind is clearly focused on one thing at a time. Today is peaceful because my channels are not clogged!

GOD'S PEACE

"The Lord will give strength unto His people; the Lord will bless His people with peace." -PSALM 29:11

Let's do some planning to help eliminate polyphasic thinking in the coming weeks. First, make a list of the eight most important things you will need to do:

1. _____

2. _____

3. _____

4. _____

5. _____

6. _____

7. _____

8. _____

Now go back over your list and number them in order of their importance. The most important task will get number 1, etc. Resolve to concentrate on that most important task first. When something else comes up, go back to work on your priority. Pray that God will give you singleness of mind which leads to peace of mind!

I am calm and peaceful, for God is directing my steps!

God's Peace

"I will lie in peace and sleep, for You alone, O Lord, make me dwell in safety." -Psalm 4:8 (NKJ)

Some time back I had the privilege of having lunch with the president of one of the largest aerospace companies. Following lunch, he took me on a tour of his large facility.

What really impressed me was the clean room. My host explained to me that the clean room is so spotless because no particle can pass through the air conditioning system into that room unless it is small enough to fit on the point of a needle. He told me something I didn't know before. The point of a needle is really flat. Put a needle under a microscope and you will see that the point is literally flat. And the largest speck that can come into the clean room will be able to rest on the flat part of the needle point!

To enter that room I had to clear security and then they had to make sure I was clean. It was fascinating, as well as a thought-provoking experience.

You should have a clean room at the center of your life. Your mind should be your own personal clean room. You should have security checks on who and what enters your room. There are some writers I refuse to read because they fill me with negative thoughts, some ideas, some practices that don't pass security. Have you been careless? I suggest you begin today to set up your clean room at the very core of your mind. A place so clean that both you and God are comfortable there. God's dwelling place!

I am careful about what enters my mind. I think only those thoughts and do those things that foster peace of mind!

PEACE OF MIND

"Let us then pursue what makes for peace and for mutual upbuilding."
-ROMANS 14:19 RSV

Imagine that you have a filter that clears everything entering your mind. What thoughts, ideas, and practices would be filtered out? Which would be permitted to enter? Think carefully about what enters your mind and then make two lists:

PASSES SECURITY	FILTERED OUT

Spend some time in prayer, talking with God about your lists. Ask for His help in filtering out all those thoughts, ideas, and practices that threaten to destroy your peace of mind. He will!

Today I accept those thoughts, ideas and practices which are pleasing to God, He is with me and gives me peace!

PEACE OF MIND

"Do not worry about your life, what you will eat or what you will drink, nor about your body, what you will put on. Is not life more than food and the body more than clothing?" -MATTHEW 6:25

Another principle that leads to peace of mind is to learn to live by the calendar, not by the clock. An enormous amount of inner agitation, emotional disturbance and turbulence, along with disruption of emotional poise and peace comes when we make mountains out of molehills.

Look at a calendar. If you try to think of the year as 365 days, it becomes unmanageable. But when you think of the year as twelve months, already time falls into order. Something else will happen to you. You will start to look at the larger picture.

A great lecturer and writer, Emily Kimbrough, tells about a lesson she once learned. As a little girl ten years old, ready to go on stage for a performance at school, she became very upset because her hair didn't look right. She got frantic—almost hysterical. Her grandmother was with her and said, "Emily, this is nonsense. You would never notice it from a trotting horse."

Emily remembered that advice. Years later she was preparing to lecture to a large audience when she noticed a run in her stocking. For a moment she felt panic; then she remembered Grandma's advice: "Nonsense, Emily, you would never notice it from a trotting horse!"

What you think is so upsetting today is just like trotting by, and a year from now nobody will even think about it, not even you. Live by the calendar, not by the clock.

Lord, help me to major in the majors as I live today!

PEACE OF MIND

"And this is the promise that God has promised us — eternal life." -JOHN 2:25

Peace of mind comes when we make our peace with eternity. Dr. Peale told of an experience he had as a young boy that shaped his life. He was living in Ohio, where his father, a former medical doctor, was a preacher.

One cold winter night his father received a desperate call to visit someone who was dying. His father hung up the phone, turned to his son and said, *"Norman, I think that since you're growing up and fast becoming a young man, you ought to go along with me."*

They drove to a part of town known as the Red Light district. The woman who was waiting showed them into the room. There, lying on a bed, was a young woman. The fingers of her childlike hands were spread apart, and lay flat and still on the sheet. She hardly stirred as her breath came in short gasps.

As the older man approached her bed he could see she was very ill. Picking up the girl's tiny hand he looked at her and said, *"My girl, you're very sick."*

Tears rolled down her face as she said, *"Sir, I was raised in a Christian home. How did I ever get here? Oh, will God ever forgive me?"* Her small body trembled as she wept, and Norman's father said, *"Little lady, do you love Jesus?"* She nodded yes. *"Can you repeat with sincerity this prayer?"* Again, she nodded yes, and prayed the Sinner's Prayer. As she said, "Amen," the most beautiful peace came over that young girl's face. A moment later she was gone.

Old thoughts and old conditions are passed away. I am at peace with God and eternity.

PEACE OF MIND

"Therefore, we have peace with God through our Lord Jesus Christ."
-ROMANS 5:1 RSV

Woven throughout this beautiful, peace-generating, love-spreading, power-producing faith we call Christianity is the theme that we have peace with God through our Lord Jesus Christ. St. Paul wrote and told the Romans, *"So now, since we have been made right in God's sight by faith in His promises, we can have real peace with Him because of what Jesus Christ our Lord has done for us."* Jesus said, *"The important thing is the your names are registered as citizens of heaven."*

There is an eternal consciousness hovering over us. It is an awareness that after this life is over, something else is going to happen. And until we can make peace with eternity, we're just not sure what will happen.

But when we do make peace with eternity, we have peace! Have you made peace with eternity? I know of only one person who can help you do that—Jesus Christ. Only He can forgive your sins. Only He can turn your life around and give you peace. Commit your life to Him today, if you haven't already done so. Then write your commitment below:

_____

_____

_____

I commit myself to God.
My heart sings a new song of peace!

PEACE OF MIND

"If anyone has a complaint against another, even as Christ forgave you, so you also must do." -COLOSSIANS 3:13

Some time ago a family came to our church who had just moved to California from New York. They said they couldn't stand another winter shoveling snow in the east. They decided to live the rest of their lives basking in the warm climate of California.

I have a better idea than that. Resolve today to spend the rest of your life basking in the beautiful climate of forgiveness, and be warmed by God's beautiful love. The spirit of forgiveness is the heart of love and leads to genuine peace of mind.

Every so often I used to spend an evening answering the telephone in our 24-hour telephone counseling center—NEW HOPE. People from all across the country call at all hours to a sympathetic ear and a heart that cares. They simply dial 639-4673. (Area code 714). These numbers spell NEW-HOPE.

Once, when I picked up a ringing phone and said, *"New Hope, may I help you?"* The voice on the other end of the line said, *"Oh, if you hadn't picked up the phone I would have committed suicide."* She went on to unveil a story of jealousy, hatred and resentment toward another woman who loved the same man she loved.

Thirty-five minutes later I said, *"You have a problem. Your biggest problem is that you need to forgive and be forgiven.""But how?"* she asked. And I had the joy of introducing her to Jesus Christ. As she invited Him into her life, her bitterness and hatred melted away. She discovered the source of peace!

As I forgive, I walk in peace!

PEACE OF MIND

"Lord, I need only one thing in this world:
To know myself, and to love God;
Give me, heavenly Father,
Your love and Your peace.
With these I am rich enough
and desire nothing more;
Sweet and humble heart of Jesus,
make my heart like yours.
Amen

JOHN XXIII

*I will try to follow your
perfect example, Jesus, Son of God!*

MORE THAN CONQUERORS

"Do not be overcome by evil, but overcome evil with good." -ROMANS 12:21

I'm collecting trophies! I hope you are. The trophies I'm trying to win are called the "More Than Conquerors" trophies. Here are some examples of how you can win one.

If you killed an enemy, you are a conqueror; if you turn your enemy into a friend, you are **more** than a conqueror!

If you pull the weeds out of your backyard, you are a conqueror; when you replace the weeds with fruit trees, you are more than a conqueror!

When you fight to overcome a hurt and do not strike back in anger at the one who hurt you, you are a conqueror; when you become so strong that troubles do not upset and defeat you, you are a conqueror; when you turn these troubles into productive and fruitful actions, you are **more** than a conqueror!

In Romans 12, Paul tells us "to overcome evil with good." When we cooperate with God, we can turn our troubles into triumphs. That always wins a "More Than Conqueror" trophy.

Cooperate with God. Here are three simple ways you can turn your troubles into triumphs:

1. Give God **thanks**—when you face a problem.

2. Give God **time**—to turn your problem into a triumph.

3. Give God **trust**—every waiting moment!

God and I are working to turn my troubles into triumphs!

More Than Conquerors

"In everything give thanks." -I THESSALONIANS 5:18

Carl Sandburg tells the story about Abe Lincoln at the age of seven. One evening, Abe walked over to his cabin door and opened it. He looked up into the face of the full moon and said, *"Mr. Moon, what do you see from way up there?"*

Mr. Moon answered, *"Abe, I see a calendar and it says 1816. I see eight million people in the United States of America. I see 16,000 covered wagons plodding slowly across the midwestern plains toward California. And, Abe, I see far to the west a wagon in the desert between two ridges of the Rocky Mountains. The wagon is broken, weeds are crawling in the spokes and there is an old dusty skeleton nearby with a pair of empty moccasins and some dry bones. I also see a sign that says, "The cowards never started!"*

Troubles? Give God thanks! The very fact that you are facing troubles is a compliment to you—you had the courage to stick your neck out and try something. When you have this attitude toward troubles, they generally turn into blessings, compliments, or tributes. When trouble blocks the road and forces you to take a detour which, in turn, spares you from an accident, then trouble becomes a blessing.

When suffering forces you to unload excess baggage in your life which you have not had the courage to get rid of before, then trouble is a blessing in disguise! Give God thanks when you face a problem!

I do not always understand what is happening in my life, but I can thank God always for He is with me!

MORE THAN CONQUERORS

"You meant evil against me, but God meant it for good in order to save many people alive." GENESIS 50:20 (NKJ)

What problem or trouble are you faced with today? Describe it briefly:

_____

_____

_____

_____

Now, use your imagination and think of all the possible blessings that could come out of that problem or trouble:

_____

_____

_____

_____

_____

_____

Give God thanks—even as you face trouble!

I will let go of anxiety, bitterness and tension and let God and His goodness take over my life!

MORE THAN CONQUERORS

"The Lord will command His loving kindness in the daytime, and in the night His song shall be with me — a prayer to the God of my life." -PSALM 42:8

Just before Dr. Poppen, one of the most inspiring missionaries I know, returned home from China, the communists had his name tagged. He was earmarked for destruction. After spending forty years in mainland China, devoting his life to Christ's service, he was now a house prisoner.

At the public trial ten thousand people gathered in the city square. Dr. Poppen was paraded onto a platform, falsely accused on many accounts, the most serious being that of treason against the state.

Following the trial, he was led to a tiny prison cell. He could not stand up straight or even lie down straight. There he remained, not knowing what his fate would be. Day after day passed, until that great man of God could take no more. He prayed that God would take him and then fell asleep.

Suddenly he was awakened as the door opened and someone whispered, *"Follow me."* He was led through a winding, dark cobblestoned alley until he found himself at the wharf. His companion said, *"See that boat? Get on quickly. It will take you to Hong Kong. When you get there, vanish. Good-bye."*

As Henry Poppen watched the China mainland disappear, he did not know what lay ahead. He was grateful to God for his freedom and he was thankful that he had given God time to turn his overwhelming problem into triumph. Give God time and you will be more than conqueror!

I am patient. I wait expectantly for God to turn my trouble into triumph!

More Than Conquerors

"Be of Good courage, and He shall strengthen our heart, all you who hope in the Lord." -Psalm 31:24

If I were asked to create a "More Than Conqueror" trophy or banner, I would include the figure of a person standing straight and tall. This person would be holding in one hand a banner upon which would be a shield, on which would be the word, **HOPE.**

That's my idea. What would you create?

Use the space below to draw a "More Than Conqueror" trophy or banner.

*Today, through Christ,
I am more than conqueror!*

More Than Conquerors

"O Lord God, who is mighty like You? You have a mighty arm. Strong is Your hand and high is Your right hand." -Psalms 89:13

When I was a young boy, I decided to put my saddle on a strange horse pastured on our farm. I rode off heading for the far reaches of our property. Everything was so beautiful. I can still see the day—sun shining brightly, puffy white clouds floating lazily across the Iowa sky, the temperature just right.

I rode along for some time, when suddenly the horse became startled at the sight of a tractor. He shied away and took off at a fast pace. I tugged at the reins, shrieked at him to stop, kicked his sides furiously—yet nothing even phased him!

Foaming at the mouth, with nostrils wide and quivering, and eyes wild with fear, he raced wildly across the gullies and blindly through the pasture. As he galloped along crazily, I bounced up and down, back and forth. All I could do was to hold on to the saddle horn for dear life. I squeezed my eyes shut and held on until my knuckles turned white. Unexpectedly, miraculously, the horse stopped as suddenly as he had begun. I opened my eyes and there we were in front of the barn door!

If life is taking you on a wild ride, grab hold of the saddle horn. Take a firm hold, because in life the saddle horn is God's mighty arm. Give God trust—every waiting moment!

I give thanks for my circumstances because God is working them for my good! I give thanks in advance!

More Than Conquerors

"We know that to those who love God, who are called according to His plan, everything that happens fits into a pattern for good." -ROMANS 8:28 (PHILLIPS)

God knows the future better than I do, therefore I trust Him! Romans 8:28 is a theme verse for my trust. Are you trusting God in the midst of your trouble? Where are you having difficulty trusting Him?

_____

_____

_____

God understands! Write yourself a letter from God about His reaction to your difficulty trusting Him. In your letter, rewrite Romans 8:28, using your difficult situation as an example of one of the things God "fits into a pattern for good."

_____

_____

_____

My faith is stronger! I can feel trust welling up within me. I am confident that God can work this out for good!

GOD'S PROSPERITY

"Blessed are you who delight in the law of the Lord ... whatever you do will prosper." -PSALM 1:1-3

I believe in God's prosperity for my life. In Psalm 1, we read that there are people who are so engrafted into God that they are like trees planted by rivers of water, bringing forth fruit every season. They live consistently productive lives! God wants your life to prosper! In the next few days look at **seven principles of prosperity for your life.**

Prosperity Principle #1: Say something positive about every person and every idea you encounter.

There is usually something wrong with every person and idea you meet. Therefore, do not discard a potentially profitable idea simply because there is an objectionable element present. Do not ignore an interesting, helpful person because of some negative quality in his or her life.

Rather, assume that you can isolate, insulate, and then eliminate or neutralize the negative elements by simply cultivating, exploiting, and capitalizing on the positive elements. Try it: What is the most negative force in your life today?

_____

Now write down every positive aspect of that force you can think of:

_____

_____

My attitude is changing. I am looking for the positives and paying less attention to the negatives!

God's Prosperity

"The Lord will give you an abundance of good things...just as He promised." -DEUTERONOMY 28:11 (LB)

Prosperity Principle #2: See the positive possibilities in every situation.

To achieve success, sell your ideas. Sell them more zealously if you have a problem. I talked with a young minister whose ideas for his church were buried under a mountain of problems, the most pressing of which was a leaky photocopier! The tight church budget could include neither a secretary nor a new photocopier.

One afternoon he struggled to print the coming Sunday's church bulletins. He succeeded only in getting ink stains all over his clothes and wasted a whole package of paper. In complete disgust he decided to wear those clothes to the board meeting that evening.

Several hours later, he was showing the mess to his board. These men were businessmen and quickly realized that they were wasting money and that it would cost even more money to wait. One man pulled out his wallet and said, *"Reverend, here is $25.00."* Another man matched that, and soon the minister had collected enough for a new photocopier.

He was overcome with joy and disbelief. Then he thought to himself, *"Possibility thinking really works!"*

Soon he picked up on some of his other ideas. He started to "See the positive possibilities in every situation." He went out visiting, exuberantly urging people to come to his church. The congregation started growing. His people saw a more confident minister. In time they purchased twenty acres for a new church complex. And it all started with a messy photocopier!

*In every situation today,
I will look for the positive!*

God's Prosperity

"God is able to provide you with every blessing in abundance, so that you may always have enough of everything and may provide in abundance for every good work." -2 CORINTHIANS 9:8 RSV

Prosperity Principle #3: Develop the daily habit of always thinking "it might work."

A maid named Matilda did this. Her employer, a wealthy woman, was concerned when she learned that Matilda had no savings for the future. She said, *"Matilda, suppose we lose our investments; suppose I have to let you go; then suppose you cannot find new work; suppose you do not have an income? What are you going to do?*

Matilda replied, *"That is all you do...suppose, suppose, suppose. There is no **suppose** in my Bible; there is only **repose.** My Bible says, 'Surely goodness and mercy shall follow me all the days of my life.'"* Psalm 23.

We get caught up in the "suppose it won't work" syndrome. It's time to change that to "it might work!"

Where in your life do you need to start affirming, "It might work!"? Take what appears to be an impossible situation that you are facing this week and think of four ways that it just might possibly work:

1. _____

2. _____

3. _____

4. _____

God wants me to prosper. Whatever I touch, in faith, will work out!

GOD'S PROSPERITY

"Light is sown for the godly and joy for the good." -PSALM 97:11 (LB)

Prosperity Principle #4: Appoint yourself president of your own "Why Not" club.

Ed is a brilliant young lawyer who recently moved to California. He and his wife, Pat, have no relatives out here, and as Thanksgiving drew near, they realized they were alone. But they also realized that hundreds of old people in the area were forsaken and lonely. So they decided to found a **"Why Not"** club. Ed was president and Pat was vice president.

They decided to have a Thanksgiving dinner for those lonely forgotten people. Ed went to one of the local hotels and asked if there was a big, empty convention banquet hall available for Thanksgiving. He explained his plan to the manager, but received a very curt "No." Undaunted, Ed asked, **"Why not?"** The manager was taken back, thought for a moment and then agreed, "All right!"

Then Ed went to some of the companies his law firm dealt with and asked them for money for the dinner. He knew they had money for charities, but received the expected, "No, we have a policy about our donations. Your plan doesn't meet our policy." **"Why not?"** Ed asked. Again, he was successful and raised the necessary funds. They made all the arrangements and then waited for Thanksgiving noon to arrive.

At 11:40, the first guest arrived—a little old lady. By noon over 300 people shared the spirit of Thanksgiving because Ed and Pat asked the question, **"Why not?"**

If someone else can succeed and prosper, **why not you?**

I am ready for the success and prosperity God has for me!

$\mathcal{G}$OD'S PROSPERITY

"Beloved, I pray that you may prosper in all things and be in health, just as your soul prospers." -III JOHN 2

Prosperity Principle #5: Honor every positive idea that comes into your mind with the D.I.N. degree.

When positive ideas come into my mind, I write them down on paper immediately. I think this is important, especially if you want to prosper—write it down. Then, in front of every good idea, write **D.I.N.** That means **Do It Now!**

Sir Alexander Fleming, a Scottish bacteriologist, discovered the life-saving antibiotic, penicillin. One morning in his laboratory, he observed that the fungus around the bacteria on a culture plate had died. He took a bit of the mold and put it in an empty glass tube for further study. The result—penicillin.

Sir Alexander observed something interesting and he did something about it immediately. He was definitely a person who believed in honoring an intriguing idea with the **D.I.N.** degree.

What could you do today about one of your positive ideas? What important step could you honor with the **D.I.N.** degree? Describe the step you will take today:

_____

_____

_____

_____

$\mathcal{I}$ lack nothing. $\mathcal{I}$ thank $\mathcal{G}$od for my prosperity as $\mathcal{I}$ act on $\mathcal{H}$is ideas and $\mathcal{H}$is riches!

God's Prosperity

"The blessing of the Lord makes one rich." -PROVERBS 10:22 RSV

Prosperity Principle #6: Practice the principle of positive expectations.

Why do some people always seem to prosper? Because they expect to prosper.

Several years ago, a minister and a group of his congregation decided at year's end to test the power of expectations. Each person wrote down his New Year's expectations, put them into an envelope, sealed them, and then agreed to meet and read them aloud at the same time the following year. The results were fascinating.

One man wrote, "In the next year all I can expect is more of the same old miserable life." What do you think he got?

A woman in the group listed ten worthy goals she expected to achieve. Nine of them had been accomplished by the time they met again. She admitted that because she expected to reach these goals, she really worked hard at them.

Another man wrote, "As none of the men in my family have survived beyond the age of sixty, I expect I may die this year." He died one month before his sixtieth birthday!

Each person in the group was surprised to see that everyone got almost exactly what they expected.

Expect prosperity! Open yourself to new ideas, knowing that your energy, your resources, your supply comes from God's bountiful storehouse of riches. You have infinite resources and therefore you have infinite possibilities.

EXPECT PROSPERITY! EXPECT THE BEST! You will get what you expect.

I am prospered by God's rich resources.
I expect prosperity!

$\mathscr{G}$OD'S PROSPERITY

"I will open up the windows of heaven for you and pour out a blessing so great you won't have room enough to store it." -MALACHI 3:10

Prosperity Principle #7: Discipline yourself to become a positive reactionary.

Dr. Norman Vincent Peale was once asked how far he would go in applying Positive Thinking. He replied, "I apply it to all situations over which I have control." I agree!

Occasions will arise in your life over which you have no control. Suppose a loved one was killed in an automobile accident. You had no control over this tragic mishap. BUT you can control your reaction!

What will you do? What will this event do to you? Misfortune never leaves you where it found you. It changes you. You can change a negative event into a positive force for good. Become a positive reactionary. Use your head. Make the best of every situation. React positively!

J. Wallace Hamilton talked about being in the desert between the Arab and Israeli sections one time when the fighting was heavy. He saw a small boy playing on a flute and said, "Come here, lad." As the boy approached him, he noticed that the flute was made from a rifle barrel. An instrument of destruction had been turned into an instrument for making beautiful music. That's being a positive reactionary. That is turning obstacles into opportunities!

Right now, the Spirit of God is working within you to open up new opportunities. Prayer puts you in tune with God's ideas and attitudes. Open yourself to His abundant prosperity.

God's spirit is changing my attitudes.
I am a positive reactionary!

PRAYER IS THE KEY

"Lord, teach us to pray." -LUKE 11:1

I believe in prayer. It is the communion of my heart with the heart of the Eternal. Prayer has the power to do several things in my life. Today, I want you to focus on the *draining* power of prayer. This is a power that enables you to drain the negative emotion out of your life.

If you want to have the abundant life that Jesus Christ came to offer you, it is necessary to drain negative emotions out of your soul—fear, suspicion, distrust, hate, resentment, jealousy, insecurity, self-pity. Jesus Christ has the power to drain these defeatist feelings from your life. In their place, He will fill you with positive ideas—love, courage, hope, good humor, cheer, optimism, enthusiasm, self-confidence.

I once experienced a conflict with a person who was a terrible troublemaker. He destroyed his wife's life; he destroyed his son's life; he destroyed the lives of many people. I tried to help him and he turned on me. It was a terrifying experience. I woke up in the middle of the night, and my heart was filled with negative feelings toward him. I thought, it is not right for me to have such negative attitudes toward another person. I am a Christian; I am a follower of Christ.

As I lay in bed, I prayed that God would drain out of me all those negative feelings. I imagined myself as a car up on the grease rack with the mechanic underneath, removing the plug and letting all the dirty old oil pour out of the crankcase. And that is exactly what Christ did with my attitude toward this man. It was a miracle!

Prayer is a miracle!
As I pray, God works!

PRAYER IS THE KEY

"I love the Lord because He had heard my voice...therefore I will call upon Him as long as I live." -PSALM 116:1,2

The late Ruth Carter Stapleton shared with our congregation her special experience in prayer. *"When my daughter started the first grade, she began to have terrible pains. Up to that time, I loved my little girl so much I never let her out of my sight. I didn't realize then that it was my insecurity that caused me to be so over-protective. So when she started school, without my constant attention, she became sick. I took her to several doctors and they all said it wasn't a physical problem, so I took her to a psychiatrist.*

"'This child has deep emotional problems,' the doctor said. 'She will need therapy four days a week for a long time. We'll put her on the waiting list and call you.'

"I was devastated. My child was emotionally ill and I was the one responsible for her problems. I took my little girl home and every night after she went to bed, I would pray over her. I waited to make sure everybody was asleep because I wasn't sure God would answer my prayers. Each night I would pray, 'Lord Jesus, bridge the gap between the love she needed and the love she got.' I never missed a night!

"Seven months later, the clinic called and said I could bring her in to begin therapy. I took her immediately and they ran tests for two days. To the amazement of everyone, myself included, the results of those tests showed my daughter perfectly normal.

"Jesus reached back into the past as I prayed, and filled the empty places. That was the beginning of my prayer life!"

Through prayer, Jesus is changing me!

$\mathscr{P}$RAYER IS THE KEY

"Search me, O God, and know my heart; try me and know my anxieties and see if there is any wicked way in me, lead me in the way of everlasting life." -PSALM 139:23,24

We receive many letters at the Hour of Power and each one is special. This letter was especially touching: *"Two months ago I did not believe in God. I tried to commit suicide four times. I hated God. My life was nothing and I didn't care. No one could help; not the doctors or my husband! Then one Sunday my husband forced me to listen to the Hour of Power. Rev. Schuller, you were talking about making your enemies into your friends. I began to think.*

"I had not spoken to my parents for years. I hated them for putting me into a foster home as a child. They had tried to contact me, but I never answered. They were on top of my enemy list!

"As I thought about them as enemies, I decided it was time to make them friends. I asked my husband to take me to see them and when we arrived, I thought they would have a heart attack. But we talked, and I forgave them. I think that evening was the nicest time I had ever had in my life. Since then, all the anger and bitterness has drained away. Jesus does make a difference!"

As you pray and allow all the negative feelings to drain out of your life, is there someone you need to call or write? Why not sit down now and turn an enemy into a friend. It's all part of God's draining system!

I allow God to drain away all negative feelings. All my relationships are an expression of God's healing power!

PRAYER IS THE KEY

"When you pray, go into your room and when you have shut the door, pray to your Father who is in the secret place and your Father who sees in secret will reward you openly." -MATTHEW 6:8

A well known Indian from New Delhi, Sulwit Shoorar, was converted to Christianity. After his conversion, he let his hair grow in curls to his shoulders, dressed in a white tunic with a gold rope vest, and wore sandals on his tanned feet.

He was asked to come to America for a speaking tour through various Christian churches. Upon his acceptance, he was given the address of a minister in New York City. Shoorar put the address in safekeeping.

When he reached New York, he gave the slip of paper to a taxi driver. The taxi drove to the address and stopped, Shoorar paid the fare, stepped out, went to the door of the house, and rang the bell.

The minister's small son opened the door and stared wide-eyed at the tall man, dressed in a white robe, with long brown hair and large, dark, warm eyes. Looking down at the little boy, the man from India said, *"My name is Sulwit Shoorar. Is your father home?"*

The boy stammered, *"J-J-Just a minute."* He ran into the house and told his father there was someone at the front door to see him. His father asked, *"Who is it? What is his name?" "I can't remember what he said, Daddy,"* the boy answered, *"but he sure looks like Jesus."*

Prayer gives me gaining power—the ability to gain more and more the attitude and mind of Jesus Christ.

Jesus is the hero of my soul. I love to talk with Him in prayer!

PRAYER IS THE KEY

"Cast your burden on the Lord, and He will sustain you." -PSALM 55:22 RSV

Prayer gives you draining power, gaining power, and prayer also gives you *sustaining* power! Sustaining power is the power to hold on and never quit in life.

One of my favorite inspirational sayings was found scratched on the wall of a basement in Germany after World War II. A Jew in hiding had scratched the Star of David on the wall along with the following statement:

I believe in the sun even when it is not shining.
I believe in love even when I do not feel it.
I believe in God even when He is silent.

That's a power-filled faith. That kind of faith can only come to the person who knows the sustaining power of prayer. When all is darkness, this person is still basking in the warm sunlight of God's presence through prayer.

If you were trapped in a dark basement somewhere, what could you scratch on the wall? Write your own trilogy of faith:

I believe in _____

I believe in _____

I believe in _____

Amen!

I sing to the Lord because
He gives me sustaining power!

PRAYER IS THE KEY

"May my spoken words and unspoken thoughts be pleasing to you, O Lord my Rock and my Redeemer." -PSALM 19:14

The president of one of the country's largest steel companies learned an important lesson one day. A man came to see him and said, *"Sir, I know you have many advisors, but give me five minutes. If what I say is unimportant, you owe me nothing. If I have helped you, your company may send me a check for whatever amount you think this advice is worth."*

The chief executive brusquely said, *"All right, you have five minutes."* The man said, *"Here is a piece of paper. List the important things you have to do today. Now, please number the items according to priority of importance."* The company president did as he was instructed.

"Now," continued the visitor, *"begin with item number one and do not work on anything else until item number one is completed. Then go on to item number two and do the same thing. If you follow this procedure, and have your executives do the same, your company will improve its management, organization and profit."* Six months later, the man received a check for $25,000.

Why not do the same thing with your prayers? Make a list of the most important things you can pray for. Then number them according to priority and pray faithfully for item number one. You will want to pray for other things on your list, but make it a point to pray for item number one every time you pray. Then be ready—God is up to something great!

The power of prayer changes my life and the lives of others!

*P*RAYER IS THE KEY

"O Lord, I pray, send now prosperity." -PSALM 118:25

Dr. Viktor Frankl gave this definition of love: *"Love is the wanting to uncover the potential in people."*

That's how God loves you! It's how Jesus loves you! He wants to uncover the possibilities within you.

Relieving power produces believing power. Believing power is the beginning of success! Because the person you see in your mind is the person you will be!

Michelangelo had a huge chunk of marble that had been cast aside by sculptor after sculptor because it was too long and too narrow. When asked what it was for, he said, "I see David." He chiselled and carved, and when he finished there was David. He saw David in the marble and he created David in the marble.

Pray right now that God will begin to reveal the wonderful potentials He has hidden in you.

*My believing power is
my beginning of success.*

ABUNDANT LIVING

"What does the Lord require of you but to do justly, to love mercy, and to walk humbly with your God?" -MICAH 6:8

One of my dear friends, the late Dione Neutra, was for over forty years the faithful, adoring wife of the internationally famed architect, Richard Neutra, who was also the architect of our first church sanctuary. After Richard died some years ago, Dione surprised everybody by developing a tremendous, dynamic life on her own. She frequently wrote to us.

She once wrote, *"You know, people are astounded at my vitality. They tell me that I am an inspiration to them. I can't understand it. Some say I don't get any older at all, but I look in the mirror and I know that is not true.*

"I am amazed. How can I be an inspiration to people? Richard was always the inspirator. How is it possible that now I can be the inspirator? I am getting old. What is true is that I have a great zest for life. My life has always had a purpose. I always have a task to fulfill. I have enjoyed what I have had to do. If I have not enjoyed it, I have been able to recognize that whatever was disagreeable to me was also a fact of life. I had to be patient and persevere. It's a mystery how I can be an inspiration.

"The other day I met a woman who was completely lost when her husband died. She did not know what to do with her life, whereas I know exactly what I want to do with the remaining years of my life. Perhaps that is my secret!"

Abundant living begins with living for a purpose!

I abide in God's abundance.
I know why I am alive.

ABUNDANT LIVING

"Trust in the Lord with all your heart and lean not on your own understanding. In all your ways acknowledge Him and He shall direct your paths." -PROVERBS 3:5,6

People often ask me, *"How can I know God's will for my life?"* And I usually answer by saying, *"That's the wrong question. The right question to be asking is 'How can I accomplish God's plan for me?'"*

You see, God's will for you is clear. He wills that you be born again. That's basic. God wants you to experience the new birth. Secondly, God want you to succeed. He has promised that when you allow Him to direct your paths, then *"whatever you do shall prosper."* (Psalm 1:3). Thirdly, God wants you to serve Him. His will is that simple.

The big question is, *"How will you accomplish His plan?"* And the key to the correct answer to that question is to identify your purpose in life. What is your purpose for living? Briefly describe it:

_____

_____

_____

I define the purpose of a Christian like this: A mind through which Christ thinks, a heart through which Christ loves, a voice through which Christ speaks, a hand through which Christ lifts, and a soul through which Christ glows.

That's Abundant Living!

Lord, show me Your plan for my life today, and tomorrow!

ABUNDANT LIVING

I have come that you may have life, and that you may have it more abundantly." -JOHN 10:10

One of the saddest sights in life, today, is to see someone buy into the empty promises of the world. It reminds me of the story told by Dr. Clovus Chappell, one of the great ministers of the South. He said, *"I remember when I was a boy attending Sunday School. One Christmastime our Sunday School class had a party. What a surprise! There was a Christmas tree with presents, and even a Santa to give out the presents. One by one we would go up and get our gifts. It was beautiful.*

"Included among our group was a mentally disadvantaged boy who was six inches taller than the rest of us. He sat there eagerly waiting for his name to be called. Gift after gift was passed out until they were almost gone. The boy was getting discouraged and was about to burst into tears.

"At that moment, Santa went behind the tree, pulled out a big gift, and read off the boy's name. A look of joy spread over his face as he grabbed the package, ripped off the wrapping and opened the box. And then despair replaced his joy. Somebody had decided to play a joke on the lad and the box was empty. The boy shook the box, then walked out of the room, his head drooping, shoulders bowed and tears pouring down his face. I'll never forget that sight!"

You say, "What a dirty trick!" Agreed! But the world plays the same trick on you and me when it promises and doesn't deliver. Only Jesus Christ can give abundant life!

Thank you, God, that You deliver on all Your promises!

ABUNDANT LIVING

"Seek first the kingdom of God and His righteousness and all these things shall be added to you." -MATTHEW 6:33

Society comes to you with beautiful packages that are really empty. Hollywood offers money, fame, or youth and it presents these empty gifts as the beautiful sources of real satisfaction. But these gifts do not satisfy.

Yet everyday we see empty promises on billboards, television and magazine ads. Identify some of these promises—perhaps the ones that are the most tempting to you:

_____

_____

_____

_____

Now look again at the verse in Matthew 6:33. Rewrite it in your own words, relating it to Hollywood's promises:

_____

_____

_____

God's kingdom comes first in my life!

ABUNDANT LIVING

"How precious is your loving kindness, O God ... for with You is the fountain of life." -PSALM 36:7-9

Whenever I am tempted to go out and buy the latest appliance, I am reminded of Dan Crawford, the man who replaced Dr. Livingston in Africa. Crawford spent twenty-eight years serving that area.

Along about his twenty-second year, Crawford thought about going home. He told the Bantu chief, "I have been here a long time, I think I will go home." The chief replied, "Where is home?" "England," Crawford answered.

Then he sat down and told his black Christian brother what England was like. He described the ships that sailed on the sea. He told him about the long trains with the locomotives that billowed out great puffs of smoke. He related the beauty of the huge bridges made of steel spanning the great rivers of his homeland.

Crawford continued, "The homes have a knob you turn and running water comes out of a pipe, right in the house. You can wash or take a bath. You can even go to a wall, push a button and light will come on in the room."

As Crawford became lost in his memories, the old chief interrupted, "Is that all?" Crawford was silent. Finally the chief said, "But, to be better off is not to be better!"

In fact, today it might even be worse. Yet all of our materialism comes into the right perspective when Jesus Christ is at the center of our lives. Abundant living is not made up of things!

I give thanks for this progressive world.
But my life centers on God
and His abundance!

*A*BUNDANT LIVING

"Happy are the people whose God is the Lord." -PSALM 144:15

What gives you the most satisfaction in life? The party is over. The guests are gone, the food trays are empty and all is quiet. What really satisfies? Think for a moment and then make a list:

_____

_____

_____

Now read again Psalm 144:15. Write your own description of "happiness."

Here is my description of truly happy people...

_____

_____

_____

_____

I sing a song of thanksgiving!

X | LEONARD STEVENS | For Commissioner

Marks
60
61
66
69

73

Jan 8 1992 Nathan
Gerry Saddoris/Robinson
Mark Conway sends
Dec 11, 1983

Bob - John 1987 Oct 19 1953

Feb. III 66

Mother (Flores) May 26 1890 - Apr 24 77-78-Gpa

Geraline Sedann Robinson 1-8-92
28 ? 3
1968 - mom
1953 - Dad
15

July 18, 1912 Harcourt Judson

July 27, 1917 Genevieve Sedann Judson ?

Gerry Robinson June 8, 1932 - 69

Jane 06 1935 Jane 06 - 14

ABUNDANT LIVING

"Give and it will be given to you: Good measure pressed down, shaken together and running over ... for with the same measure that you use, it will be measured back to you." -LUKE 6:38

E. Stanley Jones made a point about the condition upon which God's guarantee of abundance is made. All of God's promises are conditional, for God must not merely give—He must give in such a way that the person receiving is stimulated, not smothered. God must not merely make a gift; He must make a person.

Abundant living does not come through constantly receiving. Abundant living depends upon abundant giving. Everyone should receive according to need, but everyone must also give according to ability. Frank Laubach puts it this way: "The human organism is a sprinkler head. By itself, a sprinkler head is not worth very much, but attach it to a hose, let the water flow through, and the sprinkler head makes flowers grow, turns grass green and creates parks where children can play.

"Your life, in God's plan, is to be a sprinkler head for Jesus Christ." Jesus said, "Out of you shall flow rivers of living water." This is God's purpose that satisfies. By comparison, all the other purposes which appear as beautiful gifts given to you by society and culture are empty promises. The only purpose that satisfies is Jesus Christ!

I feel a growing generosity within me. I want to share all that God has given to me!

ORGIVENESS

"There is forgiveness with You, O Lord."
-PSALM 130:4

"To the Lord our God belong mercy and forgiveness."
-DANIEL 9:9

"Forgive us our debts, as we forgive our debtors."
-MATTHEW 6:12

"Whenever you stand praying, if you have anything against anyone, forgive him, so that your Father in heaven may also forgive you." *-MARK 11:25*

"Father, forgive them," Jesus said, "for they do not know what they do." *-LUKE 23:34*

"I bless the holy name of God with all my heart. Yes, I will bless the Lord and not forget the glorious things He does for me. He forgives all my sins."
-PSALM 103:1-3 (LB)

I am living today controlled by my God ~ inspired positive ideas!

*F*ORGIVENESS

"...we see God's abounding grace forgiving us." -ROMANS 5:20 (LB)

An esteemed English clergyman told J. Wallace Hamilton, "The turning point came in my life when I was 17 years old. I always had trouble with my brothers and sisters. I was called the "black sheep" in the family. We were always fighting each other.

"One night they were all picking on me until I could stand it no longer. I jumped up and cried, 'I'm getting out of here!' I ran up the stairs and there, suddenly in the darkened hallway, I ran into my grandmother. She had been listening to it all. She stood there in the hallway and stopped me by putting her hand on my shoulder. With tears in her eyes she said only a few words to me, but they changed my life. She said, *"John, I believe in you."'*

Right now, imagine God putting His hand on your shoulder. He says to you, "I've heard everything, and I want you to know, I *believe in you!*"

What a great moment that is! Faith is born anew as you experience His acceptance and forgiveness.

God, you believe in me!
Thank You for that thought.

FORGIVENESS

"God can be depended on to forgive us..." -1 JOHN 1:9 (LB)

Write God a "Thank You" note for His gift of forgiveness:

Dear God: _____

_____

_____

_____

_____

_____

_____

_____

God has forgiven me, and is forgiving me!

FORGIVENESS

"For you, Lord, are good and ready to forgive." -PSALM 86:5

Legend tells us that the beautiful Helen of Troy, over whom many battles were fought, was lost after one of the battles. When the army returned to Greece, Helen was not on any of the ships. Menelaus went to try and find her, at great personal peril. He finally found her in one of the seaport villages. She had been suffering from amnesia. Forgetting who she was, she had stooped to the lowest possible level and was living as a prostitute.

Menelaus found her in rags, dirt, shame, and dishonor. He looked at her and called, "Helen." Her head turned. "You are Helen of Troy!" he said. And with those words, her back straightened and the royal look came back. She had been redeemed!

You may be deflated and dishonored in your own eyes because you don't realize who you are. You are a member of the royal family. When you accept Jesus Christ into your life, you are a member of the family of God. You are no longer a lost soul. You have been forgiven and have recovered your honor!

I am a member of God's family!

*F*ORGIVENESS

"Now is the time to forgive." -2 CORINTHIANS 2:7 (LB)

My Forgiveness List:

I find it very hard to forgive _____

_____

for _____

_____

Because God has forgiven me, I want to forgive _____

_____

_____ . I will let _____ know

_____

by_____ and saying_____

_____

_____

_____

_____

With God's ability,
I am a forgiving person!

FORGIVENESS

"He who forgives an offense seeks love." -PROVERBS 17:9 RSV

Express your joy today in forgiveness by learning a special poem, easy enough for anyone. The first line is one word — **forgiveness.** Line two has two words which describe forgiveness. Line three is three words long and contains action words or phrases about **forgiveness.** Line four has four words that describe your feelings about **forgiveness.**

Forgiveness
God's Gift
Sets me free
So glad it's possible

Now affirm:

The more I forgive, the more love I experience. Thank you, Lord, for Your forgiveness.

FORGIVENESS

"Let all bitterness, wrath, and anger be put away from you, and be kind, tenderhearted, forgiving one another, just as God in Christ also forgave you. -EPHESIANS 4:32

During the World War I, the German armies swept over Belgium, destroying many of the cities. One day after the war was over, a Catholic nun, with a group of her little students, paused at a small Catholic shrine at the edge of the village. They knelt and began to repeat the Lord's Prayer. But they couldn't utter one phrase.

Around them was the rubble and the ruin, the resentment and the hurt of the war years. The small group started again, "Forgive us our trespasses as we..." They could go no further—until from behind them came a strong man's voice—"As we forgive those who trespass against us." They looked around and saw King Albert! With his great spirit of forgiveness, he led the way.

Christ, our King, shows us how to conquer resentment and hurt. It was our King who cried from the cross, "Father, forgive them, they know not what they do."

Perhaps you need to forgive someone. God can help you be a forgiving person. And He will replace your bitterness with love and kindness.

You, Lord, are helping me now to forgive others as You have forgiven me.

GOD IS ABLE!

"Now glory be to God who by His mighty power at work within us is able to do far more than we would ever dare to ask or even dream of—infinitely beyond our highest prayers, desires, thoughts, or hopes." -EPHESIANS 3:20

What do you do when you reach the spot where the burdens of life become just too heavy and are more than you can bear? How do you "get hold of yourself" when your whole world seems to be falling apart at your feet? Where do you turn when there are no answers and you're tempted to blurt out those negative words, "...but there's no way?"

Remember that God is **ABLE!** When you don't know how to handle the burdens of life, God is able! The Christian faith offers hope. And that hope is based on the power of God!

Do you feel weighed down by something today? Perhaps it is a burden within your own life, or a problem that is caused by someone else—a relative, neighbor or associate at work. Now use possibility thinking and list several ways in which God could possibly lift your burden:

_____

_____

Now read, again, Ephesians 3:20 and dare to believe that God is able to do far more than you ask.

God is Able!

God is Able!

"Lift your eyes on high and see who has created these things ... by the greatness of His might and the strength of His power, not one is missing."
-ISAIAH 40:26

As a small boy growing up on our Iowa farm, I had very few toys. Those were the Depression years and the Dust Bowl years. What few toys we did have were either handmade or were treasured items salvaged from some junk pile. One of my most treasured toys was an old chipped piece of a magnifying glass. I used to sit in my overalls by the riverbank, and when the fish weren't biting, I would take this piece of magnifying glass and focus on the tiny leaves of the plants, or on a tiny ant or ladybug. I would sit for hours fascinated by the life all around me. How did God imagine making such tiny things and at the same time, such large animals as elephants and dinosaurs?

How big is your God? Get out the magnifying glass of faith today and focus on God's creation. The same is true of God's power in your life. God is able when you focus on the power of God within you. I assure you, you will be able to face anything that comes your way today.

Lord, You are so much bigger than my problem. You are able to help me overcome. I focus on Your power today. Already I feel stronger!

$\mathscr{G}$OD IS ABLE!

"The Lord will give strength to His people; the Lord will bless His people with peace." -PSALM 29:11

After the last earthquake here in California, a person said to me, *"Dr. Schuller, after that earthquake and the Southern California fires, WHERE is God?"* I answered him quite easily. I said, *"Listen, turn on the evening news tonight and you will see God's hand in an incredible way. So many lives were miraculously saved. There is story after story of sovereign rescue."* God is eternal. God is omnipotent. God transcends the human family.

And God uses the human family to do His work in the world today. If you want to see the work of God in a very real way, look at the human family. He created human beings in His image We receive divine thoughts and ideas and impulses. We receive motivation and encouragement to become God's redemptive body in the world today.

Do you want to see God at work in the world in a way that you can really see and touch and feel? Look at what happened after the earthquake. I listened to the story of one man who survived the disaster where the apartment complex was leveled, crushing the entire first floor. He said everyone who was able desperately searched for survivors, even putting themselves in danger to reach those who were trapped.

Where is God? What is He doing? What kind of a God is He? Look around you. When the earth trembles and shakes, you'll be shocked at how generous people are. They will volunteer their hearts and their hopes and their hands. Where is God right now? All over the world. He's loving through human hearts. He's speaking through faces. He's healing and redeeming lives. Is He in your life? Are you a Christian? He wants to motivate you. He is asking for your help. He needs you. Embrace Him now. Where is God today? Let Him be in you.

*Lord, here are my arms,
hug and lift someone with them.*

$\mathscr{G}$OD IS ABLE!

"For I know whom I have believed, and am persuaded that God is able to keep that which I have committed to Him until that day." -II TIMOTHY 1:12

I have been inspired by the story of George Smith, the Moravian missionary. All of his life he wanted to be a missionary to Africa. Everything he did was directed towards that goal.

He finally finished his preparation and set sail for Africa. His lifelong dream and calling was now a reality. But he was in Africa only a few months when the government expelled him from the land. When he was expelled, he left behind only one convert—an old woman. George Smith died while still a young man. Until the day he died, he prayed for Africa and for the people he had come to love.

Think of it! All of his life was spent in preparation for a ministry that lasted only a few months and then died he a young man. But one hundred years later, the seed planted in the life of one old woman had multiplied into 13,000 happy African Christians!

Anyone can look at the externals—anyone can count the seeds in an apple. But only God can count the apples in a seed! Only God knows the end from the beginning. God is able! You are able as you possibilitize through your faith and multiply what God is going to do!

*I anchor myself in God and
I feel secure and strong.*

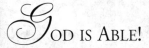OD IS ABLE!

"Now to Him who is able to keep you from stumbling, to God our Savior be glory and majesty now and forever. Amen." -JUDE 24

The parable of the sower (found in Matthew 13:18-23) gives two important insights as to how you can have a multiplying faith.

First, it is important to listen to the Word of God with an **expectant attitude.** Repeat again the words of Jesus, "But with God, everything is possible." (Matthew 19:26).

Second, **act as if it is possible.** The sower must sow the seed. He must go out into the field and work. Now this means that you must act-as-if-you-believed that "With God, everything is possible!" How?

Where do you want God's power focused in your life today? Describe how you would live and act IF God's power was focused on that point of your life:

_____

_____

_____

_____

_____

_____

Lord, help me to live as if I believed everything is possible with You!

GOD IS ABLE!

"He is also able to save to the uttermost those who come to God through Him." -HEBREWS 7:25

The first time I traveled to Russia, I visited the Museum of Atheism in Luvov. And I prayed that God would allow me to say something to our young Communist guide.

As the tour ended, I looked at her and said, *"Before I say good-bye, I have good news for you." "What's that?"* she asked. And I answered, watching her eyes very carefully for any reaction, *"God loves you, even if you don't believe in Him. You may be an atheist. You have that freedom—you have that right. But that doesn't change God one bit. He still loves you even if you don't believe in Him."* She gasped.

To this day I feel that was one of those sacred times in my life when an off-the-cuff comment was prompted by God's Holy Spirit. I believe that Spirit-directed comment powerfully burned its way into a consciousness, and will never leave that girl's mind! I dare to believe with all my being that she was cybernetically tattooed with that concept. I have no doubt in my mind that she has become a believer!

When God's Holy Spirit prompts you to do or say something, pay attention. That powerful thought or action can be used by God to bring about seemingly impossible changes! God is able!

Today I will be sensitive to the special messages that come from God.

GOD IS ABLE!

God's Spirit is flowing into me now,
for my conscience is clear.
I have made the right decision.
I am not afraid of problems.
I will face changes calmly and serenely
for God is with me.
He will help me.
If I must go through difficult times,
He will rescue me.
I feel His Spirit of confidence surging in
my heart now.

With Him I cannot possibly fail.
"If God is for me who can be against me?"
I have a strong feeling that
everything is going to work out just beautifully.

Thank you, God.
Amen.

*God is real,
and He will give
me His ideas.*

$\mathcal{G}$OD CARES!

"Blessed are those who mourn, for they shall be comforted."
-MATTHEW 5:4 RSV

As a pastor, I am in the specialized work of dealing with the hurt, the lonely, the suffering, the sick and the dying. For over twenty years I have trudged the soft, green lawns of cemeteries with my arms around wives, husbands, fathers, mothers, relatives and friends. I have sat in hospitals and wept with those who were weeping. Believe me, I am not blind to the reality of suffering.

William Saroyan once said in a television interview, "Sorrow is a cloud which hangs over everyone, always in this life." None of us escapes the very human pain and heartache that comes when we, or someone close to us, suffers.

But, I have good news! Jesus said it: "Blessed are those who mourn, for they shall be comforted!" In the words of the great church hymn, "Earth has no sorrows that heaven cannot heal."

It is possible for the vacant spot in your life to be filled with a new love. It is possible for your brokenness to be tenderly repaired and restored, or replaced. It is possible to make a comeback after heartbreak. It is possible because GOD CARES!

Surely the Lord is in my sorrow and pain and I believe God cares!

God cares!

"Is anyone among you suffering? Let him pray ... the effective, fervent prayer of a righteous person avails much." -James 5:13-16

Too many of us will simply not slow down long enough to hear God's voice until we enter the valley of suffering. If your suffering turns you to God, does it not become a blessing?

The prophet Isaiah wrote, *"The year King Uzziah died I saw the Lord!"* (Isaiah 6:1). Many a father and mother have been converted to Christ through the death of a child. But what good is that to the child, the cynic asks. Jesus Christ answered that question when He said, *"Except a grain of wheat fall into the ground and die...it bears no fruit."* (John 12:24). *"He who believes in Me, though he may die, he shall live."* (John 11:25).

There is no birth without birth pangs. And there is no entrance into eternal life except through the birth experience the world calls "death".

Are you facing trials or troubles? Rejoice, for God is illuminating your path. He is conditioning you for a life of more effective service.

In love's service only broken hearts will do!

GOD CARES!

"The very hairs on your head are numbered. ... Do not fear, you are of more value than many sparrows." -MATTHEW 10:30 & 31

William Cowper needed a miracle. He attempted suicide more than once. He put a rope around his neck and the rope broke. So he walked to the river, where he knew of a deep spot by the bridge, but there were so many people on the bridge, he could not jump. He went back home where he took an ornamental sword off the wall and put it to his chest. He threw his body down on it, but the point of the sword hit a rib bone, snapped the sword in two and suddenly, William Cowper called out, *"Lord, forgive me! and at that moment,"* he said, *"Jesus Christ came into my life. I sensed His presence. It was powerful. It was real."*

He was born again. He wrote a poem and it became a great hymn of the church.

Years later, a tornado destroyed our house and we lost everything except the clothes on our back. We went to the little country church in Iowa for a special prayer meeting. What hymn did we sing? We sang the hymn with the words written by William Cowper, who - with Jesus in his heart - wrote:

> **God moves in mysterious ways.**
> **His wonders to perform;**
> **He plants His footsteps on the sea,**
> **and rides upon the storm.**
> - WILLIAM COWPER

God cares! He is in the miracle business and He has a miracle to match my situation today!

GOD CARES!

"Blessed be the God and Father of our Lord Jesus Christ, ... the God of all comfort, who comforts us in all our troubles, that we may be able to comfort those who are in trouble." -II CORINTHIANS 1:3, 4

John Wesley was perplexed when once talking with a farmer friend, he noticed a cow with its head over a stone wall. He asked the farmer, *"Why would that cow be trying to look over the wall?"* The farmer answered, *"Well, that's simple. She's looking over the wall because she can't see through it."*

Life is full of problems, setbacks, rejections, disappointments, discouragements. Even your prayers may seemingly go unanswered. You reach a point where you think God has forsaken you—prayer is ineffective and God no longer seems real. You've run into a stone wall!

What do you do when you run into a stone wall and feel you just can't cope anymore? You stand there patiently and look over the stone wall. *"We can rejoice, too, when we run into problems and trials for we know that they are good for us; they help us learn to be patient. Patience develops strength of character in us and helps us trust God more each time we use it until finally our hope and faith are strong and steady. Then, when that happens, we are able to hold our heads high no matter what happens and know that all is well, for we know how dearly God loves us, and we feel this warm love everywhere within us because God has given us the Holy Spirit to fill our hearts with His love."* (Romans 5:3-5).

I am able to rejoice in my sufferings because God is at work in me.

OD CARES!

"When you walk through the Valley of Weeping it will become a place of springs where pools of blessing and refreshment collect after rains!"
-PSALM 84:6 (LB)

Perhaps you are suffering a deep hurt or sorrow right now. Or someone close to you is walking through the Valley of Weeping. These hurts and sorrows can, and will, become springs sending forth blessing and refreshment—that's God's promise! Believe it! Live it!

I am sure that someone close to you needs your encouragement today. Take the theme verse for today and rewrite it in your own words or in a way that would personalize it for a friend. Then take the time to share it with someone:

_____

_____

_____

_____

_____

_____

_____

Through my tears, I really believe God is creating pools of blessings and refreshment.

God Cares!

"Come to me, all who labor and are heavy burdened, and I will give you rest." -Matthew 11:28

I recognized them in the crowd. They were longtime friends from the Midwest. As they walked towards me, I recalled what had happened to their only children, two sons that sad summer morning years ago. Their two boys were having fun on the lake when their makeshift raft fell apart and the youngest boy drowned. Then, only two years later, their other son was killed as he was pinned under a tractor that tipped over in the field.

I greeted them and then asked, *"How did you find strength to carry on?"* The mother answered bravely, *"Someone in a far-off state sent me a letter with a simple affirmation. It said, 'God still loves you!' I repeated that over and over and I still believe it!"* Her eyes sparkled as she talked. Her husband stood there smiling through tear-filled eyes.

The three of us held hands and prayed. I watched them as they walked off—tall and trusting souls. God's iron-pillared people!

Saint Paul understood. He wrote, *"What can ever keep Christ's love from us? When we have trouble or calamity, is it because He doesn't love us anymore? ... NO ... despite all this, overwhelming victory is ours through Christ who loved us enough to die for us."* (Romans 8:35-37).

"God still loves me!"

GOD CARES!

"When you pass through the waters I will be with you; and through the rivers, they shall not overflow you; when you walk through fire you shall not be burned, and the flame shall not scorch you. For I am the Lord your God!" -ISAIAH 43:2,3

During the World War I, a soldier in the trenches saw his friend out in no-man's land—that ground between his trench and the trench of the enemy. His friend lay there wounded.

The man asked his officer, *"May I go, sir and bring him in?"* The officer refused saying, *"No one can live out there, and if you go I will only lose you as well."*

Disobeying the officer, the man went to save his friend, for they had been like brothers throughout the war. Somehow, he managed to get his friend on his shoulder, stagger back to his trench, only to fall mortally wounded with his friend.

The officer was angry, *"I told you not to go. Now I have lost two good men. It was not worth it!"* With his dying breath the man said, *"But it was worth it, sir, because when I got to him he said, 'Jim, I knew you'd come.'"*

The distinct message of the cross of Jesus Christ is this: God will come to you when you cry out to Him, even to the point of giving His life to prove His faithfulness to you.

Lord Jesus, when I look at Your cross I know You care for me.

GOD CARES!

"I who speak in righteousness, am mighty to save." -ISAIAH 63:1

St. Augustine spoke from the depths of a deep spiritual experience. As a wild, wanton, rebellious youth he deserted God, religion and faith. It was only when the emptiness of his life threatened to swallow him that he falteringly turned to God. He briefly prayed, *"O God, forgive me of all my sins—but not yet."*

And back he went to spend his youthful energies in immorality. Again, the hollowness of his unholy life overwhelmed him. With a sinking feeling he prayed again, *"O God, forgive me for all my sins—save one."* And again he left the place of prayer only to run again with the hares and dash with the hounds.

But total peace comes only from total commitment. And so he came back to the God Who made him. Deeply, sincerely, humbly, resolutely he surrendered his life to Christ praying, *"O God, forgive me for ALL my sins — and do it now. AMEN!"*

Try praying this prayer. Mean it, and forgiveness, freedom and fellowship will dissolve your tensions like the warm summer sun evaporates the morning dew in the meadow.

I now have total peace with God, for I am totally committed!

OD SAVES!

"Lord, I believe; help my unbelief!." -MARK 9:24

How do you define "sin?" I was asked that question by a reporter recently. My answer was very simple: Traditionally, sin has been defined as "rebellion against God, an inner warfare between the self and God."

But think of sin as a golf ball. There is the outer skin. Then there is the tight inner workings, and finally at the core of every ball is one solid, little, hard rubber pellet. The skin of sin is rebellion. The core is much deeper. What is the core of sin? It is our innate, inherited, negative self-image!

The negative self-image is responsible for any and all sin. God's toughest job is making you believe you are a beautiful, wonderful person through redemption and salvation. Believe God when He tells you how great you are!

What do you have trouble believing? Where in your life do you lack self-confidence and the feeling that you are an attractive person made by God? Write it down:

_____

_____

_____

Now cover up what you have written with the words, "God Loves Me!"

Because God loves me,
I believe in myself!

GOD SAVES!

"The Kingdom of God is at hand. Repent, and believe in the Gospel."
-MARK 1:15

I once spent an evening with one of America's foremost psychiatrists, Dr. Karl Menninger. We were playing chess together in the Chicago home of a mutual friend, W. Clement Stone.

I was about to make my second move when the giant-minded Menninger glared at me over the chessboard and asked, *"Dr. Schuller, do you preach 'repentance'?"*

I was taken aback, wondering what that question could possibly have to do with chess. Before I could answer, Dr. Menninger went on, saying, *"Nothing will bring healing quicker to people than repentance. They are sinners. People know it. They are responsible for their own guilt! And they will never be healthy until they confess and repent before God."*

I was reminded of St. Paul's words to the men of Athens: *"... Now He (God) commands all people everywhere to repent."* (Acts 17:30).

Deep within, I know the presence of God that is mine through Christ Jesus.

OD SAVES!

"Whoever walks blamelessly will be saved." -PROVERBS 28:18

Have you ever been in a church where the minister scolds the people? He rebukes them, slaps his hands and pounds his fists, verbally crucifying those listening to him. I have attended churches like that. And the amazing thing is that the people go out and tell the preacher, "Oh, that was a great sermon, Reverend."

These people enjoyed being verbally spanked. They do not understand what the grace of God means. They do not really believe that when Christ died on the cross, He paid the price. All we have to do is accept!

But then, all of us have areas of our lives where we are still trying to earn God's forgiveness. There are some things in your life that you are still trying to hide from God. My message to you is that God knows and He still loves you!

Now write your prayer as you thank God for setting you free.

Dear Lord, _____

_____

_____

_____

_____

Let me, O Lord, like a little child, dare to confess and then run with open arms to You. Amen.

God Saves!

"If anyone hears My voice and opens the door, I will come in and dine with him and he with Me." -REVELATION 3:20

I once spoke with a young woman who showed me a beautiful diamond ring that a certain young man had just given her. She was excited about the commitment she had made to the future with this young man.

I told her, *"You know what it means when you accept that diamond engagement ring. It means you make a commitment to him and he makes a commitment to you. There is a growing relationship between the two of you and you both begin to build your whole future on that commitment. You trust him and he trusts you. Now you share secrets with him that you wouldn't share with anyone else, including me."* Then I told her, *"You know, becoming a Christian is pretty much like receiving that diamond."*

She nodded her head and replied, *"I understand and I want to make that same kind of commitment to Jesus Christ."*

God offers you a "diamond" to wear on your heart, and accepting it is as simple as opening a door when you hear someone knock. Invite Jesus Christ into your life and enjoy a future rich in a trusting relationship with the Eternal and Almighty God.

God, I want a special relationship with You, therefore, I commit my life and future to You.

$\mathcal{G}$OD SAVES!

"This is the victory that has overcome the world — Your faith." -I JOHN 5:4

There is a beautiful redemptive story I once heard about Abraham Lincoln:

Abe Lincoln passed a slave market in South Carolina one day. As he passed, he saw a beautiful young black girl being brought to the block to be sold. She wore a vicious, angry look. He couldn't stand the sight of it, the humiliation that she was being exposed to, the shame that was being brought to her. When the first bid came, he raised his hand and found himself bidding to buy this slave girl. In the end, Abe won the young girl. With anger, she looked at him and said, *"Okay, what are you gonna do with me?"* And he answered her, *"I'm going to free you. Go where you want to go. Be what you want to be. Live where you want to live. Do what you want to do. Be free. Go. I don't need you. I bought only one thing — your freedom."* For the first time, she smiled and said, *"If I'm free, I gonna go with you."*

That's the way I feel about Jesus Christ. Salvation means freedom.

And you can know it today. Are you oppressed by shame, resentment, condemnation, alienation, or isolation? These are terrible oppressors. Then you are not free. You are not saved.

You can know salvation. Jesus came not only to free you from hell after you die, but from hell before you die. You can be free.

*I am free today
because I choose to believe!*

GOD SAVES!

"Restore to me the joy of Your salvation." -PSALM 51:12

I remember as a child rubbing a furry, soft peach against my cheek. It felt so soft and good. But, when I turned the peach over, the backside was all raw and rough. It had been scraped by the scratchy splintered inside of a wooden bushel basket. As I looked at it I realized there was absolutely nothing I could do to restore its soft luster.

You can take a violet blossom that feels just like velvet. You can pluck it, throw it down and trample it under your foot. But, when you pick up the crushed velvety violet, nothing can restore it to its original beauty.

You cannot redeem or replace the scraped and bruised side of a fuzzy peach or crushed violet blossom. But, God can restore your soul like new again! It is possible! It is happening all the time!

That's what the whole story of Christianity is about. God sent His Son, Jesus Christ, into this world. As He said in Luke 19:10, *"The Son of Man has come to seek and to save that which was lost"* (NASB).

*I sense God's power restoring
and strengthening me. He is smoothing
the rough places in my life.*

OD WILL!

When it looks like I have failed
      I ask, *"Lord, what are You trying to tell me?"*

Failure doesn't mean I'm a failure.
      It does mean I haven't succeeded yet!

Failure doesn't mean I have accomplished nothing.
      It does mean I have learned something!

Failure doesn't mean I have been a fool.
      It does mean I had enough faith to try!

Failure doesn't mean I have been disgraced
      It does mean I dared to adventure!

Failure doesn't mean I don't have it.
      It does mean I have to do something in a different way.

Failure doesn't mean I'm inferior.
      It does mean I am not perfect!

Failure doesn't mean I've wasted my life.
      It does mean I have an excuse to start over again!

Failure doesn't mean I should give up.
      It does mean I must try harder!

Failure doesn't mean I'll never make it.
      It does mean I need more patience!

Failure doesn't mean You have abandoned me, God.
      It does mean YOU MUST HAVE A BETTER IDEA!

"In everything you do, put God first,
and He will direct you
and crown your efforts with success."

PROVERBS 3:6 (LB)

GOD WILL!

"Your young people shall see visions, your old people shall dream dreams."
-ACTS 2:17

The fear of failure keeps most people from believing that God can, and will, make their dreams come true. They are afraid to try. I often think of Christy Wilson, that great missionary to Kabul, Afghanistan. The major industry in Kabul was raising sheep, and the major problem in raising sheep was a disease caused by a worm that gets in the intestines of the sheep when they eat snails.

Now ducks love to eat these snails, but Christy noticed there were no ducks in Afghanistan. He wrote to a friend in the states and asked for some fertilized duck eggs. Twenty-four fertilized duck eggs were sent. His friend said, *"They will hatch, provided the eggs are not dropped, they get there on time and the temperature stays warm. In other words, it will take a miracle."*

By the time they arrived in Kabul, some were broken, cracked and smelly. Christy said, *"We'll just have to pray that we get a least one male and one female."*

You can guess what happened: only two eggs hatched, a male and a female. They multiplied and eventually wiped out the snails and the sheep industry boomed. God took Christy's dream and worked a miracle because he decided to try.

I have a dream. I am testing it
to see if my positive dream is God's dream!

GOD WILL!

"Unto You, O Lord, I lift up my eyes, You, who dwell in the heavens."
-PSALM 123:1

The second important principle that will help you grab hold of God's dream is to *Eye it.* Once your dream has passed the first test, you know it is a dream that God has placed in your mind. Now you must visualize your dream. Write it down, outline it, or draw a picture. When you can see it in your mind, it becomes a fact!

Try it! Now *Eye it!* Write it down or draw a picture of your dream in the space below.

Today my dream is becoming a possibility because I can visualize it!

GOD WILL!

"In Him we live and move and have our being." -ACTS 17:28

Now you know that your positive idea is God's dream for your life. You've eyed it ... either by writing it down or by drawing a picture. Now it's time to buy it! You make the commitment to be totally sold on the idea. You are willing to pay the price. Every great idea has a price tag attached to it.

I have found that when God has given me a great dream, there are always some negative thinkers around who will criticize the dream. Every time we have moved ahead to do something great for God, I have been so convinced that it was God's idea that I would have gladly died for the success of the dream. Nothing can stop you when you know that it is God's dream for you!

Have you bought it? Are you committed to your dream as a good steward of God's great riches? Write out your commitment to the positive, life-changing dream you described yesterday:

I am ready, Lord, and I am eager to move ahead with our dream!

God Will!

"They that wait upon the Lord shall renew their strength, they shall mount up with wings like eagles; they shall run and not be weary; they shall walk and not faint." -ISAIAH 40:31

Try it! Eye it! Buy it! Now it's time to *Fly it*! This simply means the time has come for you to put strong wings on your dream and start moving! Like a little boy with a kite, start running and see if your dream can catch the wind.

Before you know it, your dream will be flying. People, who you never dreamed would help, come to your support. It's true. Positive ideas and dreams attract support from the most unexpected sources! But you must begin.

How? Simply make a list of the first three things you will need to start to make your dream a reality. Then start doing it.

To make my dream a reality, I will begin by:

1. _____

   _____

2. _____

   _____

3. _____

   _____

I can sense it~my dream is happening.
God is giving me strength, wisdom,
and power right now as I put wings to my dream.

God Will!

"If you have faith as a mustard seed, you will say to this mountain, 'move' ... and it will move and nothing will be impossible for you."
-MATTHEW 17:20

The fifth principle that will give you the confidence that God will help you make your dream come true is to *Tie it down.* **DON'T QUIT!**

One of the elders of our church suffered a severe heart attack some years ago. It was a twenty-five minute cardiac arrest. When they got him to the hospital he was in a comatose condition. The neurosurgeon said, *"There's no hope for him. Even if he lives, he'll be a vegetable."*

I came to his bedside shortly after his attack and remembered what Dr. Smiley Blanton, the eminent New York psychiatrist, once said, *"There are vast undamaged areas in the most severely damaged brain."* I believed him, so I said to my special friend, *"Stanley, this is Dr. Schuller. You're going to get well."*

And a tear rolled down out of his eye! It was the first sign of hope! And Stanley grabbed hold of a dream, even in his comatose condition-the dream that he could recover.

Several months later, Stan's wife drove him to church and he walked around without crutches! I ran to him and hugged him. He said, *"Pastor, you're great."* I answered, *"Stanley, God is great!"*

Don't quit! Only you can kill God's dream for you. He will not let your dream come smashing down.

Lord, I feel like shouting because I am confident that together, we will succeed!

GOD WILL!

"You have a mighty arm; strong is your hand, and high is your right hand." -PSALM 89:13

I enjoy the inspiring story of the Chinese farmer who had one son and one horse. One day the horse ran off to the hills. Everybody came and said, *"Oh, you lost your horse; what bad luck!"* The old Chinese farmer replied, *"How do you know it is bad luck?"* And sure enough, that night the one horse came back and led twelve wild stallions with him. The one son closed the gate and the farmer had thirteen horses.

The neighbors came again and exclaimed, *"Oh, what good luck!"* The old farmer answered, *"How do you know it is good luck?"* And sure enough, as the one son was to break one of the wild stallions, he was thrown off and broke his leg. The neighbors lamented, *"Oh what bad luck."* Again, the Chinese farmer questioned, *"How do you know it is bad luck?"*

A short time later a Chinese warlord came through town and drafted all the able-bodied young men and took them off to war with him. Those young men never returned. But the farmer's one son was spared and he lived a full, long life.

Trust your dream to God. Your dream is God's dream and His purpose is to turn you and me into good stewards of His rich resources.

Lord, my eyes are on You and I will not be distracted from my positive, life~changing dream.

TALKING WITH GOD!

"You have heard; See all this. And will you not declare it? I have made you hear new things from this time." -ISAIAH 48:6

There are four kinds of prayer. One type of prayer is called "petition." When you draft a request and go to God and say, *"God, I want this,"* that's petition. For many people, this is the only kind of prayer they know.

How much of your praying would you estimate is spent in petition?

There is a second level of prayer called "intercessory prayer," which means to intercede on the behalf of someone else. You pray for me and my needs, and I pray for you and your needs. We are both praying to God to help somebody else. This is intercession.

How much of your praying would you estimate is spent in intercessory prayer?

There is a third kind of prayer called "praise and worship." When people who know God, love God and are so thankful that they pour out their hearts in reverent words say, *"Thank you, God,"* this is praise and worship.

How much of your praying would you estimate is spent in praise and worship?

But there is a fourth kind of prayer, Frank Laubach said, *"Two-way prayer is the highest form of prayer."* And that's the kind of prayer I want to consider with you the next few days.

Thank you, Lord, for the exciting ideas You are sending into my mind right now.

TALKING WITH GOD!

"Call to me and I will answer you, and will show you great and mighty things which you do not know." -JEREMIAH 33:3

Imagine that you are in a little boat near a sandy beach. You throw out an anchor and pull on the rope until you feel the sandy shore slide underneath. Then you step out onto the shore. What have you done? Have you moved the shore to the boat? No, you've moved the boat to the shore.

That's what real prayer is ... not moving God to you in order to **get** something, but moving yourself closer to God in order to **become** something. Now you are close enough to listen to what He wants to say to you.

Too many people think of prayer as a panic-stricken plea to God, the all-powerful Doctor, to get an immediate solution to their problem. Two-way prayer is much more. It involves listening to God as much as it does talking to God. God told the prophet Jeremiah, *"Call to me and I will answer you."* That's two-way prayer.

Who's been doing the talking in your prayer times? Describe what prayer is like in your life:

_____

_____

_____

_____

Lord, today I am listening.
Already I can begin to hear You as You
answer the questions I have within.

TALKING WITH GOD!

"Be still, and know that I am God." -PSALM 46:10

I had never seen an avocado. Even though I went to college and took three years of postgraduate work, I had never heard of an avocado!

Then I moved to California and all kinds of people gave our family what I thought were the biggest, most luscious, most unusual pears I'd ever seen. I tried every way to eat them, but finally gave up and ended up throwing them away. Fortunately, someone finally discovered my ignorance and showed me how to enjoy eating an avocado.

So many people have thrown away prayer the same way I threw all those avocados away. They talk to God and it doesn't work. So, they just give up. Let me describe how you can enjoy the experience of two-way prayer:

Begin by relaxing, closing your eyes and blocking out the distractions of the eye and the world. Meditate and focus your mind on something or some scene that will calm you. Then, when you are relaxed, quietly wait until you feel the stillness of God's presence with you.

Now ask the Holy Spirit to control your thinking so that God's thoughts and ideas will come into your mind. Then begin, in a humble, expectant attitude to ask God questions. As you ask each question, pause and wait for God to answer your question.

Lord, it's hard to shut off the noise around me, but I sense Your stillness and I am hearing Your voice. Thank you!

TALKING WITH GOD!

"Rest in the Lord, and wait patiently for Him." -PSALM 37:7

They had three beautiful children. When the fourth was born, they were all excited. And then they found out the child had Down's Syndrome. The mother said to me, *"Dr. Schuller, we looked at this situation and saw it as an enormous, terrible problem. Our first reaction was one of anger, then bitterness, then self-pity. It was terrible.*

"Then we heard you talk about two-way prayer and asked, 'Lord, could there be any good in what has happened to us?' And we waited. We had a thought and the thought was very strong. 'Yes.' Then we asked, 'God, what good could possibly come out of this problem?' And this sentence came to my mind ... I will teach you a new dimension of love! Wow! That changed everything! What has happened in our lives since then has been a miracle."

Two-way prayer is going into a quiet place to talk to God and ask Him questions. You don't spill out your problems necessarily. You don't make a lot of statements. You don't ask for demands. You don't go forward with pitiful appeals. You go with questions and wait patiently for God to answer. This is mountain-moving prayer!

My spirit is refreshed and renewed as I am quiet before the Lord.

TALKING WITH GOD!

"I will bless the Lord who has given me counsel; my heart also instructs me in the night season ... because He is at my right hand, I shall not be moved." -PSALM 16:7,8

There is mountain-moving power in two-way prayer. In order to see the mountain-moving power at work, you must see the mountains. A mountain-moving prayer notebook will help you see the power available through two-way prayer. Start below and then continue to add to your list in a separate notebook.

MY QUESTION   GOD'S ANSWER   STEPS TAKEN BY ME

Today, I am taking the steps God is telling me to take in order to move mountains.

Talking With God!

"The Lord is near to all who call upon Him in truth." -PSALM 145:18

I once spent several hours with Dr. Viktor Frankl discussing the variety of forces within us that we do not understand, including the mysterious but powerful force of meditation.

We do not understand this great force, but meditation, when effective, is the proper harnessing by humans of divine laws created with the human structure for holy and high purpose. Now, this great force of meditation can be destructive when used improperly. But, Christian meditation has been practiced for centuries, all the way back to the psalmists and the patriarchs. You don't need to pay a fee or find a guru. Possibility thinking meditation and two-way prayer meditation both focus on Jesus Christ. Thinking of Jesus Christ, repeat the words, "I AM" with each breath as you relax. This will help in closing out the distracting sounds while in meditative prayer.

Two-way prayer meditation really works. It creates a mind-set where God can send His signal through to you. You can achieve a sense of oneness with God. He is so close to you that He literally speaks to you!

*I feel a quietness within my spirit~
no distractions, only God and me,
talking together.*

Talking With God!

"The word is near you, even in your mouth and in your heart."
-*Deuteronomy 30:14*

Some of you are going to make major decisions today. It may affect your family, your job, or your destiny. Try two-way prayer! *"But,"* you protest, *"how do I know that what I hear is God speaking to me?"* Let me suggest four steps you can take to answer that question.

First, repeat your question in two or three different two-way prayer conversations. If the answer you have received is from God, it will be the same each time.

Second, "possibilitize"... Believe that it is possible for God to speak to you because you have asked Him to speak to you. Believe that!

Third, compare your answer with what God has already told you in His Holy Bible. God's message to you in two-way prayer will not be different than His message to you in scripture.

Fourth, "actualize" ... The purpose of two-way prayer is to get God's message into your mind so that you can go out and act. Do what God wants you to do to make your life and your world a more beautiful place.

Let's try it now, again. Close your eyes and begin to meditate. Relax and be very informal and open with God. Ask Him questions about your major decisions. When you finish, write down God's answer.

Thank you, Lord, for Your messages that come from the deepest, unexplored, unfathomable seas of silence. I am listening. I will act.

ELF-LOVE

"Lord, you have crowned us with glory and honor." -PSALM 8:5

Once when I challenged an impossibility thinker to become a possibility thinker, his answer provided me with a new revelation. *"It's not worth the effort,"* he said. As he spoke to me, I studied his eyes and I knew he didn't mean what he said. He really meant to say, *"I'm not worth it."* I immediately dropped the idea of converting him into a possibility thinker.

Instead, I went to work attempting to build up in his mind a picture of his enormous worth as a person. Then little by little, when he began to stop hating himself and started liking himself, he came alive. He became a possibility thinker!

I can boldly say to you, no matter what has happened in your life, you are not a complete failure, a hopeless sinner or a total washout. I can't begin to count how many times I have heard people in my study tell me those exaggerated distorted and destructive lies. Every time, I was able to see and point out worthwhile qualities in the person who was condemning himself unfairly, unreasonably and unlovingly.

God loves you and so do I! And it is good and right for you to say, "God loves me and so do I!" Every time a negative or critical thought about yourself enters your mind today, repeat that sentence to yourself.

God loves me and He knows all my secrets. Because God loves me I can love me!

$\mathcal{S}$ELF-LOVE

"Pursue righteousness, godliness, faith, love, patience and gentleness ..."
-I TIMOTHY 6:11

Saint Paul warned his readers at Rome that they were to *"Be honest in your estimate of yourselves."* (Romans 12:3). It is not positive Christianity to put yourself down! But it's a lot easier than being honest about your good qualities. Today is a good time to begin making an honest list of your good characteristics. Start by listing at least six good and positive qualities about yourself. If you find it difficult, ask someone close to you to help you and write down everything they say.

A POSITIVE ESTIMATE OF MYSELF:

1. _____

2. _____

3. _____

4. _____

5. _____

6. _____

*$\mathcal{I}$ am a person of value for $\mathcal{G}$od has
created me and loves me.*

ELF-LOVE

"You are the salt of the earth ... You are the light of the world."
-MATTHEW 5:13,14

It is a majestic sight to see the good earth bearing a heavy harvest of grain and corn. Every piece of land put to good use.

Then there are the bleak and barren foothills of the great Rocky Mountains. These rugged peaks greet the traveler like granite sentinels standing guard at the gateway to the west. When you begin to climb the twisting road that winds like a snake up the mountainside, you finally reach a point where you can look to the west and see the beautiful but seemingly unproductive mountains, and to the east where unfolding below, on the endless plains, is the rich farmland with little lakes and rivers shimmering. What a contrast!

Once when I travelled through the mountains, I made the mistake of pointing at them and commenting to a shop owner, *"What a lot of worthless land."* The young man looked up at me and firmly stated, *"That is not wasteland. There are minerals in those rocks and there may be oil. We believe there is uranium in those mountains, also. We just haven't found it yet!"*

Jesus looks at you and sees the tremendous potential that can be unlocked in you if you will only believe in yourself.

I am somebody! I feel the greatness
within me stirring as I believe in myself
as Jesus Christ believes in me.

$\mathcal{S}$ELF-LOVE

"I will praise You, for I am fearfully and wonderfully made; marvelous are Your works." -PSALM 13:9 & 14

I heard of a teacher in a public school in one of the inner city areas who said to her students, *"Today, we are going to study 'identity'."* She went up to a little boy and said, *"Johnny, we're studying 'identity.' Who are you?"* He stood up and said, *"Well, I know my name is Johnny. I also know I'm good—'cause God don't make no junk'!"*

Johnny was one of God's super-living-people. He was confident because he knew he was God's creation. When you know you are God's child, you know who you are!

Johnny had a good answer to an important question—"Who are you?" The psalmist David had an answer in Psalm 139. If that teacher walked up to you today and asked the same question, how would you answer?

Write down you answer:

_____

_____

_____

_____

I am God's friend, God loves me.
If God has chosen me for His friend, I
must be a marvelous person. I am!

ELF-LOVE

"Yes, I have loved you with an everlasting love; therefore, with loving kindness I have drawn you." -JEREMIAH 31:3

It has been more than a quarter of a century since I wrote my first book, *Self-Love, The Dynamic Force of Success,* and later I retained, at my own personal expense, George Gallup, to study the subject of self-esteem in the United States of America. His findings were phenomenal:

1. People with high self-esteem tend not to get angry.
2. People with high self-esteem have incredible comeback power, despite unimaginable negative experiences.
3. People with high self-esteem are highly productive.
4. People with high self-esteem are less likely to struggle with substance abuse.

You are what you believe yourself to be. **I am** are the two most important words that will shape your life. **I am** *valuable* ... **I am** *smart* ...**I am** *needed* ... **I am** a *blessing.*

I am!
The two most important words
that will shape your life.

If you believe you are no good, the chances are very strong that you will play that out. But if you believe that you are loved, you will become lovable.

You are a human being. You are not just a biological accident, unwanted, devalued. You are **someone** God wants to use. He wants to do something beautiful with the one life you have.

"Be Someone For Somebody"

MOTHER TERESA

ELF-LOVE

"Many waters cannot quench love, nor can the floods drown it."
-SONG OF SOLOMON 8:7

A rebirth of self-worth awaits you. When that happens you will be:

> **Poised,** not **tense ...**
>
> **Confident,** not **confused ...**
>
> **Bold,** not **timid ...**
>
> **Enthusiastic,** not **bored ...**
>
> **Successful,** not **failing ...**
>
> **Energetic,** not **fatigued ...**
>
> **Agreeable,** not **cantankerous ...**
>
> **Positive,** not **negative ...**
>
> **Self-forgiving,** not **self-condemning ...**
>
> **Self-respecting,** not **self-disgusting.**

Now, for your exercise today, repeat the affirmations of the positive descriptions for your life... **I am** poised, **I am** confident, etc.

I AM! The two most important words that can shape your life. **I** *am* **loved. I** *am* **wanted. I** *am* **important.** *I am* God's! Discover true self-love. Come alive! Get motivated! Discover God and all that He has for you today.

God is alive, whether you believe in Him or not. God loves you, whether you love yourself or not.

*It's a happy day today
because God loves me!
I love myself too!*

ELF-LOVE

"Love is of God, and everyone who loves is born of God and knows God."
-1 JOHN 4:7

I attended the commencement of one of the Christian colleges nearby. In the small select group of outstanding students were three persons who immediately stood out from the others. One was an African-American man, one was an Indian, and one was a blind girl with a white cane.

All three of them graduated Magna Cum Laude! Along with other honors and distinctions, all three were listed in *Who's Who in American Colleges and Universities*. And, I am sure that all three could have been miserable failures, blaming their disadvantaged childhood, or a prejudiced society. But the fact was, three people, each with strikes against them, made it to the top!

Some people make victims of their disadvantages—others become victimized by their disadvantages. What is the difference? The African-American man, the Indian, the blind girl—all had one thing in common. They believed in themselves because they believed in the power of Jesus Christ. They believed that Jesus Christ could change their life and their situation.

When you believe in Jesus Christ—believe that He loves you and died for you—you also begin to believe that with Him you can reach the top! You deserve to reach the top!

Because I have self-love, I have self-worth. I have the confidence to turn my problems into personal triumphs.

$\mathcal{S}$ELF-LOVE

"Tomorrow...I will stand at the top of the hill, with the rod of God in my hand." -EXODUS 17:9

Many of you have read the story of Tara, the daughter of a close friend of mine. Tara suffered a brain injury which left her in a coma. It looked as though she would be an invalid all her life. Years later, she could see, she could hear, she could speak, but she could not walk.

Then one day her dad called with exciting news. For the first time Tara got on her hands and knees and began to creep. He excitedly said, *"She held herself up for about 30 seconds on her own hands and knees."* Tara experienced a new perspective—previews of great things to come. She raised her head and saw things in a way she had not seen them before. She had a *peak to peek* experience!

Tara's peak experience was like a mountain-top-experience. Her peak was holding herself up on her hands and knees. As she did this, she had a peek experience—a peek or a glimpse of possible future experiences. Today, although Tara is limited to a wheelchair, she continues to explore new things. She has learned to travel alone by plane to distant cities. She is an amazing possibility thinker.

A peak experience is a positive, self-affirming experience. It is a self-expanding experience that tells me **"I CAN."** And the **I CAN** always leads to a new consciousness, or a peek of what I can be and do.

Today, with God's help, I will climb my mountain and see what great things God has planned for me.

PEAK TO PEEK

"I will lift my eyes to the hills. From where comes my help? My help comes from the Lord who made heaven and earth." -PSALM 121:1,2

Have you ever noticed how some people's lives seem to be one success unfolding upon another? Every new achievement seems to be one up on the last success. That's the incredible way their life unfolds. The achievement level continues to escalate and climb. How do you explain it? Knowingly or unknowingly, these persons have tapped into a vital principle that I call the "peak to peek" principle.

Now a peak experience gives you a new vision of greater accomplishments that you can experience and attempt. A peak experience affirms to you who you are and leaves you with an awareness that you are more than you ever thought you were.

For a child, creeping is a peak experience. Later when the child stands with two feet and takes the first few faltering steps and succeeds, this also becomes a peak experience.

When you stand at the top of the mountain you can see a new dream from your new vantage point. The dream gives rise to desire, the desire gives rise to the daring-to-do. Then daring-to-do gives rise to the deciding-to-begin! And that's the road to success!

The Bible says that God blesses faith. Have faith in your dream.

I am daring to dream God's dream for me today. I feel exhilaration of climbing God's mountain!

EAK TO PEEK

"I am the Lord, your Holy One ... who makes a way in the sea and a path through the mighty waters ... I will even make a road in the wilderness."
-ISAIAH 43:15, 16, 19

What have been the peak experiences in your life? Think back over the past few years and make a note of those experiences which have inspired you and given you a vision of what God has in store for your tomorrows. Write down at least three vision-expanding, success-producing experiences:

1. _____

_____

2. _____

_____

3. _____

_____

*Today, God is at my side and I am
beginning to see new valleys to explore.
By faith, I am succeeding!*

Peak to Peek

"Where can I go from Your Spirit? ... If I ascend into Heaven, You are there. If I make my bed in Hell, behold, You are there. If I take the wings of the morning and dwell in the uttermost parts of the sea, even there Your Hand shall lead me." -PSALM 139:7-10

The self-centered person has to grow in unselfishness before God will say "GO."

The cautious person must grow in courage before God will say "GO."

The reckless person must grow in carefulness before God will say "GO."

The timid person must grow in confidence before God will say "GO."

The self-belittling person must grow in self-love before God will say "GO."

The dominating person must grow in sensitivity before God will say "GO."

The critical person must grow in tolerance before God will say "GO."

The negative person must grow in positive attitude before God will say "GO."

The power-hungry person must grow in kindness before God will say "GO."

The pleasure-seeking person must grow in compassion for suffering people before God will say "GO."

And the God-ignoring soul must become a God-adoring soul before God will say "GO."

I'll go where You want me to go, dear Lord, I'll do what You want me to do.

PEAK TO PEEK

"I will sing of your power. Yes, I will sing aloud of your mercy in the morning ... to you, O Lord, my strength I will sing praises." -PSALM 59:16, 17

A psychologist and I were talking about a person we were both interested in helping. This person's whole life was one set of problems after another. He was what you would call a "born loser."

The psychologist was right on when he said, *"The trouble with this person is that he has never had a peak experience. He's never had an experience in really succeeding. So he's convinced that he is a born failure."*

This young man failed in school, failed in teenage relationships, failed in sociological relationships, failed in his first job, got fired from his second job and landed in a reform school. And that's been his basic lifestyle all along. His last peak experience was when he learned to walk!

How can he have a peak experience? There is no way it can happen without the kind of dynamic religious experience we call "establishing a relationship with God." That's where he must begin.

Has it been a long time since you had a peak experience? Where do you begin? I suggest you begin by making sure that your relationship with God is solid and strong. You can only stand on the mountain peak with God! He gives you a peek at your tomorrows!

From the peak I can see greater possibilities!

PEAK TO PEEK

"Be confident of this very thing, that God who has begun a good work in you will complete it." -PHILIPPIANS 1:6

A few years ago I knew I had to get out and run. I wanted to run. I knew I should run. But I wasn't in the mood to run the six miles I used to.

My home is six miles from the church, so I got into my running suit and decided, *"I'm only going to run halfway from the house to the church."* When I got to that point, what could I do? I couldn't hitchhike home. I had to finish, there was no other way.

I use this principle a lot in my life. When I know there is something I should do, and can't see doing the whole thing, I only make the commitment to go as far as the point of no return; then I'm caught—I have to complete the job.

Some of you may be afraid to begin climbing your mountain. You don't think you can finish. You're thinking—"Can I make it? Can I succeed?"Decide to begin and then decide to keep going. Don't worry about the top, just decide to get started. The key is in deciding to begin.

What's keeping you from climbing to your mountain peak? What are you involved in now that could be a peak experience for you?

I am climbing to the peak. I can feel the clean air and I will keep going until I reach the top!

PEAK TO PEEK

"I will instruct you, says the Lord, and guide you along the best pathway for your life; I will advise you and watch your progress." -PSALM 32:8 (LB)

When the idea is not right,
God says, "NO!"

When the time is not right,
God says, "SLOW!"

When you are not right,
God says, "GROW!"

When everything is right,
God says, "GO!"

I will enter into an adventure with God with a positive heart!

$\mathcal{P}$EAK TO PEEK

"It is God who works in you, both to will and to do for His good pleasure."
-PHILIPPIANS 2:13

How do you succeed? You succeed by "hook and by crook!" Now before you misunderstand me, let me explain the meaning of that phrase—by hook and by crook.

I fish once in a while, but there has never been a time when the fish jumped into my boat. I'm a great believer in positive thinking, but the fish simply will not jump into the boat. I have to try. I must make the effort. I have to throw the fishhook into the water.

That's the *hook* in our phrase. The hook means I do everything I can-- then trust God to do the rest. The hook is a balance between trying and trusting.

The crook refers to the shepherd's staff and the curved handle. This is a very handy tool for the shepherd. If one of the lambs start to stray, he reaches out with his long staff and with the curved end gently nudges the lamb back to the flock.

Or if one of the sheep falls into a ravine, or another difficult place, the shepherd hooks his crook underneath the lamb and lifts it to safety.

So the *crook* in our phrase means that as we try and make the effort to succeed, Jesus Christ, our Shepherd, has His crook at hand to guide us and rescue us from danger. So we can succeed by hook and by crook!

By hook and by crook I am becoming what God wants me to be!

DISCOVER YOURSELF

"You are close beside me, guarding, guiding all the way." -PSALM 23:4 (LB)

God has been helping you discover the person you can be by hook and by crook. Stop and reflect back on your life. Where has God helped you use the hook? Where has He used the shepherd's crook?

God used the *hook* in my life when He _____

_____

_____

_____

_____

God used the *crook* in my life when He _____

_____

_____

_____

_____

_____

Today, a more beautiful me is coming through. More and more, I am becoming the person I want to be!

DISCOVER YOURSELF

"How beautiful upon the mountains are the feet of the one who brings good news, who proclaims peace, ... and salvation." -ISAIAH 52:7

I found myself returning back to Russia some time ago. This time my wife joined me on the visit. We were touring Leningrad together when we met a very sharp young Communist woman. I was so impressed with her that I could easily picture her as the wife of some future premier of that country.

She asked, *"What kind of work do you do?"* *"Well,"* I answered, *"I am a minister."* Then I prayed and asked God what I could say next. What he inspired me to say to her is equally applicable to you. I continued, *"You know, I have studied both theology and psychology for some years now, and I can declare as a fact this principle: Any person—whether a Capitalist, a Communist, a Russian or an American—any person will change and will become more beautiful inside if he or she will become a believer in Jesus Christ. That's a fact!"*

She was speechless as her face revealed for a moment that she was captured by this authoritative, unchallengeable law which can be scientifically proven.

You will become a more beautiful person when you become a beautiful believer in Jesus Christ. There is a more beautiful you waiting to come through!

Thank you, God, for doing something beautiful in my mind, my heart, and in my life today!

Discover Yourself

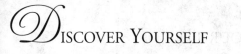

"For we are His workmanship, created in Christ Jesus for good works ..."
-EPHESIANS 2:10

I know I would not be as good a person as I am if I were not a follower of Jesus Christ. How about you? What kind of person would you be if you were not a follower of Christ? Let's take a positive inventory:

Without Christ, I would be	With Christ I am becoming

God's power now flows through me,
quickening, strengthening and
developing joy and beauty within me!

$\mathscr{D}$ISCOVER YOURSELF

"Let the beauty of the Lord our God be upon us and establish the work of our hands for us." -PSALM 90:17

"I must tell you my story," the 63 year old woman said to me. "I was 13 when I became an atheist. I had experienced something terrible and I prayed and prayed to God about it. But instead, my problem became worse than before. So then and there I decided there was no God.

"My husband and I have now been married for 42 years. All these years he was a believer and faithfully attended church. But I would never listen to him. I don't know how he put up with me.

"But," she continued, "one Sunday morning after my husband left for church, I watched you on the Hour of Power. Something about the way your eyes twinkled kept me from turning you off. You talked about Jesus and His love. I felt something inside that seemed very real. I still couldn't believe in a God, but as I continued to listen, I prayed and invited Jesus into my life. I changed right there! I could hardly wait to tell my husband when he came home."

By this time, both she and her husband were crying as they went on to describe the beautiful person she really was. Almost fifty years as an atheist, and only recently she has discovered faith, and in the same process she discovered herself! When you are related to Jesus Christ, you can discover the beautiful person you really are!

Jesus Christ makes both me~~and my day~~ beautiful!

$\mathcal{D}$ISCOVER YOURSELF

"Ask, and it will be given to you! Seek, and you will find! Knock, and it will be opened to you." -MATTHEW 7:7

"How do I get close to God?" Those words came from a corporate executive sitting next to me in a plane. *"Have you ever asked Jesus Christ to come into your life?"* I asked. He replied, *"No, that sounds too simple. I'm sorry, I can't buy that."*

"Well," I said, *"it is simple, just like the simplicity of sunlight everyday, a child's hug and kiss or the blossom of a flower. When God does something He doesn't make it complicated. Why don't we pray right now about it?"*

"Right here?" he questioned. *"Why not?"* And so we held hands and prayed, and this great big tough executive was crying with real tears rolling down his face as he said, *"It's true, it's real!"*

Have you ever discovered this? What is holding you back from trusting God for some problem or inviting Jesus Christ to come into your life? Try to describe it in words:

_____

_____

_____

_____

Now look at what you have written. Don't try to make it complicated. Believe in the simplicity of God's solution! Believe!

I am simply thrilled today as God works in and through me!

Discover Yourself

"Stand fast therefore in the liberty by which Christ has made us free ..."
Galatians 5:1

"Hi! How are you?" I asked the young girl behind the candy counter in the lobby of a hotel. *"I don't really know,"* she replied. *"You don't look very enthused,"* I commented.

As she handed me my newspaper, she said, *"I'm not very happy. I left Vietnam with my three small children after my husband was killed in the fighting. I miss my country and the rest of my family, but I can't go back."* And tears began to flow down her cheek.

"Do you have a faith or religion?" I asked. *"I'm Buddhist,"* she replied, fighting back the tears. *"But I don't practice my religion."*

"Do you mind if I share with you what Jesus Christ means to me?" I asked again. When she asked what I meant, I continued, *"Well, He's the only religious leader Who ever said, 'I love you so much I will die for you.' He died on a cross for you and me, but He rose again and lives today! He's alive! That's why I follow Him and I feel love inside of me because of what Jesus does for me. Would you like to become a follower of Christ?"*

Hesitating at first, she said, *"I think so. Nobody has ever asked me before. Yes, I would."* And so in the lobby of the hotel she invited Jesus Christ into her life. Her face was absolutely transformed!

Now I am free of all negative thoughts! Thank you, Lord, for the added blessing of freedom.

It's Possible

"Your word has given me life." -PSALM 119:50

You can enjoy living, but not until you learn to let go and let God handle your life. There are three areas of life that can get you down. First, **the stresses of life**. Then **the sins of life**. And finally **the successes of life**. And I've had experience in all these areas, so I know what I'm talking about. I want to give you three sentences that you'll want to remember:

Let God's care handle your stress.

Let God's cross handle your sins.

Let God's control handle your success.

Lord, leaning on your love liberates
me and lifts me to triumphant living.

It's Possible

"If you have faith, and don't doubt, you can do things like this and much more." -MATTHEW 21:21 (LB)

John Roebling was the engineer with the idea of bridging the river and tying Manhattan Island with Brooklyn. It was a fabulous idea, but all the bridge-building experts and structural engineers said it was impossible. Some agreed that the river might be spanned, but that a 1,595 foot span would never stand up against the winds and the tides. But John Roebling and his son, Washington, figured out how the problems could be solved and how the obstacles would be overcome.

And then, as construction began, John Roebling was killed on the job and in the same accident, Washington suffered the bends underneath the water. The son survived, but was left with permanent brain damage, so that he never walked or talked again.

Everybody said to forget the project. But not Washington. He developed a code of communication by touching one finger to the arm of his wife. And he communicated the dream through her to the engineers on the project. For thirteen years, Washington Roebling supervised construction that way. And finally, in 1883, traffic streamed across the completed Brooklyn Bridge. When Washington Roebling was told the news, he wept for joy. The impossible dream became a reality!

God, You are helping me right now discover the great possibilities You have planted within me.

It's Possible

"Do you believe? You will see greater things than these." -John 1:30

Everyone is faced, from time to time, with problems that appear to be impossible to solve. A key to successful living is to plan everyday with two questions: 1) What is the biggest problem I'm facing today? 2) What will I do about it today? Ask these two questions everyday and you'll be surprised where you're at a year from now! Briefly describe your "impossible problem":

_____

_____

_____

Now I want you to practice "possibility thinking". For some of you, it may seem futile and very difficult. But I want you to make the effort! Look again at the problem you just described. Now complete the following statement:

IT MIGHT BE POSSIBLE IF_____

_____

_____

The "if" is fading away and I can feel my faith growing. I believe it is possible!

It's Possible

"Be faithful until death, and I will give you the crown of life!"
-Revelation 2:10

It's possible for God to turn a tragedy into a triumph, and this is what happened on a dark night during the Civil War.

The Berkshire Boys found themselves at the edge of the stream where they were caught off guard by the Confederates. Fleeing across the bridge to the other side, the commander discovered that he had left his sword in his tent. Before he could start back, a teenager named Johnny Ring said to him, *"Colonel, let me go for it, sir."*

Johnny Ring ran across the bridge, retrieved the sword and started back. When he reached the bridge, flames were licking at the edges of the boards, but he ran across without hesitating, and dropped the sword at his commander's feet. He was badly burned, and lay there dying. Colonel Conwell, an atheist, looked at him and wept, saying, *"Johnny, I'm sorry, I'm sorry!"*

Johnny replied, *"Don't be sorry, sir. I'm not afraid to die. I know Jesus Christ and I'll be all right."* With his dying breath he asked, *"Colonel, are you afraid to die?" "Yes,"* replied the commander.

Beside Johnny's body that night, the commander knelt down, and in a great moment alone, he invited Jesus Christ into his life as his Savior. As he knelt, he made a vow that he would become the minister that Johnny wanted to be. He told God that he would work sixteen hours a day—eight for Johnny and eight for himself. Conwell became one of the great ministers of his day.

*I am an instrument of God's
mighty possibilities.*

It's Possible

"God who is in you is greater than he who is in the world." -I JOHN 4:4

After becoming a minister, Colonel Conwell began to lecture across the country. His lecture was entitled, "Acres of Diamonds." He said, *"There are acres of diamonds in the problem that you have before you right now."*

He delivered that lecture over 6,000 times and earned more than six million dollars. With that money he built Temple University, in Philadelphia. He believed "It was possible!"

What great thing is God attempting to do through you? An interesting experience is yours if you will complete the following sentence:

If I knew I couldn't fail, I would _____

_____

_____

_____

_____

_____

God is greater than my failure and success.

It's Possible

"Faith is the substance of things hoped for, the evidence of things not seen."
-HEBREWS 11:1

I'll never know to what extent being born on an Iowa farm made me the possibility thinker I am today. I don't think anything is more exciting than experiencing springtime on a farm.

I remember the many years when Dad needed all the grain of last year's crop to feed the cattle and the livestock. But there was one little corner of our corn bin where there was grain, and Dad would never touch it. I would say to him, *"But, Dad, you still have some grain in there."* And he would say, *"No, that is next year's seed corn, and I cannot use it to feed the cattle."* So he saved it. Then the spring came. How desperately he needed every kernel to feed the livestock. But what did he do? He buried it in the ground.

Now suppose my father had studied the odds. Let's suppose he said, *"Let's see, I've got a basket of corn. If I feed it to the cattle, I know it will be productive. I can be sure of it. There is no risk. On the other hand, I can plant it in the ground, but that's filled with risk. Weeds could choke it, birds could eat it, it could rot, or the hail and winds could destroy it just as it starts to grow. It could be worthless. It's risky to put it in the ground. But it just might multiply a hundredfold!"*

Don't wait because something is risky. Break loose and begin before it's possible. Only then will your dream really become a possibility!

I am making my decisions on God's ability, not on my ability.

It's Possible

"All shall speak of the might of your awesome acts and I will declare Your greatness!" PSALM 145:6

I have occasionally been criticized for my "slogans," but they have been an important part of whatever success I am today. I remember sitting in the bank at twelve years of age as my father conducted some business. I sat there and memorized the slogan on the bank calendar. Over the years I have changed it a bit to read:

> **GREAT PEOPLE ARE COMMON PEOPLE**
> **WHO DARE TO MAKE**
> **UNCOMMON COMMITMENTS TO GOD.**

God's great people are great because of their commitment to a goal. They are committed to some beautiful God-inspired dream. I invite you to become one of God's great people. Make a commitment today. Write it down so you can look back at it for inspiration when the going gets rough. Take the risk!

MY COMMITMENT

_____

_____

_____

My problems are possibilities. My obstacles are opportunities because I am committed to God and to greatness!

THE FUTURE

"If anyone serves Me, him will my Father honor." -JOHN 12:26

The surgical ward was a crude shop. The heat was stifling. The odors almost overwhelmed the visiting American minister, Dr. Evans. But the steady missionary doctor kept at his task with untiring skill.

After seven hours the missionary doctor stood up, faced Dr. Evans, and announced that the job was done. They walked back to the modest office and Dr. Evans asked the missionary doctor, *"How much would you have been paid for that operation in America?" Probably five hundred dollars,"* the doctor answered.

Evans said, *"I'm curious. How much do you get for that operation here?"* The doctor picked up a dented copper coin from his desk and said, *"Well, to begin with—this. The patient came into our mission holding this coin and with tears in her eyes asked me, 'Doctor, do you suppose this would pay for an operation?' I looked at her and said, 'I think so.'"* The doctor went on as tears filled his eyes, *"Most of all it makes me feel so good inside knowing that my hands have been the hands of Jesus Christ healing a sick woman for a few hours."*

What about the future? If you want a full life, you have to pour it out. Involvement is the only indulgence that really satisfies!

My faith removes limitations and replaces the fear of the future with the activity of love.

The Future

"If I ride the morning winds to the farthest oceans, even there your hand will guide me." -PSALM 139:9

As I watched, I noticed that some daring swimmers were trying to see if they could "ride the waves," the huge mountainous waves which came crashing in on the beaches. As I watched, several of these would-be-swimmers got into the water and stumbled through the foamy shallows, but they were too slow. They were overtaken, upset, flattened and sent sputtering into the surf by the liquid mountain.

Farther out in the deep, I saw a skillful rider of the surf as he carefully watched the wave as it was building, swelling and rising. Instead of running from the wave, he rode the graceful curve of the growing mountain of water. Instead of being flattened, he was lifted! Instead of being made low, he rose high and was carried far!

Every trouble has vast built-in opportunities in which to grow, to learn, to serve, or to be cleansed. Imagination can turn your bed of trouble into fruitful pastures. Your time of lying low can become your morning of spiritual refreshment. Wait patiently for the Lord. He will not mock your waiting. God will not laugh at your praying. Suddenly, you will feel the mighty hand of God underneath you and all around you, as He lifts you and guides you into your future!

I feel a mysterious, calm, quiet, tranquil assurance for the future rising deep within my being. What a relief. Thank you, Lord!

THE FUTURE

"No eye has seen, nor ear heard, nor have entered into the heart of anyone the things God has prepared for those who love Him." -1 CORINTHIANS 2:9

Gideon, a great Old Testament leader, wanted to be certain about his future, so he put out some wool on the threshing floor and asked God to make the wool wet and the floor dry. His fear was so real that when God answered Gideon, it wasn't enough. Gideon had to repeat the process again another night asking God to do just the opposite.

If Gideon feared the future, then you do not need to be ashamed if you have fears about your future. Gideon did something constructive about his fear. Write down what it is about the future that creates within you a feeling of fear:

_____

_____

_____

Now read over what you have written, and then read the verse for today. Can God handle your future? Believe He can—God CAN!

My future is my friend because God is in my future just as He is with me now.

THE FUTURE

"I would have lost heart unless I had believed to see the goodness of the Lord in the land of the living." -PSALM 27:13

I like the attitude of my neighbor. She and her husband worked, saved, and in their fifties bought a lovely home near ours. Suddenly, one week after they moved, her husband died of a heart attack without warning! And she was left alone with a new home.

I stopped and talked with her one morning. She was out in the yard surveying the boxes, barrels and unpotted plants. The morning sun was bright and she looked wide awake as she took stock of the work that needed to be done. *"Do you know what gives me great strength?"* she said to me. *"It is the certain assurance that it was my husband's time to go. It was God's will. And it is His will for me to get these plants in the ground and things unpacked!"*

And she meant it! I watched her as she helped the neighborhood children collect old newspapers for the local school. She was laughing and having a grand time. Soon after that, she was in our home for coffee and said, *"Oh, sometimes I cry—but it was God's will. And I know He loves me. He does nothing wrong."*

Her life has not stopped. Her future is alive.

This one thing I know~
God is for me! I am not afraid!

THE FUTURE

I have a strong, serene feeling
that God is planning something good
for me today. I cannot explain it,
but I have a deep feeling that
wonderful things are in store for me.

I am expecting God to surprise me
with His tender mercy.

Thank you, Lord,
for today and
each of my tomorrows!

*I am learning to
really enjoy life!*

 The Future

"I will be your God through all your lifetime...I made you and I will care for you." -Isaiah 46:4 (LB)

The hand of the Almighty is never far away. No wonder you can trust the future! And when you cannot see any good, only stark, naked, cruel, brutal tragedy in a catastrophic situation, then you can expect God to come and show mercy!

As an unexpected gust of wind comes under the weary wings of a storm-drenched bird, to lift the pitiful creature to higher altitudes where it can soar in new strength, so God comes with His unannounced invasion of mercy!

Often, God will use people as His messengers of mercy. I am certain that you can recall times when God sent someone to you at the right moment with words of encouragement. Perhaps God wants to use you in that way today.

Stop and relax. Enter into two-way prayer with God. Ask Him if there is someone He would like you to visit, or call, or send a note of encouragement. Write down that person's name:

_____

_____

What does God want you to do?_____

_____

_____

God, here I am. Use me as the bearer of mercy to someone who is hurting today.

The Future

"The desert shall rejoice and blossom as the rose; it shall blossom abundantly and rejoice, even with joy and singing. -ISAIAH 35:1 AND 2

As I returned from New York, the giant jumbo jet circled into the landing path at Los Angeles. As we completed our cross-country flight, those last miles presented a kaleidoscope of scenery: Catalina Island laying off the coast in the dark blue Pacific; the white surf on the Southern California beaches; the snow-capped mountains surrounding the Los Angeles basin; and beyond those majestic mountain peaks, the vast expanse of desert.

Whenever I have made the same flight I have frequently noticed a tiny square patch of green in the middle of that seemingly endless desert wasteland—a thriving little farm surrounded by a thirsty monster of shifting sand. Will the defenseless little ranch be swallowed up by the parched desert on some future flight? I doubt it. For this fertile oasis draws its life from deep wells that tap a subterranean river. Far to the west, the snow on the mountains melt and the water streams silently down the eastern slope, draining deep into the sand to feed the subterranean river. The future of the ranch is quite safe, for it has a secret alliance with the mountain!

So it is with you. You may be like an island surrounded by an unfriendly sea, a patch of green in a desert wasteland. But your life is in the care and keeping of God Who keeps watch over His own.

My roots run deep and tap into God's rich supply. I can feel God's confidence surging within. I have nothing to fear!

GOD-POWER WITHIN

"Seek first the kingdom of God ... and all these things shall be added to you." -MATTHEW 6:34

You can explode with achievement if you have God-power within you. This is absolutely true. It can be reduced to a simple lesson in what I call religious mathematics, or the mathematics of faith.

Faith is a mathematical power! It subtracts weakness; adds power, divides difficulties, multiplies possibilities! What a way to live!

You can see this principle at work in the life of Jesus Christ. He was the most successful person Who ever lived. He never had a negative, defeating thought. I try to think positively, but there are times when I become negative.

Now someone will say that Jesus was a failure because He died on a cross. But nothing could be further from the truth. The key is in your definition of "success." I define success as "fulfilling God's plan for your life." Success is achieving what God wants you to achieve.

Jesus was the world's greatest success because He did what God wanted Him to do perfectly. Don't be afraid of success! God wants you to succeed!

Through the activity of God's power within me, I succeed with every endeavor!

GOD-POWER WITHIN

"O the depth of the riches both of the wisdom and knowledge of God!
How unsearchable are His judgements, and His ways past finding out!"
-ROMANS 11:33

Earlier in our devotions, we considered goals that were long-range—what shall I do with my life? Now it's time to become more specific. What short-range goals could you set? Remember, they should still be big enough to include God, but they should be specific enough for you to be able to reach them by the end of one week. Take the time to stop and think, and then write down one or two goals you could reach in seven days:

In one week, I _____

_____

_____

_____

_____

Now that you have stated your goals, are they big enough that you need God's help? I hope so! Spend some time today talking with God, asking Him to help, for inspiration, for courage, and for a plan to reach that goal.

Today, I begin a new venture. Trusting
God for the strength, the courage,
the inspiration, and the help I need to
reach my goal.

GOD-POWER WITHIN

"For we walk by faith, not by sight." -ROMANS 5:7

In 1950, Ralph Johnson Bunche, a well-known American statesman, won the Nobel Peace Prize, the first awarded to an African-American. What was the secret of his climb to national and international success and acclaim?

He was born in Detroit, Michigan. His mother died when he was very young. His father, a butcher, supported the family until his death soon thereafter. Ralph Bunche was left an orphan at the age of twelve.

When his parents died, Ralph left Michigan and came to Los Angeles to live with his grandmother, Lucy Johnson. She was such an inspiring woman that near the end of her life, her writings were put into a limited publication entitled, "Believe in Yourself." I want to share with you something from that book.

In the first chapter she says, *"Believe in yourself. Never say I am going to try, but, rather, I am going to do."* There is sound advice in those two sentences. They hold the seed of self-confidence. And that trait is one God wants you to have.

Mrs. Johnson continues, *"You must not only believe in yourself, you must believe in other people, too."* Faith is not just directed towards God, but in successful people, faith is also directed to other people. She notes how often faith is emphasized in the Bible. *"Read the Bible,"* she added, *"and control your destiny!"*

Small wonder that Ralph Bunche attained such distinction. He had Lucy Johnson as his grandmother and the example of her faith in Jesus Christ!

I feel the reservoir of God's strength welling up within me!

GOD-POWER WITHIN

"And I will give you a new heart and put a new spirit within you."
-EZEKIEL 36:16

Where the Crystal Cathedral now stands, there was originally a large walnut grove. In the fall these walnut trees dropped their leaves. Those that didn't fall off were blown off by what we call in California - the Santa Ana winds. These are strong winds that periodically come whipping through Southern California.

I was walking through our barren walnut grove one day, and I saw here and there a dead leaf still clinging to the branch. The strong winds hadn't blown them off. The winter rains hadn't washed them off,

Sometimes we have problems like that. They just seem to hang on and the winds will not blow them off. The storms will not wash them off. But wait - in a little while new sap will come from the deep roots, surging through the trunk into the branches and a new bud will push the dead leaf off. *Every dead leaf that still clings on through the wintertime is doomed because new life will push it off in the spring!*

Depressed? Deflated? Defeated? New life can come to you! But you can't do it alone. God's power within you gives you new life. He will push off the old and make room for the new.

I shall not be defeated today if the strong winds of trouble come. God's power within me will give new energy.

GOD-POWER WITHIN

"Do you see that faith works together with works, and by works, faith is made perfect." -JAMES 2:22

The late Joe Frazier, former world heavyweight boxing champion, is a good example of Christian dreaming and planning. He was a dedicated Christian who read his Bible nightly and attended church regularly. He credited his success to faith in God.

As a young boy, Joe dreamed of becoming a boxer. He was inspired by Archie Moore, one of the greatest boxers of our time. Archie Moore, had a program called "ABC—Any Boy Can." That program inspired Joe Frazier to start.

He had no money, so he had to improvise. He got an old sack and filled it with sand and he had a punching bag. That was the beginning of a dedicated, disciplined plan which ultimately led to Frazier's becoming the United States' boxing representative for the Olympic games held in Tokyo in 1964.

He worked hard, prayed and believed. And even with a broken thumb, Frazier won the gold medal. He firmly believed that success depends on your roadwork. I agree. You must be willing to do your roadwork—month after month, year after year, hurdle after hurdle. That's called working your plan!

Frazier admitted that many times he wanted to stop midway in his daily eight mile runs. He knew that no one would know the difference. But then he realized that he would only be fooling himself and that is the last person he wanted to deceive. Therefore he kept on running!

Whatever hurdles you face, keep on running!

*My future is bright,
because I am working my God~inspired plan!*

GOD-POWER WITHIN

"It is God who arms me with strength and makes my way perfect. He makes my feet like the feet of a deer and sets me on my high places." -
PSALM 18:32,33

Pat Nordberg's life hung by a thread in surgery for hours. Miraculously, she survived. But as a result of the surgery, she was left an aphasic. She had a partial loss of her ability to speak along with the loss of her memory for words.

She was faced with enormous problems to overcome. In her aphasic condition, she began helping as a volunteer with mentally disabled children. This work inspired her with a dream; she would become a counselor and psychologist, specializing in working with mentally disabled children.

She dared to believe that with God's power within she could do it. She started with a detailed plan. She figured that she would have to regain her muscle coordination, so she spent two years taking Hawaiian hula lessons. She built up her strength to the point where she could take her driving test and get her license—step two. Now she was ready to tackle college.

Pat earned her degree. Her dream became a burning desire. She succeeded. Today she is a counselor of aphasic children and their parents. Great things occur when you plan your course step-by-step!

God's power within me gives me strength. I am reaching my goal!

God-Power Within

"Uphold my steps in Your paths, O Lord, that my footsteps may not slip."
-PSALM 17:5

A few days ago I asked you to set some short-range goals. Did you? Now it's time to evaluate your progress. How are you doing? Did you arrive at your objective? Did you get partway there? Describe how you feel about your progress:

_____

_____

_____

If you didn't reach your goal, it's time to restate your goal. Don't let the seeds of discouragement defeat you just as you're beginning to succeed! If you did reach your goal, it's time to make some new ones. Use your faith, and the power of God within, to reach farther than you ever have before. Stretch your faith. Remember, beginning is half done!

My next goal is:

_____

_____

_____

_____

I am anticipating success. My path is clear. Step~by~step, God is giving me the power to reach my objective!

ENTHUSIASM FOR TODAY

"As for me I trust in you, O Lord; I say, "You are my God." -PSALM 31:14

Dr. Norman Vincent Peale once asked a surgeon, *"What's the most exciting operation you have ever performed in your career?"* The doctor thought a brief moment and replied, *"You know, there is one surgery that stands out. It changed my life.*

"There was this little girl with only a ten percent chance of survival. When I went into the operating room, there she was, a tiny little thing under the sheet, with an ashen gray face—so frail, so weak and helpless.

"Just as the nurses were going to prepare her for the anesthesia, I walked up to her and she looked at me and said, 'May I say something, doctor?' I said, 'Sure, honey.' 'Well, doctor,' she enthused, 'every night before I go to sleep I always pray a prayer. May I pray now?' I said, 'Of course.'

"Now I was having troubles of my own at that time with my son," the doctor continued, *"and I was a very unhappy person. I stood there and told her to go ahead and pray, and to remember her doctor, too.*

"She prayed, 'Jesus, tender Shepherd, hear me. Watch your little lamb tonight...and Jesus, bless the doctor, because he's got troubles, too.' That broke me up. I turned away from the operating table so that nurses wouldn't see my tears. I prayed like I never prayed before, 'Oh God, if You ever use me to save a life, use me now to save this little girl!' She survived surgery, and I found Jesus!"

*I will trust you, O Lord,
for You are my God!*

ℰNTHUSIASM FOR TODAY

"One thing I do, forgetting those things where are behind I reach forward to those things which are ahead." -PHILIPPIANS 3:13

JESUS CHRIST IS ALIVE! And He gives you and me enthusiasm for today!

When you think about <u>yourself</u> ... trouble **grows.**

When you think about <u>Christ</u> ... trouble **goes!**

The exciting good news is that Jesus Christ has liberated us through the power of His Holy Spirit living within you and me. He cares about what is happening in your work, your dreams, your marriage and your family!

What can Jesus Christ do for you? I submit He can do for you what He is doing for me. He can reach you wherever you are; He can redeem you no matter how trapped you feel; He can unlock your possibilities and assure you of your worth—of the meaning and purpose of your life!

When you respond to His reach, you'll discover real enthusiasm for living! You will enjoy a better life, a happier life, a fuller life. He can reach you wherever you are!

Jesus Christ is reaching me with His confidence and enthusiasm.

ENTHUSIASM FOR TODAY

"Be renewed in the spirit of your mind." -EPHESIANS 4:23

When the melody goes out of your life, when the sun is gone, when a bell no longer rings, and life is flat and dull, when you've lost enthusiasm for living and you no longer have a dream, what do you do? The answer lies in a beautiful passage in the Bible, Ephesians 4:23: *"Be renewed in the spirit of your mind."*

Recite this verse out loud right now: *"I will be renewed in the spirit of my mind."* Say it one more time: *"I will be renewed in the spirit of my mind."* Say it often. Say the verse with energy. *"I will be renewed in the spirit of my mind."*

The young stewardess on an airplane recognized me and said, *"Dr. Schuller, if I can have a few moments I'd like to talk to you."* She began to pour out her life's story. She told me how she was married for three and a half years, and how her husband was unfaithful to her, and beat her up. She said, *"I thought to myself, 'If I can't beat him, I'll join him.' So I started running around."*

Then, of course, the guilt spilled out. She said, *"I feel so guilty. Can you help me?"*

I said, *"I think I can point you to One who can help you."* Then I introduced her to my best friend — Jesus Christ.

She took hold of my hand, we bowed our heads and I prayed for her. When I finished, the tears were rolling out. She had a dream again that her life can be clean, noble, beautiful and honorable. She was renewed with fresh enthusiasm!

*Jesus Christ, take my guilt away
so I can be enthused again!*

ENTHUSIASM FOR TODAY

"I will praise the Lord with my whole heart." -PSALM 111:1

He had no religion, never did have, according to his testimony to me later. But that morning he flipped the TV dial trying to check the weather, and for a moment watched this minister from Los Angeles being interviewed on a talk show. He listened a bit, then continued his search for news of the weather, and then turned off the set.

Later that morning, he couldn't stop thinking of the minister on TV. All he could remember was the fact that he was speaking that night at the Hilton Hotel.

Finally he called the Hilton in San Francisco. Yes, there was a convention. Yes, there was a Dr. Schuller speaking. NO, he could not get a ticket, it was a closed meeting.

Undaunted, the man got into his car, drove to San Francisco and went to the meeting. When he arrived, the usher was not at the door. He walked in and sat down in the back. He heard me say, *"God is reaching out to you. A hundred times each day God reaches out to you but you don't recognize that it is God. He wants you to discover the enthusiasm He gives for living!"*

That young man decided he needed God to come into his life. And in that moment God reached down and filled him with a new joy, confidence and enthusiasm.

Today I sense God filling me with a new joy!

ℰNTHUSIASM FOR TODAY

"Imitate me, just as I also imitate Christ." -1 CORINTHIANS 11:1

Enthusiasm is contagious — especially when its source is a positive faith in a positive God. My enthusiasm was transmitted through a TV set and into the mind of a man who searched until he found where I was speaking. God used that instance to draw that man to Himself.

Saint Paul was so enthusiastic about Jesus Christ that he wrote to the believers in Corinth and said, "Imitate me just as I imitate Christ!" That's enthusiasm!

Who are the enthusiastic people in your life? Are there Christians who inspire you by their enthusiasm and faith? Write their names below along with a brief description of the attractiveness of their enthusiasm.

NAME	THEIR ENTHUSIASM INSPIRES ME BECAUSE
_____	_____
_____	_____
_____	_____
_____	_____
_____	_____
_____	_____

My enthusiasm is growing. I can feel joy within me this day!

ENTHUSIASM FOR TODAY

Put on the new you which was created according to God, in righteousness and true holiness." -EPHESIANS 4:24

Michelangelo is credited with creating forty-four statues in his lifetime, but he only finished fourteen of them. Now most of you are familiar with the fourteen he finished—David, the Pieta, and Moses, to mention a few.

But the thirty he never finished are very interesting. I have seen many of them...a huge chunk of marble out of which he had sculptured an elbow or the beginning of a wrist. The rest of the human form is still locked up in the marble.

Another chunk shows a leg with the thigh, knee, calf, heel and foot clearly chiseled out of the hard stone, but the rest of the body is still locked within. And then another one shows the head and shoulders of a man, but the rest of the body is still frozen inside.

When I saw these unfinished masterpieces in a museum in Italy, the thought struck me, "Of all the tragedies in life, the greatest tragedy is for a person to live and die and never be told what his possibilities are." And then I thought of the possibilities still locked within me, and my enthusiasm for God's releasing power grew.

You and I are unfolding masterpieces in the hands of God—the Master Sculptor!

Unlock the frozen possibilities still within me, O God, and be at work in my life!

ENTHUSIASM FOR TODAY

O God, when a life has been so richly blessed as mine has been, it is not right for me to be crying! I confess that I am responsible for my moods. I have no right to selfishly indulge in negative feelings of self-pity. It's time for me to change my mental dial, Lord.

You are helping me.

This will be the moment when the sun breaks through the parted clouds, like springtime returning after winter.

Thank you, Lord! The dreary, depressing, disconsolate mood disappears like the morning mist in the glowing sunshine of Your love.

And joy moves in!

And hope begins to build up within me!
And a beautiful feeling of enthusiasm is surrounding me now!

Thank you, God, for the great things You are doing within me now in this moment of prayer.

Amen.

*I am living today controlled by my
God~inspired positive ideas!*

Never Be Afraid

"I am the door. If anyone enters by me, he will be saved and will go in and out ... " -JOHN 10:9

It happened one night in France. There was a Halloween party and a hundred happy young people were having a ball. Somehow a fire started— no one ever knew how. People ran but were unable to find the exits. Most of them died.

In that hall there were doors built for one purpose and one purpose only ... namely, to get out in time of danger. But those doors were unseen. They were covered with curtains.

Early the next morning as firemen checked through the burned out building, they pulled what was left of the curtains aside and found the doors. *But the doors had been nailed shut to prevent party crashers.* And the result was that people perished!

Somebody dreamed of a building, and planned a safety door.
Others were afraid and hammered the door shut!
Jesus Christ is God's door ...
into a closeness with God
  into salvation,
  into eternal life,
into a life where there is no fear at all!

"I am the door!
Don't hammer me shut! Open me! Walk through!
I will never forget your name!
 I will never forget your face!
You are mine!"

*The bottom line of my life
is faith, not fear.*

NEVER BE AFRAID

"Fear not, for I have redeemed you;
I have called you by your name; you are Mine.
When you go through the waters and great trouble
I WILL BE WITH YOU.
When you go through rivers,
they shall not overflow you.
When you walk through the fire you shall not be burned,
nor the flame scorch you.

For I am the Lord your God, your Savior...
you are precious in my sight
you have been honored, and I have loved you.

Fear not, for I am with you."

ISAIAH 43:1-5

My future is in God's hands,
so I am not afraid!

Never Be Afraid

"Be of good courage, and He shall strengthen your heart, all you who hope in the Lord." -PSALM 31:24

Courage belongs to those who know God, says the psalmist. And I say we need to continually affirm God's power to protect us. Today we're going to create a litany which affirms our faith in God's power, so that we need never be afraid. In the blank spaces, write down some situation that strikes fear in your heart. When you have finished, read your litany of courage and praise. You need never be afraid!

When I _____
... I will put my trust in God.

When I _____
... The Lord gives me courage!

When I _____
... The Lord is my light and salvation!

When I _____
...My heart shall know no fear! God will save me!

When I _____
... God will send the help I need!

When I _____
... I am expecting the Lord to rescue me!

When I _____

*I am brave, for God's power
is greater than any situation
I could possibly face today.*

Never Be Afraid

"Behold, the Lord's hand is not shortened that it cannot save. -ISAIAH 59:1

Imagine for a moment that you are lined up along a street waiting for a parade. It has been said that Jesus Christ is going to pass by.

As He comes down the street, you can hear the applause. Most of us, perhaps all of us, would applaud Him.

"That is Christ."

"He is wonderful."

"Isn't He great?"

But watch! From time to time, there are those who do not applaud. They break through the rope, dash into the middle of the street, and for a moment take hold of His hand...

Jesus looks at them, with His face close to them.

Something happens between them and then they slip back and once more stand at the curb. Now they are changed. And the biggest change of all is a boldness, and a fearlessness, that transforms them into exciting, enthused, world-changers!

It is not enough just to applaud, to admire, to respect, and to adore. We must break out and take hold of His hand for a moment! And as He looks at us, our fears will vanish! We know Him—the Creator of the universe. And He knows us!

*I feel my courage growing as I
reach my hand out to God.
He knows who I am! And comes to me!*

Never Be Afraid

"The Lord is the One who goes before you. He will be with you. He will not leave you ... do not fear nor be dismayed. -DEUTERONOMY 31:8

The people who lived next door to us had three Doberman pinschers. The huge dogs welcomed us soon after we moved in. They were marvelous, beautiful creatures, but ferocious. I kept at least ten feet between me and the fence. When I did my running they would see me, and as soon as I came near their yard they came racing after me, teeth bared, foaming at the mouth. I'm alive because of the fence!

My daughter, though, walked over to our neighbor's yard to play with their daughter and the Dobermans never bothered her. I kept saying, *"Honey, you'd better watch out for those big dogs."* And she answered me, *"Dad, those dogs are trained."* I replied, *"I know they're trained, but be careful!"* But she persisted, *"Dad, you just don't understand. Those dogs are trained only to bite somebody who is running. That's why they never bite me!"*

Now I've never experimented with that theory, but I do know this: After all my years as a pastor, I can confidently say that most, if not all, of our fears are the kind that are trained to strike at our hearts only when we run away from them. Face them, and we find they are not enemies at all. They are shadows in our path—it's that simple! Face your fears and they fade away!

I will bravely face my fears today for God is with me!

NEVER BE AFRAID

"Do not be afraid. Stand still and see the salvation of the Lord which He will accomplish for you today." -EXODUS 14:13

A couple of days ago you created a litany of praise affirming your confidence in God's power. In that litany, you listed several things that create fear within you. Go back to that list and choose one of those fears that you might have to face today. Describe it:

_____

_____

_____

Today, instead of running, reacting, or hiding, you are going to FACE YOUR FEAR! Stop! Turn around and look your fear in the eye. Now write down three positive steps you are going to take, today, to face this fear and conquer it. As you do, claim the promise of God in Exodus 14:13 for God will be with you!

1. _____

_____

2. _____

_____

3. _____

_____

I am not afraid. God is with me and together we are invincible!

NEVER BE AFRAID

"The Lord will fight for you, and you shall hold your peace."
-*Exodus 14:14*

I love the story about old Doctor John McNeil, who was a famous American preacher some years ago. He said, "When I was a lad in Scotland I used to work late, and in order to get home I had to walk a long distance. I had to go several miles through a little village and then through a narrow canyon where criminals and thieves were known to hide.

"One particular Saturday night I walked as fast as I could. My heart was pounding in my teenage chest, for the night was as black as a wolf's jaw. Not a star was shining. The moon was dark. There were no lights in the sky.

"I rounded a bend in the road in the most desolate, the most forsaken and the most frightening part of the whole canyon. Suddenly, there was a call in the night! For a moment my heart stopped. The call came again, it was my father's voice. He was coming out to meet me at the worst part of the canyon. 'John! It's you!' he said.

"In a moment his large hand was on my shoulder and his heavy footsteps were falling at my side. I was home right then and there!"

You are always home when your Father comes to meet you. For God has promised, "I will be with you!" He knows you. He calls you. And He is with you! You need never be afraid again!

*I need never be afraid again,
for You walk with me all the way.*

TRANQUILIZE TENSION

"For God is not the author of confusion but of peace."
-1 CORINTHIANS 14:33

"Relax, Dr. Schuller, just relax," my golf instructor told me. "Why, I'm quite relaxed," I assured him as I gripped my club fiercely, as if it were a sword.

"Feel the muscles in the back of your legs," my teacher continued, adding, "I dare say that every muscle in your body is tense right now. I can see it—even your cheek and lip muscles are tensed up! You've got to relax!"

I waited and he kept right on preaching to me. "All right, Dr. Schuller, mentally unwind. Loosen up the muscles on your forehead. Now relax your eyebrows, now your cheeks, now your tongue and your mouth. Now your whole face. Good!" He added his encouragement, "Now keep on relaxing your muscles across your shoulders. Feel the soothing, balmy relaxation flow like warm water over your whole body. Let the tension drip away. Now breathe deeply and exhale slowly. Do it again."

It all sounded silly, but as he repeated this process, and I agreed to do what he suggested, it really worked! I relaxed so much the golf club fell out of my hand!

Well, I never learned to play golf very well, but those lessons did make me aware of tension I never sensed before. And only as we become sensitive to the presence of tension will we begin to do something about it!

God didn't create us for tension. Instead, He has provided us with tension tranquilizers. And He is the source of all tranquility!

I feel tension slipping away as I focus my thoughts on God's tranquil peace.

TRANQUILIZE TENSION

"I will lie down in peace and sleep, for you alone, O Lord, make me dwell in safety." -PSALM 4:8

Now, before we can attempt to
paralyze the destructive effect of tension,
sterilize the reproductive effect of tension,
tranquilize the seductive effect of tension, we need to ...
Sensitize ourselves to the reality of tension, and
Analyze what gets us so uptight and tense.

I GET TENSE AND UPTIGHT WHEN:

1. _____

2. _____

3. _____

4. _____

5. _____

THE MAIN CAUSE OF MY TENSION IS:

_____

_____

My tension becomes more tranquil
as I focus on God's prescription for peace.

TRANQUILIZE TENSION

"My peace I give to you; not as the world gives do I give to you. Let not your heart be troubled, neither let it be afraid." -JOHN 14:27

In my world travels, I have run across all kinds of trinkets, tricks and techniques for relieving tension—everything from "worry beads" to a rubbing stone. But I find nothing that can compare with the peace that Jesus Christ brings into the human heart.

Gilbert Chesterton, after wandering far and wide in his lifetime of free thinking, came back at last to faith. He said, *"It was like a man setting sail from England to discover some great new land. Into the fog he sailed, for days and days— confident that he would make some great new discovery.*

"Finally, as the fog lifted, he saw land, and coming to an exotic shore he ran up and down the beach. He hoisted the English flag with dreams of naming this new land after himself. But in his running across the beach, he turned a bend and noted, with shock and dismay, that this was only the other side of England. Trying to escape England—he only came back to where he began."

Trying to turn away from Christ, through centuries and cultures, human beings come back to Him again and again! For only Jesus Christ can bring true tranquility.

Lord, I turn to You and feel the warm rays of Your love filling me with peace of mind and heart! Thank You!

TRANQUILIZE TENSION

"Remember the Sabbath Day, to keep it holy." -EXODUS 20:8

Traditionally, Sunday was a very great creative day of quietness for faith, for fun and for the family, for the church, and for the community. Something happened. And I make this statement here and now based on research that I have done, and that is, in the past fifty years we have seen a growing, deepening sense of depression in the widespread epidemic of emotional ailments like anxiety, and stress, with its effect upon the human organism. This emotional epidemic of negative, mental, and spiritual problems in our country has risen sharply in proportion to our forsaking of that one day in seven as a useful day of healing.

How can you use it? First, use it as a day of **rest.** You need one day in seven to rest the heart, the system and the body. And then use it for a day of **retreat.** Retreat from the tension-producing inputs that you have to be exposed to the rest of the week.

I remember when our oldest daughter, Sheila, was about four years old, and her neighborhood playmate came to the house one Sunday asking if Sheila could come out and play. I wasn't prepared for that, and I said, *"No, not today, but she can play tomorrow and the next day, but not on Sunday."* I wanted that one day completely different so that she would be exposed to just the family and friends in church. Sunday is a day to regroup. I mean regroup your thinking and get your act together again.

You need one day in seven to rest, to retreat and to regroup. Go to church.

*Lord, thank You for the church
where I find rest and can regroup my thinking.*

$\mathscr{T}$RANQUILIZE TENSION

"Therefore, if Christ makes you free, you shall be free indeed." -JOHN 8:36

God's first tension tranquilizer is FREEDOM. Nothing tranquilizes like real freedom—shoes off, running barefoot on the windy and sandy beach, alive and free!

But real freedom is found in the commitment of responsible inter-personal relationships. We often think of freedom as total freedom—freedom without responsibility. That's the kind of freedom the prodigal son experienced, and the end of that road is utter loneliness and despair.

Real freedom comes within a relationship, like the relaxing freedom that comes the moment you run into the arms of a caring, loving God. At that point you can say good-bye to the "I'm trapped" tensions; the "I'm boxed-in" tensions; the "I'm stuck-in-a-rut" tensions.

Have you experienced real freedom? Describe a time recently when you experienced this kind of freedom and write down what that freedom felt like:

_____

_____

_____

God, as I run to Your arms,
I experience the joy of real freedom ...
the freedom to become!

Tranquilize Tension

"Forgive, and you will be forgiven." -LUKE 6:37

Forgiveness—God's healing tranquilizer number two!

Forgiveness is the flow of divine love through your spiritual consciousness. It is God, real and alive; A Powerful Positive Emotion flowing through you. Deep Peace and Power surge instantaneously through your soul.

Tensions flow out when you take and give forgiveness ...

Detection tension—"what if they find out?"

Exposure tension—"what if people tell on me?"

These terrible tensions are gone when you experience God's forgiveness.

Hostility Tension, Anger Tension, Resentment Tension, Retaliation Tension—all these leave you as you begin to practice forgiveness. Here is a tranquilizer that really tranquilizes!

HE WHO FORGIVES ENDS THE TENSION!

All sorts of mental battles cease at the peace table of Divine Forgiveness. Whom do you need to meet at that table? God? A parent? A child? A friend? A co-worker?

Stop now and in your mind visualize a table ... a Divine Forgiveness Table. And seated at that table is you ... and God ... and _____. As God forgives, your heart is filled with forgiveness towards that other person. *"Forgive us our sins, just as we have forgiven those who have sinned against us."* (Matthew 6:12).

*God's tranquilizer of forgiveness
fills me with peace!*

Tranquilize Tension

"For Christ himself is our way of peace. He has made peace between us... by making us all one family." -EPHESIANS 2:14 (LB)

Freedom, Forgiveness and Fellowship are the three sacred tranquilizers that really tranquilize. Fellowship is that deep, serene, trusting experience that is available between you and God, and between you and your friends.

Fellowship with God—Divine Fellowship—how easy it is to empty the cup of this relaxing drink! How it relieves. Suddenly, loneliness, tension and rejection-tension are gone. When we experience acceptance by God, and enjoy fellowship with Him, faith, hope and love flood our being. All tension is gone!

When we experience fellowship with God we also desire fellowship with the family of God. And in that fellowship together, we can experience the healing power of God's Spirit working. For in the fellowship of the family of God, we discover that we are not alone, our troubles are not unique, our hurdles can be conquered!

It's time to come to the party. Join other believers as they worship the God you believe in. Your tensions will vanish as you come inside to the church of your choice and enjoy fellowship with the Family of God!

Through my church I can experience the tranquilizers of freedom, forgiveness and fellowship!

LIBERATE YOUR IMAGINATION

"To whom then will you liken me? Or to whom shall I be equal"' says the Holy One. Lift your eyes on high, and see who has created these things ... He calls them all by name. By His greatness and power ..." -ISAIAH 40:26

It's exciting to me to realize that I am made in the image of God. What does that mean to you? To me, the image of God means that I share with Him His most distinctive qualities-including His Creative Power! God is Creative! He is Cosmic Imagination! When you look at the splendor of God's creation, you know that one of the primary features of His image is His Creativity!

Only human beings share the gift of creative imagination with God. You have it. I have it. But for many of us our imagination is locked up in a cage. And we cannot dare to dream to become the persons we could become until our imaginations are liberated!

I remember listening to one of the American POW's who had just returned from Vietnam. He had been held captive by the Vietcong in a tiger cage. These cages were made of bamboo, and were about six feet long, four feet high and two feet wide.

This POW told how, one night, he managed to work one of the bamboo rods loose. Soon he had another one loose and then another, until finally he slipped out of the cage and made his escape. As I listened to him, I thought of the mental tiger cages that hold our creativity captive. Our potentially powerful imagination is imprisoned in a tiger cage of our own mind!

It's time to liberate your imagination and discover the dreams God has for your life!

I am made in the image of God! I share His creative power. He is at work helping me liberate my imagination!

LIBERATE YOUR IMAGINATION

"Strengthen the weak hands and make firm the feeble knees and say to those who are fearful-hearted, 'be strong, do not fear!'" -ISAIAH 35:3,4

There are five bars in our mental tiger cages that must be loosened. Let's look at them.

First, our **frights** restrict our imagination. Nothing holds people back more than the fear of failure. And no fright more than this one keeps us from really imagining the person we could become.

What failure are you afraid of today? What is it? _____

_____

It is possible for us to overcome our fears! We overcome our fears when we realize that our fears do not come from God and hence they are not to be trusted!

Don't surrender your life and your future to fear. In the name of Christ, command any fears to *get out!* Work your imagination free from imprisoning any unreliable fears by first of all recognizing that God is stronger than any fear. Then boldly repeat out loud this affirmation:

With God's help, I will not fail,
so I command all my fear of failure to be
released from my mind today.

Liberate Your Imagination

"I will bless the Lord who has given me counsel' my heart also instructs me in the night season ... therefore my heart is glad." -PSALM 16:7-9

The second bar in our mental tiger care is our **nights.** I'm thinking about the dark times of life; the experiences that hurt us. Both our **frights** and our **nights** can imprison our imagination.

I met a man on the way to the airport in North Carolina. He was filled with enthusiasm. He said, *"Dr. Schuller, you would never have known me a couple of years ago. Christ has transformed my life!"*

He went on to tell me how he had been raised on a farm outside of Charlotte. As a young man he said, *"There must be a better life than this. The work was hard and I could barely make a living by farming. I borrowed all I could,* he said, *"and set up a business selling farm machinery. Four farm machinery businesses went bankrupt that year and mine was one of them. I was penniless, with no trade or skill except farming, but I wasn't ready to go back to farming."*

"What happened?" I asked. *"Well, I took a job in a post office doing menial work. But I felt trapped. I was so depressed I would often go into the rest room and bawl like a baby. This went on for eight years!*

"One day a fellow came into the post office and asked me why he never saw me smile. He told me, 'You can smile, for God loves you!' That man introduced me to Jesus Christ and gave me the courage to start another business. My dark nights are over!" he affirmed.

My faith in God turns my night seasons into days of gladness.

LIBERATE YOUR IMAGINATION

"It is good to give thanks to the Lord ... to declare Your loving kindness in the morning, and Your faithfulness every night, O Lord." -PSALM 92:1,2

What experiences in your past are holding you back? Is it a setback, a hurt, a failure, a defeat, a reverse, a rejection? Refuse to surrender leadership of your future life to past hurts! If you're afraid of getting hurt again, you'll never break free.

Stop a moment, today, and write down one or two experiences in your past that could be called "night" experiences:

_____

_____

_____

Now look at those experiences carefully and positively. What good things were you able to learn from those experiences?

_____

_____

_____

Now affirm that you are a child of the day—darkness and night are no longer a part of you!

The past is past. I am alive, today, and living in the light. I am filled with possibilities for today!

LIBERATE YOUR IMAGINATION

"Your gentleness has made me great, you enlarged my path under me; so my feet did not slip." -2 SAMUEL 22:36,37

The third rod that binds our imagination in mental tiger cages is the **light.** How can that be, you ask? How can success bind us?

It's easy to see how some people can be restricted from becoming the great people they should become by the hurts of life, but it is just as true that some people are bound by the highlights of life.

SUCCESS IS NEVER SETTLED!

That means there are always greater things that you can and should do. If you attain a goal, and become so enamored with the glory and the honor and the laurels that you stay at that level—then your imagination is being blinded by the light of the success in your life.

But the light of God is meant to show us the path to greater possibilities and richer experiences. When you are tempted to stop along the path of life and enjoy the view, resist that urge. Step forward and move onward to new and greater heights. Don't let the light of your victories cause you to become a failure.

God, keep enlarging my path of success so that I can help others along the way.

LIBERATE YOUR IMAGINATION

"Let patience have its perfect work, that you may be perfect and complete, lacking nothing." -JAMES 1:4

The fourth rod in our mental tiger cage is our **blights.** I don't think anything keeps people from becoming the people God wants them to be more than perfectionism.

Consider the limiting, lowering, negative influence of these statements: "I can't do it." "I'm not as good as others." "I'm not beautiful." "I'm not smart."

What's your favorite excuse? Write it down:

_____

My publisher challenged me once with this point: *"Dr. Schuller,"* he said, *"you've got to prove to people that it's not talent that makes them reach the top." "But talent is terribly important,"* I argued. *"After all, I can be a possibility thinker, but I can't sing like Beverly Sills."*

He insisted, *"You do some more research, Schuller!"* and I did. I discovered that in every profession you will find that the people at the top are not the most talented people in their professions. ***The people at the top have learned to ignore their blights!***

Now rewrite the sentence above. Or better yet, write a new sentence that affirms the great, unlimited potential God has placed within your life!

_____

_____

Success is being the person
God wants me to be!

LIBERATE YOUR IMAGINATION

"Can you search out the deep things of God? Can you find out the limits of the Almighty? They are higher than the heavens." -JOB 11:7,8

The fifth rod in our mental cage—our **sights.** They are too low or too short. We don't think long enough or far enough. Just because we can't reach our objective in five months doesn't mean we can't do it in the next five years.

One of my favorite stories is about the man fishing off of a pier. He would catch a fish, measure it, and if it was ten inches or less, he would throw it in the bucket. If the fish he caught was over ten inches, he threw it back!

Another person, observing this ritual, thought the fisherman was crazy. Finally he asked, *"Why do you throw the big ones away and keep the little fish?"*

The fisherman answered, *"My frying pan is only ten inches across."*

Now you may laugh at that, but the news I have for you is this: You and I are that fisherman! The big ideas God sends our way are tossed out. We only keep the smaller ones.

As you liberate your imagination, God is going to stretch your dreams and your thinking. Remember, God loves each of us, but He is not satisfied with any one of us!

Do you dare to pray this prayer? "Dear God, help me catch the dream of the person you want me to be! Even if the dream is bigger than I've ever imagined before." Amen.

God, don't let me be so scared that I try to throw Your dream back!"

Winning Is Beginning

"He who deals with a slack hand becomes poor, but the hand of the diligent makes one rich." -Proverbs 10:4

To really succeed in life, you must be able to solve two problems: (1) How to get **started!** And (2) How to **never quit!** These two problems are the only ones you need to solve in order to become the person God wants you to be!

You didn't think when you got up this morning that this would be the day your life would change, did you? But it's going to happen! Because the only thing that stands between you and grand success in living are these two problems—getting started and never quitting! You can solve your biggest problem. You can get started right here and now.

I don't know what idea is in your mind, but I know that everyone has some idea of something that he or she should be starting and hasn't. Maybe it's to lose weight. Maybe it's to get started on an exercise program. Or maybe it's to start a new business. Maybe it's to join the church. Maybe it's to say "yes" to God. Maybe it's to read the Bible.

Now ... what will you do with that idea? Whatever you do, don't waste it! Begin to do something about it today!

Maybe you just need to write down your idea:

_____

_____

My decision today will become tomorrow's reality.

WINNING IS BEGINNING

"Then the Lord said to Moses, 'Quit praying and get the people moving!'"
-EXODUS 14:15(LB)

I remember visiting Hope College, in Holland, Michigan, while my son was a student there studying for the ministry. He's a great young man and I'm very proud of him.

Bob and I walked around the campus, our arms around each other's shoulders, and I said to him, *"Bob, do you know the most important thing I learned on this campus? I don't think it was Greek or Hebrew. I don't think it was history or psychology. The most important thing I learned while a student on this campus I learned right there in that room."* And I pointed to the room where I took History 101.

"The coach was the professor," I continued. *"One day in the middle of the semester he asked, 'How many of you students have started your term paper?' And not a hand went up. I've never forgotten what happened because I am indebted to him—and so are you,"* I enthused to Bob. *"He paced up and down across the front of the classroom—just like a coach. He didn't say a thing, but everyone knew something was coming. He was getting ready!*

"Finally he stopped, turned and faced the class. In a loud voice he said, 'I don't care if you all flunk this course and forget everything you have ever learned on this campus. But don't ever forget the sentence I'm about to say to you now, Then he paused and bellowed it out:

"'BEGINNING IS HALF DONE!'"

Today, with God's help, I will begin that project I've been putting off!

Winning Is Beginning

"Neglect not the gift that is in you ..." -I TIMOTHY 4:14

Today I ask you a most important question which is:
How do you treat ideas?

Treat your idea tenderly...
> It can be killed quickly.

Treat your idea gently...
> It can be bruised in infancy.

Treat your idea respectfully...
> It could be the most valuable thing that ever
> came into your life.

Treat your idea protectively...
> Don't let it get away.

Treat your idea nutritionally...
> Feed it well.

Treat your idea antiseptically...
> Don't let it get infected with the
> germs of negative thoughts.

Treat your idea responsibly!
> Respond! Act! Do something about it!

DECIDE TO DECIDE!

*Knowing each idea is a gift from
God, I shall receive it as a
sacred responsibility.*

Winning Is Beginning

"Never be lazy in your work but serve the Lord enthusiastically."
-ROMANS 12:11 (LB)

Go back to the September 24 devotion and look at the idea you wrote down. Are you still excited? Then it's time to get started! Set up a file, start a notebook, open a special account, but do something!

As I started to write my first book I remembered a teacher's negative remark to me. She had said, *"Bob Schuller, I think you can make a living talking, but don't ever try to write."* But as the negative thoughts that surrounded her comment moved through my mind, I also remembered that "Beginning is half done." So I took out a piece of paper and typed the title of my book on it. I bought a loose-leaf binder, and stuck the title sheet in it. And before I knew it, I had written a book!

What can you do today to begin? Write it down:

_____

_____

_____

What can you do this week to keep moving on your idea?

_____

_____

_____

*Now that I've started, I'm half done.
And I can feel enthusiasm building
within me. I know I can finish!*

Winning Is Beginning

"Whatever your hand finds to do, do it with all your might ..."
-*Ecclesiastes 9:10*

When faced with a God-inspired idea, **insecure people hibernate.** They run away from good ideas. They're afraid they might fail or that it might cost too much. Like a bear feeling the first whisper of a winter wind, they rush off to hide.

Lazy people luxuriate. They just don't pay much attention to the idea. They just want to enjoy the pleasures of the moment. They say they'll get serious later on, but seldom do anything different.

Wounded people commiserate. They say, "Oh, its a good idea, but I couldn't do it. I've tried before and failed." They have a long list of "I've tried but..." excuses that seems endless.

Foolish people procrastinate. They put things off and say, "Later on when I'm ready. But I'm not ready yet." And the difference between the high achiever and the low achiever is that the high achiever almost always makes the decision before he's ready to move! Don't wait until you're ready or you'll never make the move.

Wise people dedicate themselves to the task and move in. They're do-it-now people. They don't waste a good moment or a good idea—especially when that idea comes from God.

Which kind of person will you be today?

Lord, I'm making the decision now to act on the idea You've given me.

Winning Is Beginning

"Our help is in the name of the Lord who made heaven and earth."
-Psalm 124:8

I've learned one important thing about beginning. I can do anything I think I can...***but I can't do anything alone!*** I've taught this, preached it, written it, tried it, and it's true. Always, I need someone to support me! Don't try to handle your dreams alone. It won't work.

Winning starts with beginning, and beginning starts when you get up and do something. And the exciting thing is that God is there with you to give you the strength and the power you need!

Write a prayer of thanksgiving for His presence within you and affirm His help as you begin to act on your dream:

DEAR LORD, I THANK YOU FOR

_____

_____

_____

_____

AMEN.

God, the two of us together
make a great team!
Watch out, world!

LISTEN AND GLISTEN

"I can never get away from my God! If I go up to heaven, you are there; if I do down to the place of the dead, you are there." -PSALM 139:7,8

"I don't believe in God anymore. There is no God. I thought so once, but He left me and I am in hell now. There is no God!" The woman saying these words to me was in a mental hospital. I talked with her at length, but failed to help encourage her. I heard soon after, that she had withdrawn and become silent.

Some months later, I returned to visit her again and found her completely transformed. What had happened? A young doctor walking through her ward had stopped to talk. *"What's your name?"* he asked. She didn't answer. *"Well my name is Dr. Heven,"* he said to her. Slowly her head raised. Her hollow eyes stared at the doctor. As he started to walk away, she touched his sleeve and asked him to repeat his name. *"Dr. Heven,"* he said with a smile.

Into her mind leaked this tiny thought: *"Dr. Heven. Heven. If Heven is here then this can't be hell. If Heven is here God must be here. God is here."*

The next morning she walked down the corridor repeating out loud a Bible verse she had learned as a child. For several days she did this, and then gradually the healing power of God's Word began to do its work. Her irrational association of heaven with Dr. Heven started to give way to rational thoughts. Soon—with a smile like a person slowly awakening from a deep and terrible nightmare—the power of God brought about a transformation in this woman's life, and when I saw her last she was fully recovered and teaching school. God can work in our lives through the smallest trickle of hope that leaks into our mind!

God is present right where I am!

LISTEN AND GLISTEN

"Why do you spend money for what is not bread, and your wages for what does not satisfy? Listen carefully to Me ..." -ISAIAH 55:2

When I was in high school I sang in a male quartet which won national honors. Later, in college, I joined another quartet, and we gave many college concerts. My first trip to California was made possible when the Hope College Quartet toured across America.

One of the things I will never forget is my high school music teacher saying, *"Boys, the key to a good male quartet is equally balanced harmony. All voices must be balanced!"* Then she went on to explain how to obtain harmony.

"Listen to yourself sing, but also listen to the other voices on each side of you," she explained. *"If the voices on either side of you are a little louder than yours, you know that you have to sing a little louder. If you hear yourself louder than you hear those on each side of you, then you are singing too loud—tone down a little. All you have to do is use your ears! Make sure you don't sing louder or softer than the voices around you. Learn to listen!"*

I have discovered that this is also an important principle in all relationships in life. The tragedy is most people only listen to themselves and to their own will and desires. And that always produces disharmony. Listen— and you will find harmony!

I relax, I still my mind, and I pray.
I listen with love!

LISTEN AND GLISTEN

"But the Lord was not in the wind ... the Lord was not in the earthquake ... and the Lord was not in the fire, but after the fire a still small voice. So it was that Elijah heard it." -I KINGS 19:11

Listen! The difference between people who are morbid, morose, melancholic and pessimistic, and those who sparkle, twinkle, are vibrant and alive is not genetic! It is mental. Glistening personalities are people who are listening. They listen to their family members, their friends and working companions, and to God Himself. And they glisten because their sensitive listening produces a deep inner harmony.

But the enthusiastic radiant person has also chosen to listen to positive voices. They have developed the habit of turning off negative sounds that vibrate through our society.

What are you listening to? Let's take an inventory of the past 24 hours:

POSITIVE VOICES	NEGATIVE VOICES

I am blocking out the negative voices around me and tuning in to all the positive resources God has for me!

LISTEN AND GLISTEN

"Incline your ear and come to ME. Hear, and you soul shall live…"
-ISAIAH 55:3

Henry Fawcett was one of the great distinguished members of Parliament in England. Gladstone appointed him Postmaster General, and he made some of the greatest contributions to England in the area of postal services and telegraphy.

The interesting fact behind Fawcett's success is this: *He was completely blind!* Here was a man who had every reason to be bitter. When he was 20 years old, he and his father were on a hunting trip. They enjoyed a very close relationship as father and son.

On this trip, the father accidentally discharged his rifle and shot his son in the face. This bright, healthy, mentally alert young boy dropped in a pool of blood. The young man lived, but he was sightless the rest of his life.

The father wanted to kill himself. Young Henry wanted to die, too. He had no hope of reading or returning to his studies. All of these negative thoughts flooded his mind day after day.

One day, Henry overheard his father crying. His father was in deep despair. Henry decided to build his father's hopes by pretending, *"It's okay, Dad. Others can read to me, I'll make it!"* He lived a lie of joy and happiness before his father, but then something happened. The lie became a reality! He had hope! His life had meaning! He was dynamically changed because he chose to listen to his own positive words, not the negative!

I shall listen to my own voice declaring only positive words today thereby releasing hope and joy in my life.

Listen and Glisten

"Let all bitterness, wrath, anger, clamor, and evil speaking be put away from you, and be kind to one another, tenderhearted ..." -EPHESIANS 4:31, 32

Two days ago we did an inventory of the types of voices we listen to each day. Today we ask the very important question: *Are you a positive or a negative voice to yourself and others?*

Do you recall when you were a positive voice to someone recently? Last week? Yesterday? Today?

_____

_____

_____

Now can you recall when you voiced a negative opinion or reaction to someone in your family or your neighbor, or church member?

_____

_____

Today, be an encourager to someone. It is a decision you can make. If you will listen to God's Word you can change the environment in your home, or your office from negative to positive. Determine, now, to say a kind word. Be a positive voice to someone today. As evidence of your commitment, write down the person's name:

_____

God's thoughts are filling me. Today I share these positive thoughts with someone. I am God's light!

LISTEN AND GLISTEN

"Loves does not behave rudely, does not seek its own ... is not puffed up ... Love bears all things, believes all things, hopes all things, endures all things." -I CORINTHIANS 13:5 & 7

This year Arvella and I will celebrate our 49th wedding anniversary. Over 49 super years! And our marriage is better today than it was when we were first married and it keeps getting better everyday. Let me share our secret.

When we came to California, our new church demanded so much time and attention that we soon realized that the many pressures were affecting our marriage. And we knew that the first priority for each of us was our marriage. So one Monday night my wife and I had a date—and that became a weekly commitment to each other —"date-night."

And so every Monday for over forty years, with rare exceptions, we have planned a special night for ourselves. And that meant that every seven days we would get our marriage, our thinking, our listening, and our communication lines clean and clear.

I compare it to the alignment of the wheels on my car. I am constantly bumping curbs or hitting ruts in the road. About every six months or so, someone will say, *"Dr. Schuller, you need to get your front wheels aligned. You're wasting rubber."*

Now if I went in every week to have my front wheels aligned, my front tires would last twice as long. I'll tell you something: My marriage and my family mean so much to me that every week my wife and I have a realignment scheduled. And the important thing is we listen to each other. As a result, we keep growing closer together!

Lord, help me to align my relationships with those whom I love today.

LISTEN AND GLISTEN

"The flowers appear on the earth; the time of singing has come and the voice of the turtledove is heard in our land." -SONG OF SOLOMON 2:12

Too often, O God, the sacred calm
of Your still small voice
is overpowered by
the roar of the traffic,
the moan of ambulances,
the wail of sirens
the growl of buses,
the rude interruption of the doorbell.

Jet airplanes, trucks, trains, television, telephones fill my everyday world with noises my ears were never designed to tolerate.

An irritating assortment of unnatural sounds drowns your silver-soft-voice. Oh, my Lord, there are birds winging and I do not see them, children playing and I do not hear them, flowers blooming and I do not enjoy them, clouds sailing silently through the soundless sea of space and I do not see them!

God, You are living and moving, and I do not feel You! Increase my awareness of the throbbing reality of the dynamic spiritual universe around me, Lord.

*God, move in the thoughts
and feelings within me now! I am surrounded
with an awareness of You that gives me
a new lease on life! Thank You, God!*

LISTEN AND GLISTEN

"Whoever listens to Me will dwell safely and be secure without fear of evil." -PROVERBS 1:33

I talked with a father, recently, who has two daughters working in very influential positions in our nation's capitol. I said to him, *"How did you ever manage to have two daughters acquire such powerful positions on Capitol Hill?"*

"It wasn't easy for me, Dr. Schuller," he answered. *"I used to take them to the capitol when they were little girls so they could see the seats of power. My one daughter graduated from high school and I wanted her to go to college. But she said, 'I'm going to get a job—I'm going to become a secretary to one of our great senators!'"*

The father continued, *"I didn't want to let her go. I didn't dare let her leave home and go out into that city without me or her mother!"*

I asked him what made him give in and this is what he told me: *"I'm a football fan and about that time I was watching my favorite team play. One of the officials threw a flag indicating a penalty—they were guilty of defensive holding! It was like a message from God saying, 'Don't be penalized for defensive holding! Don't hold your daughter back. Let her become what she was meant to be!' So I let her go with my blessing!"* he added.

Some of you are guilty of defensive holding. The person who listens to God and is open to His beautiful dreams is never penalized for defensive holding! Listen to Him and you will glisten!

God gives me the ability to listen and to choose the happy way, the right way, the way of joy!

Exalt Courage

"I take pleasure in distress for Christ's sake. For when I am weak, then I am strong." -II CORINTHIANS 12:10

What is courage? We can all understand what courage is when we see a soldier fighting for our freedom as he heads for the front line. We can understand courage when we see a fire truck speeding down the street and the fireman climbing high on his ladder. We can understand courage when we see a police officer rushing through the black of night to protect someone.

But there are other levels of courage. There is the courage to love, or the courage to forgive, or the courage of commitment.

What does courage mean to you? Create a special courage poem using the following format. The first line is one word—the title. Line two has two words which describe the title. Line three has three words and is an action phrase about the title. Line four has four words that describe your feelings about the title. Line five is one word that restates the title. Try it, using the word **Courage** as the title.

COURAGE

_____

_____ _____

_____ _____ _____

_____ _____ _____ _____

_____

I face today with courage~ God's courage! I feel His power flowing through me!

*E*XALT COURAGE

"Watch, stand fast in the faith, be brave, be strong." -1 CORINTHIANS 16:13

There is not a city in America where you cannot pick up a telephone and dial for the correct time. In many cities you can even dial a number and receive the weather forecast. Along the coast, you can dial a number and find out the condition of the surf.

And no matter where you live in this country you can dial the area code 714, and the letters NEW HOPE anytime, day or night, and the phone will ring in the Tower of Hope on the Crystal Cathedral campus. You can talk with a trained counselor in America's first 24-hour church telephone counseling program.

But did you know you could dial for courage? You don't have to remember any numbers, all you need to know is one letter—"C!" You can dial for courage when the doctor's report comes back and the cancer is malignant; or when your husband leaves you; or when you lose a precious child. You can! *Dial "C" for courage!* The "C" stands for Christ. All you need to do is turn to Him and courage will come to you from a Source that transcends you.

God is listening. And He always gets our message. He gives us what we need. That's what Jesus Christ can do for you! Dial "C" for courage today!

God has given me a courageous, all-conquering spirit. He has given me the spirit of Jesus Christ. I am confident!

EXALT COURAGE

"The godly are bold as lions!" -PROVERBS 28:1 LB

The judge was campaigning for reelection and was running on his record of integrity. He was a distinguished and honorable gentleman of no small charity. And his opponent was conducting a vicious, mud-smearing, unfair campaign against him.

At a news conference, a reporter stood and asked the judge, *"Your Honor, do you know what your opponent is saying about you? Would you care to comment?"*

The judge looked at his campaign counselors and the chairman of his committee. Then he looked at his audience and calmly replied: *"Well, when I was a boy I had a dog. And every time the moon was full, that old hound dog would howl and bark at the things he saw in the bright face of the moon. We never did sleep very well those nights. He would bark and howl at the moon all night long."* With that he concluded his remarks.

"That's beside the point," his campaign chairman impatiently said. *"You haven't answered your critics!"* The judge explained, *"I just did! When the dog barked at the moon, the moon kept right on shining! I don't intend to say anything back to my critic. I'm going to keep right on shining—quietly and calmly, like the moon!"*

That takes courage! That's the courage required to sail to the top and not worry about what people will say if you succeed or if you fail. Only God can give you that kind of courage!

I'm shining, Lord. I can feel Your courage within me.

Exalt Courage

"He who tills his land will be satisfied with bread." -PROVERBS 12:11

It is often the fear of the unknown that saps the reservoir of courage in many of us, even though we may strongly desire to succeed. W. Clement Stone pointed out that it takes time to succeed and it takes time to fail, so why not decide to succeed? Get started!

When your courage starts to fade as you face some difficult task or situation, repeat ***Do it Now!*** to yourself over and over again. Develop the habit of saying ***Do it Now!***

Let's Do it Now! Finish each of the lines below and then repeat aloud what you have written, and repeat the words Do it Now!

WHEN FACED WITH _____

DO IT NOW!

WHEN MY COURAGE FADES BECAUSE _____

I WILL DO _____ NOW!

WHEN UNCERTAINTY HITS ME BECAUSE _____

_____

I WILL DO _____ NOW!

DO IT NOW!

Exalt Courage

"There is no fear in love, for perfect love casts our fear." -I John 4:18

"Here I am!" the young voice called out to the stranger walking by. The little girl was barely two years old, lying in bed hugging her teddy bear. Both of her tiny legs were hanging in the air, in traction.

"Well, hello!" the new friend enthused. *"I have brittle bones,"* the tiny girl responded quickly. *"This one is broken. Last time it was that one,"* she said as she pointed to her right leg. *"I've had 22 fractures!"*

By the time she was six, Charlotte had been in and out of the hospital 85 times. Because of a rare disease her bones would break very easily. By the time she was ten she had had over 200 fractures.

"I only saw her cry twice," a close friend of the family said. *"Once when she had to miss her sister's wedding because she fractured her arm. The other time was when she made a community appeal to urge people to give so crippled children could walk."*

Charlotte never weighed more than fifty pounds, but she pushed through high school, chose a university with ramps (before there were laws demanding handicap access) for wheelchairs, and graduated four years later Cum Laude! She went on to law school and passed the state bar exam! All fifty pounds of her. She had courage! She was so much in love with life that she fought every day! Courage is the back side of the coin of love!

Courage fills my mind and heart, for I know that God is my strength!

EXALT COURAGE

"Great is the Lord and mighty in power: His understanding is infinite ... the Lord takes pleasure in those who trust him." -PSALM 147:5 & 11

Why do we exalt courage? Because every person who chooses to be brave inspires the rest of the human race! The entire human family is exalted, honored and dignified when someone fights a brave battle.

Lillian Dickson and her husband felt called by God to go to the island of Formosa. When they arrived, they talked to a government official in Social Services. He looked at this young and naive couple and laughed, *"Look, go back to America. You can't possibly succeed here. There is no way!"*

He stood up and walked over to the window and pointed outside. *"Look, you can see the ocean. Helping people here in Formosa is like trying to change the ocean one bucket at a time!"*

Young Lillian Dickson got out of her chair and said, *"Well, then I am going to fill my bucket!"* and they left the room. Fifty plus years later, her husband dead, Lillian was still filling her bucket. She established over one thousand churches, schools and hospitals. It all happened because she and her husband had the courage and the willingness to fail!

If they had turned around and gone home, no one would have blamed them. But they stayed and faced possible futility. And Formosa is a better place today because of their courage!

Today I will courageously speak only words of hope to encourage others to have more courage!

EXALT COURAGE

"By my God, I can leap over a wall. As for God, His way is perfect."
-II SAMUEL 22:30,31

What is courage? Courage is not the absence of fear. Courage is deciding to go ahead even when you're scared stiff.

If you make a decision where there's no risk involved, it does not require courage. If you are moving ahead and you know you cannot fail, that doesn't take any courage.

Do you want to stay where you are the rest of your life? God has bigger and better things for you and me, but we'll never advance until we take a chance.

Taking a chance means you run the risk of possible failure, real hurt. Courage! Somebody said to me, *"But some people have it and some people don't."*

Courage isn't a gift. Courage is a decision. Courage is that scary emotion that motivates you to make the right decision. Courage is always a choice!

Courage is something I can never lose. Because courage is something I can always choose. Courage is when you know it's what God wants you to do.

I've got that courage, and I get it, frankly, from Jesus Christ. If you believe that God is alive, that He loves you, that He's forgiven you and that He has a plan for your life, automatically you have courage.

"Thank You, Lord, that You are giving me courage. You have called me to make daring decisions, to put my feet on a road, and only You know where that road will lead, only You know how far it will take me. Lord, touch me and let me know that the beginning of success is when I reach up and put my hand in Yours and decide to walk faithfully with You all through life. Amen

I am living, today, controlled by my God-inspired positive ideas!

Scars Become Stars

"To the weak, I became weak, that I might win the weak ..."
-I Corinthians 9:22

A guide said to me one time some years ago in the Netherlands, *"See that huge concrete plug in the dike? We had a leak there one time and the sea rushed in. Many people perished in the floods. But we plugged it with concrete—steel-reinforced concrete—and it'll never break there again."*

A doctor said to me one time as he pointed to a nurse walking down the hall, *"She's the best nurse we have. She works so hard and is so dedicated to the patients."* Then, almost as an afterthought, he added, *"I guess it has something to do with the fact that when she was a teenager she spent ten months on her back in this hospital."*

Before my secretary, Lois Wendell, died of cancer, people would often tell me how much she had helped them as they faced uncertainties of an operation. *Where she was weak, there she became strong!*

You can turn your scars into stars. Your hurts can become halos. The principle here is that if you want to live an emotionally healthy and happy life you must discover how to handle the hurts that come. St. Paul assures us that our weaknesses can be turned into blessings for others.

God helps me turn my scars into stars!

Scars Become Stars

"O Lord, you are my God. You have been a strength to the poor, a strength to the needy in distress." -ISAIAH 25:4

There are several types of weaknesses. Some relate to hurts caused by other people. Some are simply caused by life and its natural processes. There are also weaknesses that relate to qualities in our personality. Perhaps we are very trusting, or our feelings are very sensitive. And because of these qualities, we find we are easily hurt.

What are some of the weaknesses in your life? Have you ever considered the potential strengths represented by these qualities? Let's list some of them and then think of all the possible strengths that could be associated with those "weaknesses:"

MY WEAKNESS	POTENTIAL STRENGTH

I can feel my attitude changing.
I am turning my former
weakness into a strength.

Scars Become Stars

"For I will turn their mourning into joy, will comfort them, and make them rejoice rather than sorrow." -JEREMIAH 31:13

Here are some sound principles that will help you turn your scars into stars. First, **don't curse life's hurts!** I hear it so often: *"He's been going downhill ever since his son died."* Or, *"She's been drinking a lot since her husband left her."* Or, *"He dropped out of high school when he was a senior because he didn't make the football team."*

There are many ways to curse our hurts, but when you curse them you become bitter. Hurts can either make us bitter or better—don't curse your hurts!

Second, **don't rehearse and nurse your hurts.** A lady called my office and asked to see me. Her husband had died two years before and she had been crying inside for two long, painful years. She said, *"Dr. Schuller, I know you are so busy. I just didn't want to bother you."* I put my arm around her and I led her into my office.

As she talked, she related everything that had happened up to the time of her husband's death—everything! She knew every detail. Finally she opened her purse and took out a sheet of paper and read to me the words of her doctor as he had explained to her the cause of her husband's death. I cried with her!

We prayed, and then I said, *"I want you to do something. I want you to tear up that piece of paper and throw it away. It's time you stopped rehearsing and nursing your hurt!"* Weeks later when I saw her again, she smiled and whispered, *"Thanks, I feel better already."*

Lord, the past is past!
Thank You for the newness of today!

Scars Become Stars

"Share each other's troubles and problems, and so obey our Lord's command." -GALATIANS 6:2 LB

You probably can't help it when the hurt comes, but you can help it if the hurt lasts. Through the power of God, and through the power of prayer, you can handle any hurt!

A friend of mine was having a problem with a business competitor. All kinds of negative emotions were beginning to overwhelm him. I suggested to him that he pray about it.

"And what do I pray?" he asked me, *"that my competitor will succeed?"* *"No,"* I suggested, *"Just ask God what you should pray and God will tell you."*

Several days later, he said, "I woke up this morning at 2:00 a.m. and I knew what I had to pray!" *"What was it?"* I asked. *"God gave me the prayer—here it is: 'Dear God, make that person into exactly the person You want him to be and cause his business to develop just the way You would like to see it develop!'* He went on, *"That completely cured me. If that guy's business succeeds, I can't be angry about it because I prayed that God's plan would be worked out."*

Now, if you have a hurt, and if you have prayed about it and your praying hasn't helped, then you have prayed the wrong prayer. Start now and ask God what you ought to pray. He'll help you disburse your hurts by placing them in His care!

My hurts are fading as I turn them over to God~ one~by~one!

SCARS BECOME STARS

"Cast all your cares upon God, for He cares for you." -I PETER 5:7

What are some of the hurts you are still carrying? Take the time to write a description below:

_____

_____

_____

_____

_____

_____

Now, look back over what you have written. Stop and commit, through prayer, each hurt to the healing power of God. Then in big bold letters, write "CANCELED" across what you have written!

I am a child of God.
Nothing can hurt me for
He takes care of His children!

$\mathscr{S}$CARS BECOME STARS

"I was hungry, and you gave ME food ...""Lord, when did we see you hungry and feed you?""Inasmuch as you did that for the least of these, my brothers and sisters, you did to ME." -MATTHEW 25:35 TO 40

One day I was watching as the elevator doors opened. I had just stepped out of my office in time to see a young mother with a little girl pulling at her skirt. The mother looked busy...she seemed to be rushed, and even a little harassed.

I asked my secretary, *"Who is she? What is she doing here at this time of day?"* My secretary reminded me that she was in charge of our Helping Hands project.

This young mother spends hours at the church collecting tin cans full of soup and vegetables. People call in to our 24-hour counseling service and say they have nothing—including no food. We have a policy that we will not give people money, but we will give them food and groceries. This young mother managed this whole operation.

My secretary reminded me, *"You remember she wrote you a letter some months ago that really moved you. She thanked God for our wonderful congregation."* I remembered. Her husband had been flat on his back for months, unable to work. She couldn't work, either, because she had a baby who became sick. The church heard about her and the ladies brought breakfast, lunch and dinner for them, day after day, week after week.

She found a way to repay their love! Time after time, when I look at a giving person, I say, **somewhere that person was hurt, and turned that hurt into a halo!**

I belong to God. All that happens to me is part of His plan for my good. I feel His strength flowing within!

Scars Become Stars

"Though I walk in the midst of trouble, you will revive me ... the Lord will perfect that which concerns me." -PSALM 138:7, 8

Some people curse their hurts, rehearse and nurse them, or disburse them by sending them on their way. The best way to turn a hurt into a halo, a scar into a star, is to turn it over to God and allow Him to turn it inside out. He will reverse it so that it becomes a star in your crown!

Write a prayer today that expresses your feelings as you turn any and all of your hurts over to God.

Dear God, _____

_____

_____

_____

_____

_____

_____

_____

_____

_____

*I give my hurts to God
and He turns them into strength!*

KNOW WHERE YOU'RE GOING

"For all the promises of God are 'YES!'" -II CORINTHIANS 1:20

The man who booted the longest field goal in the history of pro football wasn't supposed to be able to do it. But no one told him that, and he did the impossible.

Tom Dempsey was born with only half a right foot and with a deformed right arm and hand. And even though he successfully overcame his handicap and played football in high school and in college, he was turned down by the professional teams. They looked at his right side and said, *"You are not professional material."*

But he refused to accept their word. He said, "I have learned never to give up. So many times in sports, I have seen things turn around because someone persevered and kept the faith. My parents taught me that kind of faith.

In 1970, in a game between the Detroit Lions and the New Orleans Saints, the Saints were about to upset the Lions. With only 11 seconds left, Detroit took the lead by one point. It looked like the game was over. The Saints had 2 seconds left and were on their own 45 yard line. In came Tom Dempsey to kick a field goal.

Up to that time the longest field goal had been 56 yards. This one would be 63 yards. The goalposts were so far away that Tom didn't even know he had made it until the official raised his arms. The Saints won because no one told Tom it was impossible!

God does not plan failure for me.
Because God says "yes" to me,
I shall say "yes" to Him!

KNOW WHERE YOU'RE GOING

"Lead me, O Lord ... make Your way straight before my face." -PSALM 5:8

Possibility thinkers begin setting goals by realistically examining their God-given talents. A story is told about a farmer who, while trying to decide his future, saw a cloud formation in the sky which formed the letters "P" and "C." He interpreted this sign to mean "Preach Christ."

He became a preacher, but because he thought he lacked the God-given talents and the necessary spiritual gifts, he failed. He concluded that the letters must have stood for "Plow Corn." So he returned to his great work of feeding a nation.

On the other side of the coin, a friend of our family is over 60 years old. Two years ago she started taking piano lessons. Today, she's good enough to be giving beginning piano lessons to little children. Because she has such a sweet, pleasant spirit, the children love her. She is a success!

These two stories illustrate some very important principles for goal-setting:

1. Discover the undiscovered talents within you.
   They are there! Look for them.

2. Realistically estimate your talent.
   It takes all kinds of abilities to keep God's world moving.

3. Dedicate your talent to God.
   He can do a lot with a little if it's turned over to Him!

4. Start today!

I am an important part of God's plan for today!

KNOW WHERE YOU'RE GOING

"God has given each of us the ability to do certain things well."
-ROMANS 12:6 (LB)

Saint Paul urges each of us to make an honest evaluation of ourselves. A helpful bit of advice in setting goals is to begin where you are. You find out where you are by checking out the talents and abilities God has given you. With that information in hand, you are ready to plan where you're going.

You can begin by listing some of the things you enjoy doing. Then write down the abilities you have that help you enjoy doing these things:

THINGS I ENJOY DOING	ABILITIES I HAVE

I am glad for all that God is planning for me!

KNOW WHERE YOU'RE GOING

"Count it all joy when you fall into various trials knowing that the testing of your faith produces patience ... that you may lack nothing." -JAMES 1:2,3

Along with your talents, you need to consider your challenges. The challenges God sends your way often appear, at the outset, as problems, troubles, or difficulties. Only as you exercise possibility thinking will you begin to discover the universal principle that every problem is really an opportunity! Thus difficulties become challenges to do something constructive, or to become bigger, better persons than ever before.

As you consider setting personal goals, consider the challenging spot you're in. If you are in the hospital, your goal today may be to raise an arm, tomorrow you'll try to raise a leg. Then your goal will be to roll over on your side, then getting up, and finally, you will have as your goal walking in the hallway—on your way home!

INCH BY INCH, ANYTHING'S A CINCH!

The important thing is your attitude toward the situation you're in right now. If you think "it's impossible," then your problem is really a problem! But if you "think possibilities," then your problem is really an opportunity for you to triumph! And triumph is made up of two words: TRY and UMPH!

Today, because of my problem, I will be able to know the joy of personal triumph! With God's help I will Try~umph!

KNOW WHERE YOU'RE GOING

"Ask in faith, with no doubting, for the one who doubts is like a wave of the sea driven and tossed by the wind." -JAMES 1:6

So far, you've considered your talents and your challenges. Before setting personal goals, you also need to consider your values.

A young lady had just finished her college education and started working. During the first months, she spent every cent she earned on clothes. Her father urged her to put some of her money in a savings account, arguing that thrift was a virtue.

She insisted that clothes "make the woman" and therefore she had to have a beautiful wardrobe. The argument reached a stalemate. Finally, the desperate girl turned to her brother and asked, *"What should I do—put the money in the bank or buy clothes?"*

His immediate reply was, *"Put your money wherever it will draw the most interest!"*

Each individual—the father, the young woman, and her brother—expressed their sense of values in their discussion. The father valued thrift. The daughter valued appearances. The brother valued his neck—he didn't want to get caught between his father and his sister.

Sometimes our values are inconsistent, like the man who had just been caught in a daring burglary. The officer asked him why he had tried such a complicated crime alone.

"Well," replied the prisoner, *"where can you find a man who's honest enough to be trusted for a job like this?"*

Today I will adopt God's value system in all my planning.

Know Where You're Going

"Set your mind on things above, not on things on the earth." -COLOSSIANS 3:2

What do you value? If you were faced with a choice, what would you keep and what would you let go of? Suppose you are suddenly faced with a fire in your home. You only have time to rescue eight items. What would they be? Write down the first things that come to mind:

1. _____

2. _____

3. _____

4. _____

5. _____

6. _____

7. _____

8. _____

Now go back through your list and think about each one. How would you rank each item? Which would be first? Why? Which one was eightth on your list? As you think about each item, what does each one say about your values? What value system are you living by?

*My values are in tune with God's values!
I am doing my part to live as God's child
in this world!*

$\mathcal{K}$NOW WHERE YOU'RE GOING

"The Kingdom of God does not come with observation; ... "see here" or "see there." The Kingdom of God is within you"! -LUKE 17:21

Deep within you lies the power of God. And God waits to give you what you need to make your dreams come true.

BELIEVE IN A BIG GOD! Then make your goals and plans big enough for God to fit into them. Simply ask yourself and God, what would be a great thing for me to do with the rest of my life? Do it now and write down your answer:

_____

_____

_____

_____

_____

_____

Decide to do it. If you need more education, get it. If it's money you need, find it! If it's talent you need, learn the skills or find someone to share your dream with that has the skills. The important thing is to begin—today!

God gives me dominion over every limitation!

Grow Faith

"If you have faith as a mustard seed, you will say to this mountain Ômove" and it will move and nothing will be impossible for you. - MATTHEW 17:20

Recently a person said to me, *"Dr. Schuller, you talk about possibility thinking, and you say that faith moves mountains. Yet I cry and bleed because my mountain has not moved. Was Jesus wrong? Did He make a mistake?"*

My immediate reply was, *"Oh, but your mountain did move and so did you. You perceive your mountain differently today than you did yesterday, last week, or last year. And you have 'moved' in your thinking, even if your faith is as small as the mustard seed."*

Faith is like a seed. A seed must be planted, to bear fruit. That's the first phase. The seed must be watered to sprout. That's the second phase. The plant grows as it is nourished — phase three. Phase four—the proper climate is needed. Finally, there is phase five — the harvest!

Next we'll talk about the five phases of faith. We'll use different words to describe each phase—that's our project in the days to follow.

Yes, I see my mountain moving today. I believe that with God all things are possible!

$\mathscr{G}$ROW FAITH

"Look at the birds of the air ... consider the lilies of the field ... O you of little faith ... seek first the kingdom of God ..." -MATTHEW 6:25-34

Yesterday, we illustrated faith as a seed. Our faith evolves and grows in much the same way as a seed planted in a garden.

Today, allow me to use the illustration of a sparrow which builds her nest for her egg.

Yes, the first phase of faith is the **nesting** phase. An egg is dropped, an idea is born, a thought comes into the nest of your mind.

But how sad if the egg is never hatched! Faith must go beyond the nesting phase. Today is the day to simply do something about the potential possibility of faith seeking to be born. When faith comes don't let it die in the nest!

What faith-thoughts are nesting in your mind today? What beautiful possibility is God seeking to bring to your attention? Stop and meditate awhile and describe where your faith is right now.

Today I will allow my newborn faith to grow.

Grow Faith

"Blessed is the one who trusts in the Lord and whose hope is the Lord, for he shall be like a tree planted by the water which spreads out its roots by the river." -JEREMIAH 17:7,8

The second phase of faith is the **testing** phase. This is the time to ask questions. And your questions will arise out of your value system. I have lectured on this to students and leaders in schools and industry, and I always emphasize that decision-making is easy if your value system is clear and unclouded.

When you know the right questions, you can know immediately if you have a good idea or a bad idea. Here are the three questions I use. Ask them of yourself and your idea:

1. Is it really necessary? _____

_____

2. Is it needed? _____

_____

3. Is it a beautiful idea? _____

_____

If you are satisfied with your answers, then your idea has passed through the second phase—the testing of faith!

My faith is growing! I am more confident as I test my idea against important questions and know that God is guiding me!

GROW FAITH

"No temptation has overtaken you except such as is common to all, but God is faithful who will not allow you to be tempted beyond what you are able, but with the temptation will also make the way of escape."
-I CORINTHIANS 10:13

The third phase of faith is the **investing** phase. Now is the time to make a commitment and move forward! You will need to commit time, money, energy—and possibly your most valuable item, your prestige, to the project.

When you have to put up risk capital, you can easily be tempted to suddenly quit. It is easy to dream dreams and test them for their value. But when you have to invest time, money, energy and prestige, faith can easily begin to falter. When it does, remember that God is faithful!. Don't fail the test of your faith by backing away from your investment.

It's easy to get cold feet when you have to risk something. But if your faith is going to grow, you must successfully pass through this **investing** phase of faith.

What will your idea cost? Make as accurate a list as possible:

_____   _____

_____   _____

_____   _____

_____   _____

_____   _____

My faith is strong as I willingly make the commitment to invest!

Grow Faith

"He who calls you is faithful, who also will do it." -I THESSALONIANS 5:24

Watch out for phase #4 — the **arresting** phase of faith. Suddenly problems surround you, troubles block you, defeat seems almost certain as you begin to think you are overextended. This is when you wonder if you've made a mistake with your investment.

The arresting phase of faith is God's way of testing us before the surge of success. Will we really be grateful? Will we be humble? Can He trust us with success?

My personal testimony is that every idea that came from God in my life took a lot of faith for me to be willing to invest my time, energy and reputation. And every time I made the commitment to invest, I inevitably ran into a problem where the whole momentum of the project was arrested just when success seemed around the corner. I was suddenly stopped in my tracks. It looked like I would sink!

In this fourth phase of faith, God is testing our **reliability** and our **humility.** So be patient when trouble comes and be thankful God is at work.

I do not believe that God will ever give you an idea that will not run into the arresting phase of faith. But remember, *God's delays are not God's denials!* Hang on! Stay with it! Keep on believing!

Today, regularly affirm:
God's delays are not God's denials!

GROW FAITH

"Tomorrow will be as today and much more abundant." -ISAIAH 56:12

It was a beautiful picture of a log cabin and the White House. Between the log cabin and the White House there was a ladder. Standing at the bottom of the ladder, looking up to the White House, was a caricature of Abraham Lincoln.

A little boy who was looking at the picture said, *"Mommy, what does it mean?"*

"It means Abraham Lincoln climbed the ladder all the way from the log cabin to the White House."

Then she added, *"Look, son, at the line that's under the picture."*

Under the picture was the line, *"The ladder is still there."*

There is a ladder for you. It can take you from where you are to where you want to go. All you need is a dream. A dream is just another word for believing that God loves you and He wants you to succeed.

If you're in a ghetto, if you're at the bottom of the ladder economically, culturally, or physically, you can climb up. You can be stronger tomorrow than you are today.

Do you want to climb the ladder from a log cabin to the White House? Probably not. But you do have some goals and dreams, don't you?

I offer these four, timeless, classical concepts to you, today, as the steps, the rungs of the ladder on success:

A — Attitude that is positive
B — Boundaries of the Ten Commandments
C — a Caring Concern for other people
D — the right Direction

They can absolutely change your life. But it starts by asking a question: Are you willing to let someone manage you? Are you willing to take direction from somebody else?

There's one person I really trust.
His Name is Jesus Christ.

Grow Faith

"I will bless the Lord at all times; His praise shall continually be in my mouth." -PSALM 34:1

The final stage of faith is the **cresting** phase. The crest comes when we reach the mountaintop and achieve success. All the problems are solved. Salvation comes. The habit is broken. The money is here! The project is accomplished! The chains are broken and deliverance has come.

Look how these five phases of faith worked in Christ's life. His idea of His ministry started to come together when He was 12 years old. He knew that God wanted Him to do something. The **nesting** phase occurred when He realized He must be about His Father's business.

The **testing** phase came when He spent 40 days in the wilderness being tempted by Satan. The **investing** phase came as He spent several years walking the plains and deserts, preaching, teaching and touching lives. He experienced great popularity with the crowds.

But then came the **arresting** phase as people turned away from Him. The agony in the Garden at Gethsemane and the tremendous shame of the cross led to Jesus crying out, "MY God, why have You forsaken me?" Dying on the cross, it looked like His dream was finished.

But then came the **cresting** phase. He arose on the third day! Easter morning was the crest! And He is alive today! Be patient. God is at work. As you keep on believing, you will reach the crest!

Almost there, Lord. I can see the top! I can feel Your Spirit driving me onward and upward. Thank you!

POWER STEERING LIVING

"I will put my law in their minds and write it on their hearts, and I will be their God, and they shall be my people." - *JEREMIAH 31:33*

Most of you are too young to have had the experience of driving a car before the wonderful invention of power steering— when driving a car was hard work.

I still remember the first time I drove a car with power steering. Wow! Suddenly, maneuvering the difficult corners was so simple, and managing my way through heavy traffic was fun. Turning the wheels and cruising the curves in the road became easy, calm and controlled.

There are some people today that seem to live their lives just like that. They make decisions swiftly, and maneuver their way though the traffic of frustration and problems with such calmness and control. With smooth power they move ahead toward their easily determined goals and objectives. I call that *Power Steering Living.*

Then there are others, frustrated and insecure, without Power Steering Living. Maneuvering through the traffic of frustration and problems is so tiresome and laborious for them. They simply cannot turn their life in any direction.

Why do some people have power steering living while others don't? Because *Power Steering people have achieved mind-clearing!* Mind-clearing produces power steering. When your mind is clear, you have the power to steer your life without any difficulty!

As I quiet myself, I feel frustration leaving me. My mind is clear now and available for God's power!

POWER STEERING LIVING

"Your word is a lamp to my feet and a light to my path." -PSALM 119:105

Look up the following verses and write down what they say to you about Power Steering living.

Psalm 1:2 _____

_____

Psalm 4:4 _____

_____

Psalm 19:14 _____

_____

Psalm 49:3 _____

_____

Psalm 119: 15, 16 _____

_____

Psalm 139:17 _____

_____

Psalm 143:5 _____

_____

As I fill my mind with thoughts of You,
O Lord, I am filled with joy!

POWER STEERING LIVING

"Whatever things are true, whatever things are noble, whatever things are just, whatever things are pure, think on these things." -PHILIPPIANS 4:8

How do you maintain the process of mind-clearing? Let me answer that question this way: All fuel needs to be filtered before it can produce power. There can be no power without fuel. Whether it's gas to an engine or thoughts that come as energy to the brain, all power-producing organisms require fuel! And all fuel needs to be filtered or the power-potential will diminish.

A good friend of mine invented and patented the Vacco filter. The fuel in all the space vehicles that carried men to the moon was cleansed through this filter. And the fuel in all the nuclear submarines, cruise missiles, nuclear generating plants, and satellites goes through this remarkable filter. It's the only filter used!

What makes this filter different? For one thing, it operates on the horizontal. And as the air and the fuel pass through, this filter traps particles as small as 1/25th of a micron. (It takes 25 microns to make a thousandth of an inch.) It can literally filter out bacteria. There's no other filter like it!

But there is something that is even greater than the Vacco filter. It can screen out something even smaller than bacteria. It can even eliminate negative thoughts. It is the power of God. He is the screen to filter out all the negative thoughts and influences that would take away your power!

Jesus Christ is cleansing my thoughts of all negative forces. Power is being restored to full capacity!

POWER STEERING LIVING

"You must put off: anger, wrath, malice, blasphemy, filthy language ... and put on tender mercies, kindness, humbleness of mind, ... forgiving one another ... above all put on love." -COLOSSIANS 3:8, 12, 13, 14

Saint Paul is very direct. His words written in A.D. 60 are still right on target!

Think, now, about how St. Paul's words can be applied to you. Remember that Power Steering Living comes from clearing your mind of all negative, replacing with the positive that comes to us from the Holy Bible, from Jesus Christ and St. Paul.

Using the verse at the top of the page, write down what best describes your mood today and how you can improve or, if need be, change it.

_____

_____

_____

_____

_____

_____

_____

_____

Negative thoughts are fading.
Pure, clean, positive thoughts are
growing stronger!

POWER STEERING LIVING

"If there is anything praise worthy, think on these things." -PHILIPPIANS 4:8

One of the best ways to tap into Power Steering Living is to concentrate on all the good things you can praise God for in your life and in the lives of those around you. That's the best formula I can give you to get rid of negative thinking. If a negative thought or idea comes into my mind, I immediately try to change my mental dial. And I do this by thanking God that my situation isn't nearly as serious as someone else's problem. There are always other people who are worse off than I am today. That works for me each time. Make today your PRAISE DAY! Make a list of everything you can praise God for and be glad about!

I PRAISE GOD FOR:

_____

_____

_____

_____

_____

_____

_____

*My whole body, soul and spirit
praise God!*

POWER STEERING LIVING

"It is good to give thanks to the Lord ... to declare God's loving kindness in the morning, and His faithfulness every night." -PSALM 92:1 & 2

E. Stanley Jones in his book, *Abundant Living*, tells how he was tested in an airplane over St. Louis when they circled above the clouds for two hours, trying to land. The ceiling was so low that they could not get under. E. Stanley had time to think, and wrote down this life conclusion: *"I am in this plane and we have been circling over these clouds for about two hours. If we do not land safely I would like to leave my last will and testament to my friends and fellow followers of Christ. There is peace, perfect peace. Apart from my unfaithfulness to the Highest, there are no regrets about the general course of my life.*

"Life with Christ is the way to live. In this hour there is assurance—there is God underneath all the uncertainties of human existence. So I rest in God. God's best to you all. Living or dying I am His—His alone. Glory! Signed, E. Stanley Jones."

E. Stanley Jones knew how to clear his mind for Power Steering Living! He also added this wise advice:

"I meet today, today. I do not telescope all next week into today. The load of Tomorrow, added to that of Yesterday, carried Today, makes the strongest person falter."

Today I will live today.
The future is in God's hands!

POWER STEERING LIVING

"As one thinks in his heart, so is he!" -PROVERBS 23:7

I read recently the documented story of a man who thought he was accidentally trapped inside a refrigerated railroad car. He became frantic, pounding on the door and screaming, but nobody heard him.

He knew that no human being could survive in that kind of an environment so he settled into a corner of the car and began to scrawl his last thoughts on the wall.

"I am becoming very cold. I do not have long to live. I can tell that death is coming close to me. I can feel it very near. These may well be my last words." And they were!"

When the refrigerator car door was opened, they found the man dead. But here's what's so amazing ... the door was not locked. The refrigeration unit had not been working for a month. There was still enough oxygen in the railroad car to sustain life, and the lowest temperature during the man's entrapment was 58 degrees! He did not die of cold. He did not die of suffocation. Only one thing killed him. FEAR!! That fear, along with the illusion that he was freezing inside the railroad car!

Psychologists are beginning to pay attention to this phenomenon. Centuries ago, God revealed to us that *"As one thinks in his heart, so is he!"* Clear your mind for Power Steering Living!

My thoughts dwell on the realization of God as the Source of my every need.

CHANGE

"Great is your faith! Let it be done for you as you desire."
-MATTHEW 15:28

Istanbul, once called Constantinople, is a beautiful city. Over the centuries, it has always been one of the great cities of the world. When you enter the harbor by ship, as I did some years ago, it is an inspiring sight to see. You enter by way of the Golden Horn and sail up the Sea of Marmara. From there you can catch the view of the sun reflected off the gold domes of the mosques that were originally built as great cathedrals. Many of them were built over 700 years ago and still stand today as glorious monuments to the people of faith.

There was a time in the ancient days when insecure rulers of Constantinople wanted to make sure that they could keep the enemy out. They performed a remarkable feat. They created the largest and heaviest chain ever built by human beings. The links are about a foot and a half long and about two inches thick. This monstrous chain was built by hand and then draped across the harbor to keep foreign ships out of their territory. People still marvel at how they were able to maneuver something so bulky and heavy.

As I listened to the story of that chain, I thought of the people who draw chains across the harbor of their minds, chains that keep out new thoughts and ideas. Chains keep us from being open to change. What chains are holding you back today from God's great plans for you?

I will be open to all the wonderful possibilities of change in my life!

CHANGE

"Cast away from you all transgressions which you have committed and get yourself a new heart and a new spirit." -EZEKIEL 18:31

Imagine your mind as a harbor. There is a channel leading in, and there is a harbor master keeping close watch on everything that comes and goes. Can you draw a picture of what the "harbor of your mind" holds today? The regrets? The grief? The self-condemnation? The fears? What wreckage of the past threatens to block the channel? When do you draw the chains across the opening? Symbolize these things in a picture, or simply list them in the space below:

Lord, I need You as my harbor master,
You are now in control!

CHANGE

"Behold, I will do a new thing ... I will even make rivers in the desert."
-ISAIAH 43:19

Musa Alami, a Palestinian, was educated at Cambridge University and then returned to Jerusalem to establish his own business. He did quite well by his own standards until the political upheaval. He had to vacate Jerusalem and live in a refugee camp along with many other poor Palestine refugees. But rather than live with that kind of a static, non-productive life-style, he decided to be a possibility thinker.

He stood on top of a mountain and gazed on the hills of Moab. He saw only one trickle of blue water flowing in the vast wasteland—the Jordan River flowing from Galilee to the Dead Sea.

With all that desert, Musa thought, *"If only there was more water."* Then he came up with an incredible and impossible idea. *"Why not dig for sub-surface water, like they did in California?"* So he talked some of his more daring friends to go out into the desert and start digging.

"You fools," people mocked. *"There is no water in Jordan!"* But Musa and his companions kept on digging. After months, they found a place where sand felt cool and seemed to change color. Could it be water? One more shovelful and the water began to seep in, covering the dry soil, and Musa was able to establish his farms in the desert—all because he removed the chains from his mind and sought change!

I relax and let the life-changing power of God flow through me!

CHANGE

"The fruit of God's spirit is love, joy, pace, long suffering, kindness, goodness, faithfulness, gentleness and self-control." -GALATIANS 5:22, 23

Inventory time! Let's do a checkup on the positive changes we have already made. Recognizing that we never reach perfection, fill in your own testimony of the changes God has already brought about in your life!

BEFORE I BECAME A BELIEVER, I WAS	TODAY, I AM BECOMING MORE

I am changing as I focus on what God is doing in my life!

CHANGE

"A merry heart does good, like medicine." -PROVERBS 17:22

I say to you, today, that the past does not bind the present! You can change! Whether you inherit poverty, oppression, prejudice, physical limitations, or whatever, you don't have to stay locked up and bound by these chains!

Some people hang on to their chains. They allow themselves to remain bound. I was born into a poor family. We had no electricity—we couldn't afford it. We used kerosene lamps!

The only gift I remember receiving at Christmas was in Sunday School. There was an orange, some peanut brittle and a few chocolates packaged in a butter box advertising the local creamery. This gift was given at our church Christmas program for all Sunday School children. We knew what poverty was! But I remember Christmas as a time to be merry, to laugh and to love.

I'll tell you why. Because I was taught that I am a child of God which make me the child of a King! Believe that God is able to change your attitude no matter what your past experience is, but you must really want to experience change. Ask Him right now to help you.

I will let go and let God take over in my life.
His presence gives me a merry heart today!

CHANGE

People
who never change their minds
are either perfect to begin with
or stubborn forever after.

So, Lord, I'm willing, wanting, and waiting
to change into the person
You want me to be.

Amen.

CHANGE

"So says God the Lord, ... who gives breath to the people and spirit to those who walk ... 'I, the Lord have called you in righteousness'." -ISAIAH 42:5, 6

I am a great admirer of Arabian horses. They are such spectacular, gorgeous creatures. Legend says that the prophet Mohammed decided that he wanted to breed the finest horses on planet earth, so he searched the world over for one hundred striking mares.

After he collected these beautiful animals, he led them to the top of a mountain where he corralled them. Directly below was a cool stream which they could only see and smell. He deprived them of water until they were wild with thirst. Then, and only then, did he lift the gate allowing all one hundred horses to gallop to the water.

All you could see were thundering, stampeding horses with tails flying in the wind, neck arched, nostrils flaring and mouths foaming, pulling themselves through clouds of spraying dust.

Just before the stampeding herd reached the water, Mohammed put a bugle to his lips and blew with all his might. All of the horses kept running except for four mares who dug their hooves into the ground and stopped. With mouths foaming and necks trembling, they froze, waiting for the next command. *"These four mares will be the seeds of a new breed, and I will call them Arabian!"* Mohammed cried out!

A common person becomes uncommon simply because he hears a different bugle call! Listen to the Lord's bugle call of greatness!

I have heard God's call and I am following His leading.

RATITUDE

"Bless the Lord O my soul; and forget not all His benefits." -PSALM 103:2

When I was a child in the 30's, a drought swept into Iowa from the Dakotas. The winds became our enemy, peeling off the dry, rich, black soil and swirling it like drifting dunes into the gullies of our fields. We prayed for rain, but rain never came. We walked around our farm with white towels over our faces to keep from suffocating in the driving dust.

Then harvest season came. My father would normally harvest a hundred wagons full of corn. But I remember the harvest that year. My father harvested a meager one-half wagon load.

You know what happened? I'll never forget it. Seated at the dinner table with his calloused hands holding ours, my father looked up and thanked God. He said, *"I thank You, God, that I have lost nothing. For I have regained the seed I planted in the springtime!"* He planted a half wagon load of seed; he harvested a half wagon load in the fall!

While the other farmers were saying, *"We lost 90 or 100 loads,"* my father told me, *"Never count the might-have-beens or you'll be defeated. Never look at what you have lost, look at what you have left!"* The attitude of gratitude releases dynamic power in the person who is thankful.

I am looking at what I have.
Lord, I am grateful for Your blessings!

GRATITUDE

"Oh, give thanks the Lord, for He is so good! His loving kindness is forever!" -PSALM 118:1

How's your attitude of gratitude working today? Are you looking at what you have or at the "might-have-beens"? Let's practice! Start on this page, and then use extra paper when this page is full, and begin to list all the things you can think of that you have and for which you are grateful. Now add the names of persons you're grateful for! When you have finished, stop, and like the psalmist, say, *"Thank the Lord, for He's so good!"*

1. _____
2. _____
3. _____
4. _____
5. _____
6. _____
7. _____
8. _____
9. _____
10. _____
11. _____
12. _____
13. _____
14. _____
15. _____
16. _____

Lord, I thought I had so little, but You have made me rich in ways I hadn't noticed before today. Thank You!

RATITUDE

"I thank You and praise You, O God, You have given me wisdom and might." -DANIEL 2:23

A friend of mine told me the story of a mother who came from Hawaii to visit the United States. She and her sons were traveling across the country by train. The little boy sat and talked with a distinguished gentleman, who later told the mother, *"You've got a fine boy there. When he grows up, he ought to be a lawyer. He's smart. In fact, he ought to go to Stanford University. When he grows up, you just let me know if I can help."*

The years passed. The young boy never forgot those words. When he graduated from high school, he wrote this man and reminded him of his promise. The man, Herbert Hoover, kept his promise. When Ike Sutton graduated, he wrote Herbert Hoover and asked him how he could express his gratitude. Hoover, a Republican, said, *"Go back to Hawaii and enter politics. Run for office as a Republican and keep running until you win."*

Hawaii has always voted heavily for Democrats. But Ike Sutton ran for office. He lost, but he kept running. Then came 1974 and he decided to run again and a miracle happened. He won!

His attitude of gratitude gave him **surviving** power. He survived eleven elections until he finally won. Gratitude gives you **surviving** power as well. Keep on keeping on until you win!

I will not give up! I have too much to be thankful for to be a quitter!

GRATITUDE

"My heart is steadfast, O God, I will sing and give praise. Awake, My glory! Awake, lute and harp! I will awaken the dawn." -PSALM 57:7,8

The attitude of gratitude releases the dynamic power that helps you survive. Gratitude also releases **reviving** power. You can find the power to start again when you feel like quitting. You can pick up the pieces and bounce back to make a comeback.

When do you feel like quitting? Think about a situation for a moment and then write down some of the pressures that cause you to feel like quitting:

_____

_____

Now identify everything about your situation for which you can be thankful. This will be difficult, but practice the attitude of gratitude and write your special thanksgiving thoughts:

_____

_____

_____

I fill my mind with thoughts of gratitude concerning God, the people I know and the circumstances that surround me!

GRATITUDE

"I press on toward the goal for the prize of the upward call of God in Christ Jesus." -PHILIPPIANS 3:14 RSV

The attitude of gratitude releases the dynamic power of surviving and reviving. Gratitude also gives you striving power. When you are revived through gratitude, suddenly you discover the energy to keep striving.

How do you strive? Saint Paul said he was pressing on toward a goal. Goals gave him striving power. He wanted to really know Jesus Christ (Philippians 3:10). He wanted to preach in Spain (Romans 15:24). He wanted his fellow Jews to believe Jesus Christ was the promised Messiah (Romans 9:11). Saint Paul had a number of goals.

What are your goals? Are you happy with your goals? If not, you're free to set new ones. Make your goals big enough for God to fit in! Ask God to help you describe two important goals for your life today. Then write them down:

1. _____

_____

2. _____

_____

Now strive onward and upward to meet your goals today—with God's help!

My eyes are clear and bright as I look at the goals God and I have set.

RATITUDE

"O Lord, You are my God. I will praise Your name, for You have done wonderful things … You have been a strength to the poor, a strength to the needy in distress, a refuge in the storm." -ISAIAH 25:1&4

I was home from college for the summer when a tornado dropped out of the sky like a slithering snake and wormed its way across our farm. We had enough warning to jump into the car and escape with our lives. But that black serpentine cloud dropped its poisonous head and sucked up all nine buildings on our farm, including our farmhouse, destroyed the crops and killed all the animals.

When we drove back after the tornado was gone, we found only white foundations remaining on a clean patch of black ground. Everything my father and mother had worked for was gone.

That night our family gathered together, and we held hands and prayed. My father prayed, *"Oh, God, I thank You that not a life was lost! Not a human bone was broken. We have lost nothing that cannot be regained. And through the storm we have kept that which is irreplaceable — our faith!"*

My father's attitude of gratitude gave him **driving** power. He went into a nearby town and bought an old house that was to be demolished. We took it apart board by board, nail by nail, and rebuilt it over the empty hole in the ground that was the foundation of our previous house.

Oh how we all need **driving power** — the ability to make bold decisions and move forward confidently in the face of tremendous odds.

I awake to a new day filled with abundant driving power. I am confident.

RATITUDE

"I thank my God upon every remembrance of you, always in every prayer of mine making requests for you with all joy." -PHILIPPIANS 1: 3&4

The attitude of gratitude releases dynamic power! Gratitude releases **arriving** power. You made it! Success is yours. The problem is solved.

Now that you have arrived, you will have also developed the great qualities of character—humility and unselfishness. Humility because you realize you did not arrive through your efforts alone. It took teamwork. Unselfishness because gratitude is nothing more than saying, *"I didn't really do it. Thank you for your help!"* Gratitude is saying thank you to this person, to your friends, your community, your country, and to God.

It is impossible to become a vain, egotistical, selfish person if you maintain an attitude of gratitude! To whom are you grateful today?

I am grateful to: _____

_____

_____

I will let them know by: _____

_____

_____

_____

The light of God illuminates my mind.
I see people who have helped me and I
am filled with gratitude.

WELCOME THE UNEXPECTED

"You have turned my mourning into dancing ... and clothed me with gladness ... O Lord, my God, I will give thanks to You forever."
-PSALM 30:11, 12

I recall a woman who had recently lost her husband. They had been married for many years and had planned to retire and travel together. They had all their plans made and were looking forward to finally realizing a lifelong dream coming true. But a month after he retired, her husband suddenly died.

All of life seemed to come to an end for this wife. She put a tombstone on her husband's grave inscribed with the words, *"The light of my life has gone out."* I am sure many of you know the feelings she experienced.

But with the passage of time and the wise counsel of friends, this woman came alive again. The unexpected and unwelcome interruption lost its sting. Two years later her pastor married her to another wonderful man and watched them as they enthusiastically anticipated building a new life.

"Pastor," she said, *"I'm going to have to change that line on the tombstone."*

"No," replied her pastor, *"I think all you have to do is add one other line ... 'I struck another match!'"*

When a crisis comes, or when your plans have to be laid aside, then God moves in and turns a tragedy into a triumph and a problem into your greatest opportunity!

Lord, give me the faith to look for a miracle ... in the unexpected events of today!

WELCOME THE UNEXPECTED

"Many, O Lord, my God, are Your wonderful works ... and your thoughts toward me ... If I could speak of them, they are more than can be numbered." -PSALM 40:5

How do you handle life's unwelcome interruptions? We all react differently. Think back over the events of the last several weeks. Did anything happen unexpectedly? Describe your unwelcome interruption:

_____

_____

Describe your feelings and reactions:

_____

_____

_____

Describe how you wish you had reacted:

_____

_____

_____

Today, Lord, I shall look at every interruption as a heaven~sent gift from You.

WELCOME THE UNEXPECTED

"A man's heart plans his way, but the Lord directs his steps." -PROVERBS 16:9

"Dr. Schuller, I believe in miracles!" said the man sitting next to me. Now when someone says those words to me, I'm ready to listen! *"Tell me more,"* I enthused.

"Well," he continued, *"I pride myself on getting to work on time. If the telephone rings when I am ready to leave the house, I tell my wife to tell them I have already left. And she always does, except for one morning.*

"The phone rang and she said, 'He's just getting ready to leave.' I was muttering under my breath as I went and picked up the phone. Of all things, on the other end of the line was the one person I was trying to avoid. Now he had cornered me on the phone.

"Because of some business relationships, I could not simply cut him off, so I had to talk. I had to keep the other guy happy.

"Finally he was finished and I hung up, still muttering to my wife. At that point, my house shook and the ground seemed like water. It was the big quake of several years ago. I checked my watch and thought to myself, I would just now be at the bridge crossing the freeway. Later I would read in the paper that the bridge over which I was to have been at that moment had collapsed."

Don't resent those unwelcome interruptions. God may be doing something beautiful through them!

God, I invite You to interrupt my well laid plans with Your wise direction.

WELCOME THE UNEXPECTED

Thank you, Father, for the beautiful
surprises You are planning for me today.
So often in my life, when it looked like
the day would be
 ... dismal,
 ... depressing,
 ... dark,
an unexpected burst of
golden sunshine
exploded through a black cloud
sending inspiring shafts of warm,
beautiful sunshine into my life.

Father, it is happening now!
I can already feel the power of
Your love, through Christ my Lord.
Amen.

WELCOME THE UNEXPECTED

"O, give thanks to the Lord, for His goodness ... for He satisfies the longing soul, and fills the hungry soul with goodness." -PSALM 107:8,9

One of the great missionaries of our day related to me the story of his conversion: While a student at Columbia University, he went through a long intellectual struggle, first as an agnostic, and then as an atheist.

Finally, while walking the streets of New York one night, he decided that if there is no God then nothing makes any sense. And he reached the point of utter and total despair.

Just then he was passing a church, and in a last desperate effort, he decided to go inside. He was numb throughout the entire service, and when the minister called for a time of prayer at the end, instead of closing his eyes, he just looked around.

And then he spotted his physics professor in the audience, praying with his head bowed. He was shocked! The thought, *"My goodness, if my professor believes in God, maybe it's not such a crazy idea after all!"* When the prayer time was over, he looked at the face of his professor and saw in that unguarded moment an aura and a spirit that was heavenly. It was, to this student, proof of the existence of God.

At that moment he bowed his head and accepted Jesus Christ into his life. The whole direction of his life was changed as a result of an unexpected encounter!

I am giving in to the miracle of the unexpected. God is making my life more beautiful and complete through every experience!

WELCOME THE UNEXPECTED

"Behold, this is our God; we have waited for Him; we will be glad and rejoice in His salvation." -ISAIAH 25:9

A few Sundays ago, at the Cathedral, I greeted a family from out of town. *"Dr. Schuller,"* the mother said, *"God has changed our lives!"* Their little boy, who was not quite five years old, added, *"Yes sir! We just found out about God!"* About that time, the whole family was kind of misty-eyed.

I said to the little boy, *"That's beautiful! Do you know what? God has a plan for you. I was about your age when I found out that God wanted me to be a preacher."* And then I touched his little nose and repeated, *"God has a plan for you!"*

He looked up at me with his big eyes and said, *"For me? For me?"* *"Yes,"* I replied, *"for you."* Then he looked up at his mother and said, *"Mommy, for me!"* And as he walked out the door I could still hear him saying to his mother, *"For me!"*

His whole life will be different because of that word and that touch. I know that for certain.

I invite you to be receptive. Today you will meet people you have never met before. You'll think it is a chance encounter. But God intends you to be a miracle in their life. In some way, because you meet, their life will never be the same. God will use you to make a miracle!

God is in charge of every encounter in my life today. I am expecting miracles to happen because He is in charge!

WELCOME THE UNEXPECTED

"And she brought forth her first born Son, and laid Him in a manger, because there was no room for them in the Inn." -LUKE 2:7

As we usher in the Christmas season, we observe all of the unexpected events that surround that familiar story. Away from home, no room in the inn, the unusual visits of the shepherds and wise men. There were so many of God's surprises for the world that first Christmas.

As you and I come once again to Christmas, let's open our hearts and minds so that we will not miss God's special surprises for us this holy season.

Anticipate God's unexpected events in your life today. Describe an unexpected encounter you experienced before. Write down how God used that:

_____

_____

_____

_____

_____

_____

I shall anticipate a special unexpected surprise from God this Christmas Season.

EXPECT MORE

"For my eyes have seen your salvation which you have prepared before the face of all peoples." -LUKE 2:30

W. Clement Stone said, *"The greatest power available to man is the power of prayer."* These are the words of an extremely successful businessman. He had learned there can be no ultimate solutions to any of our problems unless we are in tune with God's Spirit.

God is the Source of all supply. It is God Who makes the seed rupture and send its tender shoot through the spring soil, reaching to the sun. And the seed is not content until it produces and multiplies.

God is also the Source of life and abundance in humans. Do you have a problem? Are you lacking anything? If your answer is "yes" to these questions, then look at your problems with new vision, recognizing that all pain, all problems, including poverty, were really not designed by God. Ask yourself, *"Is the problem due to disharmony in my own life as it relates to people, to society and to God Himself?"* If so, then I urge you to get in tune with God's Spirit through creative prayer.

Begin by praying, *"Dear God, help me to see my blind spot. Open my eyes and my thinking to see Your salvation."*

Our text today is the joyous exclamation of a devout man, named Simeon, who, through prayer, knew he would see the Christ Child with his own eyes before his death. As he held the Holy Babe in his arms, his joy was complete.

I shall keep focused on the true meaning of Christmas this year.

EXPECT MORE

"Ask, and it shall be given to you ... for everyone who asks, receives."
-MATTHEW 7:7,8

If you could have **anything** you asked for this Christmas what would you ask for?

This is the question our family asks each other as we put up the Christmas lists on the side of the refrigerator. Write down anything you want ... add color and sizes too. Of course the lists always include outlandish and impossible requests, but it makes for lots of fun. Last Christmas our son-in-law asked for a new sports car. He described the model and the color. So Mrs. Schuller and I found a toy car identical to his wish. Those Christmas lists are so revealing of each of our family.

What you and I ask of God reveals how much faith we have in God's abundance. Jesus said,"I am come that you might have..."He wants you to be among the haves, not among the have-nots! You can expect more out of life.

Become a possibility thinker today. Make your Christmas list today for God, and add to the end of each sentence ... **"IT'S POSSIBLE!"**

I believe that God in heaven is waiting to give good things to those who ask Him, so I shall ask in faith today!

EXPECT MORE

"And my soul shall be joyful in the Lord; it shall rejoice in His salvation."
-PSALM 35:9

There were still seven shopping days left before Christmas. As I passed the room of my youngest daughter, Gretchen, I noticed she was sitting on the floor surrounded by envelopes and sheets of clean stationery. On closer inspection, it looked like she was busy writing letters. Now Gretchen never writes letters, so naturally my curiosity was aroused.

"Gretchen," I exclaimed, *"what are you doing?"* Caught by surprise, she looked up at me with a big smile and said, *"Oh, hi, Dad. I'm writing my thank you notes."*

"You're what?" I asked.

"I am starting to write my thank you notes for Christmas now, so you and mom won't have to bother me about it after Christmas," she explained.

A little confused at this point, I continued, *"Gretchen, how can you write thank you notes for presents you haven't received? How do you know who to address them to or for what you'll be receiving?"*

"Oh," she enthused, *"I've got that all figured out. I'm going to say, 'Dear Friend, thank you for your wonderful gift. I'm enjoying it very much. Love, Gretchen.'"*

I laughed at her ingenuity and said, *"But, Gretchen how do you know you will enjoy all the gifts?"* *"Oh,"* she countered, *"I just know I'm going to."*

That's what you call advance planning. But her anticipation produced within her a spirit of joyful expectancy. She was living in the arena of goodness. When you expect good things to happen to you, your attitude will change. Your spirits will soar, your face will beam and you will be filled with joy and enthusiasm for the day.

I am giving lovingly to others and
I am richly blessed in return!

&xpect More

"*For unto us a child is born. Unto us a Son is given. And His name will be called Wonderful, Counselor, Mighty God, Everlasting Father, Prince of Peace.*" -ISAIAH 9:6

A child is born.

A seed. A snowflake. A mosquito. An atom. A baby. All five have something in common. All five, by themselves, are very insignificant. But in each case, their effect can be multiplied to create an unbelievable power and impact.

The snowflake stopped Napoleon in his invasion of Russia. A snowflake defeated him at Waterloo.

The mosquito halted the construction of the Panama Canal.

One seed turned into a fruit tree, which turned into an orchard, which turned into a fruit-bearing, food-serving industry that fed a nation.

The atom, harnessed as a bomb, ended World War II, and probably was responsible, more than anything else, for ushering in the longest era of international peace without a world war, since the Pax Romana.

The seed, the snowflake, the mosquito, the atom, —but a Baby born in a manger in Bethlehem surpasses the impact and influence of all.

In less than a month all calendars will observe his 2000th birthday. His name? Wonderful, Counselor, Mighty God, Everlasting Father, Prince of Peace. I call Him my Friend and Savior.

What will you expect from this Baby, the Christ Child, this Christmas? His miracles are as abundant as ever. His powerful love moves mountains.

I shall believe in the miracle-working power of Jesus Christ today.

EXPECT MORE

"And when they opened their treasures, they present gifts to the Christ Child; gold, frankincense and myrrh." -MATTHEW 2:11

The car we were riding in was obviously a very expensive automobile. I commented to the driver, *"It looks like you're doing very well."* *"Yes,"* he said, *"by the grace of God, I am prospering."*

He then told me his story. *"Eleven years ago, at the age of 52, I didn't have a dime. I was broke, but I had a dream. I wanted to run a restaurant and make a success out of it without getting involved in the liquor business. Everyone told me it couldn't be done.*

"I read a book on ways to succeed through having the right attitude. The author said to never let a problem stop you. I needed money, so I went to a wealthy lumberman and presented my dream to him. Miraculously, he agreed to invest in my dream! Today I have six restaurants and my net worth is over a million dollars!

"But the exciting thing is what just happened recently. I have always been a tither. Last year, competing restaurants went up on both sides of my place. On top of that, the energy crisis forced us to eliminate our advertising lights. So my advertising source was cut and competitors were moving in. And then my pastor made an appeal to our church to double our tithe for the year. My wife and I prayed about it, doubled our tithe, and now here's the exciting news—last week my accountant said we doubled our business and doubled our net profits! God keeps working miracles!"

*I commit my financial assets to God.
He is my miracle worker!*

EXPECT MORE

"Let each one give as he purposes in his heart, not grudgingly or of necessity, for God loves a cheerful giver." -II CORINTHIANS 9:8

Christmas is a time of giving and sometimes this tradition can cause stress, but think of what the act of giving does for us. We all know people who are wealthy, but who have no joy. In giving, we discover a deep joy and feel good inside.

W. Clement Stone, a friend of mine once said, *"I've discovered that super rich people who do not really give generously, and who do not look upon their wealth as a stewardship from God, usually come to the end of their lives filled with bitterness, frequently committing suicide."*

His statement reminds me of the Dead Sea. Fresh water comes from a brook and fills the Sea of Galilee, which is alive with fish. And then the Sea of Galilee takes that water and gives it to the Jordan River, which turns the desert into a rose and makes it the land of milk and honey. And finally, the Jordan River gives its water to the Dead Sea. The Dead Sea is dead because it does not give itself away!

This is a universal principle. If you want to live a life filled with joy, you have to give. Giving is the key to prosperity. Giving is the key to joyful living!

Because I give, I am rich in joy and know that I am in God's loving care!

EXPECT MORE

"Every good and perfect gift is from above, and comes down from the Father ..." -JAMES 1:17

It's time to check and double check your Christmas list of giving. Of course you've remembered each one in your family. Even if you have had a quarrel, Christmas is a time to mend relationships, so check your list again. Whom have you forgotten?

Now, whom will you remember to present a gift to that you never have before? The neighbor boy who cuts your lawn? The checker at the supermarket who has looked so sad lately? How about God? Where does He fit on your Christmas list?

My Christmas Giving List to Special People:

1. _____
2. _____
3. _____
4. _____
5. _____
6. _____
7. _____
8. _____

I shall not forget God this year because His gifts to me are more than I can count.

EXPECT LOVE

Lord, make me an instrument
of Thy peace.
Where there is hatred, let me sow love;
Where there is injury, pardon;
Where there is doubt, faith;
Where there is despair, hope;
Where there is darkness, light;
Where there is sadness, joy;
O Divine Master, grant that I may
not so much seek to be consoled, as
console; to be understood, as to
understand; to be loved, as to love.
For it is in giving, that we receive;
It is in pardoning, that we are pardoned;
It is in dying, that we are born to eternal life.

Amen.
St. Francis of Assisi

EXPECT LOVE

"Perfect love casts out fear." -1 JOHN 4:18

For countless numbers of people, the "Merry Christmas" greeting is a stab to the heart, because emotions of grief and tragedy surface to the top, making this season almost unbearable for them. Among the tragedies I have witnessed in my years of counseling as a pastor are those of broken relationships where there is no love, only fear.

One day, shortly before Christmas, Mary came to see me about her marriage and I asked her the question, *"Why did you ever marry him in the first place?"*

She answered, *"When we first met he proposed marriage,"* she said. *"But I didn't love him and said 'No.' His answer was, 'If you don't marry me, I'll kill myself.'*

"I thought he was kidding. But he attempted suicide and ended up in the hospital. I felt guilty so I went to visit him. While there, he pleaded with me to marry him and this time I agreed."

And for 24 unhappy years she lived in the fear that if she left he would try to commit suicide again. Her marriage was based not on love, but on fear. And fear produces horrible results. Love produces miraculous rewards!

Christmas is more than carols, ringing of bells, laughter and get-togethers. Christmas is the celebration of God's perfect love in coming to earth to cast out fear. *"For God so loved the world that He gave His only Son..."* This Christmas know the true meaning and it can be a Merry Christmas for you and yours.

Because of God's love of His gift of Jesus Christ, I am free this Christmas to be a loving person!

EXPECT LOVE

"The greatest is love." -1 CORINTHIANS 13:13

> *"Love came down at Christmas,*
> *Love all lovely, Love Divine;*
> *Love was born at Christmas*
> *Star and angels gave the sign.*
>
> *Love shall be our token*
> *Love be yours and love be mine."*

These words penned by Christina G. Rossetti in the 1800's gives the newborn Christ Child the name, Love. Yes, God's love came down to earth at Christmas to show each of us how to love.

But how do we describe "love?" The word love is so rich that it almost defies definition. Truly Christ was all love. He spoke love. He healed in love. He changed people from sinners to saints with His love. He gave His life in love. How do we begin to love as Jesus did? St. Paul continued in the footsteps of Christ in his description of love in I Corinthians 13. Write your own description of love from what you know of the life of Christ and from the words of St. Paul:

Love is _____

Love is _____

Love is _____

Love is _____

Love is _____

May the love of Christ be born in me this Christmas.

Expect Love

"Though I speak with the tongues of angels, but have not love, I have become as sounding brass or a clanging cymbal." -I CORINTHIANS 13:1

I recently saw, on a friend's desk, a little prayer. It read, *"Lord, today help me to make my words tender and sweet. Because tomorrow I may have to eat them."*

That thought reminded me of what a director of nurses told me. She expressed a very profound concept when she said, *"When I train nurses, I say to them, 'Your words have the power to heal. The way you talk, your tone of voice as you touch, the way you listen, the way you offer encouragement builds hope and always puts healing strength into a patient. You create a mental atmosphere in which God can perform His healing ministry."*

The beauty of the Christmas season is the tradition of the Christmas carols and joyous Christmas greetings. Have you noticed how the atmosphere is lifted because of these positive sounds that surround us? Today let's add to the beauty of this holy season by using our voices to tell people how special they are. Whom do you know who needs a word of love today?

What a gift you can give with your loving words.

*O God, lead me to someone today
who needs to be loved.
Speak Your words through my voice.*

Expect Love

"He who does not love does not know God, for God is love." -1 JOHN 4:8

I spoke to a teacher recently who teaches third grade students. She relayed to me this story:

"The other day, I told my students to say, out loud, 'I am special! All together, one, two, three.' I heard one lone voice echo in the silent room. No one would join in this simple, yet profound statement. I encouraged them. 'Come on.' Still no one would repeat the self-affirming phrase. Finally, I went to each student and asked them why they wouldn't join me. A message came through loud and clear. They simply didn't believe it. And they couldn't repeat such a strong statement when they didn't believe it. You see, Dr. Schuller, most of those children come from horrendous home situations where there is tremendous brokenness. Nearly all of them are lacking either a mother or a father. Many have parents and siblings trapped in drug and alcohol abuse or immoral behavior, some of which is committed before the eyes of these little ones. They just don't believe much of anything that has to do with them or their world bringing something good or special to them."

This is a classroom right here in America. Children not believing that they are special. They don't go to Sunday School. They don't go to church. The adult in the house, where they live, doesn't go to church.

When you know Jesus Christ, you know you have value.

Christmas means you are loved! You are special! God came to earth to show you that you are His child.

I am special. I love myself because God loves me!

Stand before your mirror each day and tell yourself this joyous affirmation!

I am living, today, controlled by my God-inspired positive ideas!

EXPECT LOVE

"Whoever believes that Jesus is the Christ is born of God." -I JOHN 5:1

Ten years ago when I traveled to London I visited Harrod's Department store. I had heard so much about this unusual place that I decided I had to see it for myself. I entered the front door, where there hung a big sign which read, *"Enter into a new world."* And believe me, that sign was true. I discovered I could purchase anything in that store, including a live elephant!

When I left Harrod's, I returned to my hotel and tried to make contact with my church office. I checked the phone directory to see how I could place a call from London to California. Then I noticed the hotel had instructions on the phone which read, *"Now you can dial direct."* Wow! *"Prepare to enter a new world."*

So I picked up the telephone and had my first experience in dialing direct across continents. I dialed the special number they told me to dial, added the church phone number and almost immediately heard, *"Crystal Cathedral, may I help you?"*

Every day we should hang a little sign in our mind that says, "Prepare to enter a new world!" And soon, *"Prepare to enter a new millennium."* Unfortunately, many people fear anything new. There is a normal inclination that we all run to the shelter of the familiar. But when we experience love, and are loving in return, we are captured by a confidence that gives us a spirit of adventure—love's reward!

This Christmas I shall adventure out into a new experience of love where God is.

EXPECT LOVE

May your roots go down deep into the soil of God's marvelous love;
and may you be able to feel and understand,
as all God's children should, how long, how wide,
how deep and how high His love really is;
and to experience this love for yourselves,
though it is so great that you will never see the end of it,
or fully know or understand it.

Ephesians 3:17-19 (LB)

A Special Christmas Prayer

*I pray that Christ will be more and more
at home in your hearts, living within you
as you trust in Him.*

THE STAR OF JOY

When they saw the star, the wise men rejoiced with exceeding great joy."
-MATTHEW 2:10

One of the beautiful symbols of the Christmas season is the Christmas star which shines from many Christmas treetops. In the Glory of Christmas Pageant at the Crystal Cathedral, the Christmas star majestically dominates the Bethlehem landscape throughout the entire pageant. I know it as the "Star of Joy," perhaps because of the joy the wise men experienced as the star guided them to the manger of the Christ Child.

Question: JOY — what is it? Can you describe joy? What gives you joy? List the events, persons, or objects which make you joyous. Does going to church give you joy? Does reading your Bible bring joy to you? How about your prayer and meditation times?

Would you describe your faith as a "joyous" faith? Christ was born to bring joy where there was gloom; to bring the sparkle back into living.

My definition of joy? **J**esus first, **O**thers second, **Y**ourself last. That spells **JOY!** Unselfishness is the key to my personal happiness.

Remember: A star is best seen at night.

THE STAR OF JOY

A Christmas Prayer

O loving Father, as the joy of the Bethlehem star bursts through the sky,
    so I come before You bringing songs of joy and praise.
I rejoice in the Good News of the birth of Your Son, knowing that
    my heart will take wing as it is filled with the love of Christmas.

With the birth of Christ in my life, I receive the gift of love in my heart.
And as the star of joy brought light to a dark world that night,
    so illuminate all negative thoughts within me with the bright light
    of faith.

For as Christmas captured God's dream of bringing me back to Him, so
    now crystallize my courage so I can dream new dreams and sight new
    stars.
And with the Christ child as my North Star, I look expectantly to a New Year,
    knowing that Your Spirit will shine in splendor in my life.

*I am living today controlled by my
God-inspired positive ideas!*

THE STAR OF JOY

"The virgin shall conceive and bear a Son ... and shall call Him Immanuel — God with us." -ISAIAH 7:14

There are usually five points in a star, so let's give the Star of Joy five points also, and name the first point **Conceive.**

When the angel announced to the Virgin Mary that she would conceive and give birth to the Messiah, she responded with a joy that is known throughout all Christendom as "The Magnificat" found in Luke 1:46-54. Webster's dictionary describes the word "conceive" as "to cause to begin ... to imagine, image."

W. Clement Stone's famous saying: *"What your mind can conceive, you can achieve."* What idea has God put into your mind today? Can you imagine achieving it?

Great joy comes when you begin to conceive that it is possible for God to come into your life. It's possible! He will show you the path of life. This Christmas believe that with God's help you can now conceive, imagine, and visualize Christ coming into your mind and heart, filling them with JOY!

I want to experience joy this Christmas, so I shall conceive the idea of Jesus Christ coming into my mind and heart now. I believe it is possible for Him to live within me.

The Star of Joy

"Behold, the star shone over where the young Child was, and when the wise men saw the Holy Child, they fell down and worshiped Him."
-Matthew 2:9, 10

Yesterday I suggested that the first point of the Christmas star of joy is **Conceive.** Today let's look at the second point of the star of joy that I call **Receive.** God's wonderful book — the Bible — not only introduces Jesus Christ to the world, but makes it very clear that if you ask Jesus Christ to come into your life, He will. The three wise men traveled from the east to see this newborn King, received Him as their King, and *"They fell down and worshiped Him."*

Through thoughts about Christ, and through ideas about Jesus that come into your mind, Christ comes into your life. Through an experience with Christ—and a love for Christ—He comes into your life. Now I can't completely explain this reality scientifically, psychologically or any other way, but it is a fact. The Bible teaches it. Try it! It works!

If you have never done it before, this Christmas invite Jesus Christ into your life. *Receive* Him and let the very living mind of Christ reach into your being.

Whether you have just invited Christ into your life now, or have invited Him in before, take the space below and describe what it means to you to receive Jesus Christ:

_____

_____

_____

Christ lives within me now!

THE STAR OF JOY

"Now may the God of hope fill you with all joy in believing." -ROMANS 15:13

Let's continue our study today on the Christmas star of joy by concentrating on the third point of the star: *Believe.* After you **conceive** the facts and **receive** Christ into your life, don't expect rockets to explode. God does not promise that your eyes will fill up with tears or that your heart will burst with emotion. Simply *believe.*

The Bible tells how the early Christians experienced trouble because of this new faith, but still they were filled with joy. The wise men from the east, after following the star and finding the Babe in the manger had to change their plans. Warned by God, they hurried back to their own country. Immediately after their joyous experience at receiving the newborn King, they were faced with a troubling situation.

Believe that God promises to act on your faith when you believe.

When faith is weak, joy fades. Are you experiencing doubts? Identify them. Write them down. Then change them into affirmations and watch your joy begin to shine brightly again.

Your Doubt	Your Affirmation
IS CHRIST IN MY LIFE?	I HAVE RECEIVED CHRIST INTO MY LIFE AND I BELIEVE HE IS THERE NOW!

Lord, give me the faith of the wise men to follow the star.

The Star of Joy

"I have come as a light into the world, that whoever believes in Me should not abide in darkness." -JOHN 12:46

Today we see the fourth point in the Christmas star of joy: *Relieve*. Joy comes when you and I relieve our minds from all negative thoughts. Fear, hate, doubt, suspicion, hostility, unbelief—all of these are negative forces that rob us of joy. Faith does not harmonize with any of these negative emotions, so we must relieve our minds of them.

I recall one chilly Sunday when one small dead spider in the thermostat at the base of the stairs in our first sanctuary knocked out our entire heating system.

If a dead spider can do so much destruction, what do you think one prejudice, or one hate, or one worry that you hang onto can do to your faith? Joy fills the vacuum left when you *relieve* your mind of negative thoughts.

Christmas is a celebration of joy. Jesus Christ came as a light into our world so we don't need to lie in a joyless environment of negative living.

If the sparkle of faith is gone this Christmas season, then today is the time to see where you have been negative, and concentrate on the joy that is available to you now!

*I relieve my mind of negative thoughts
by thinking of the joy Jesus Christ has for me.*

THE STAR OF JOY

This thing I have spoken to you, that your joy may remain in you, and that your joy may be full." -JOHN 15:11

And now we complete the Christmas star with point five: *Act-chieve.* I've deliberately misspelled the word achieve ... ACT-chieve. That's the key!

ACT! Be like a sprinkler head and let the water of joy flow through you. Be like a fountain pen and let Christ, like beautiful ink, write His message through your life.

What are your dreams? What would you like to achieve? What could you do that would bring you great joy? Do it! Dare to be a dreamer and then dare to ACT!

Write down one of your dreams that, when accomplished, would bring you joy:

_____

_____

Now write down the first step you must take to ACT-chieve your dream. Now, **do** it with God's help:

_____

_____

Our star of joy ... it is only complete when all five points are there. Joy is present when we **conceive, receive, believe, relieve, and ACT-chieve.** It takes all five. Live by them and Christ's joy will fill you to overflowing.

ℰxpect Miracles!

"For there is born unto you this day a Savior, who is Christ the Lord."
-*Luke 2:11*

O Lord, we come! We come to celebrate
Your coming to earth as a Babe in a manger.

Open our eyes that we may not miss the
wonder of this holy Christmas night.

O Lord, we come for we need to hear
again Your words of peace, of joy, and hope.

We come, Lord, great and small, rich
and poor, to look, to listen, to sing
and kneel in awe and wonder.

Open our hearts and make there a
manger for the Christ child. Amen.

Expect Miracles!

*"It is more blessed to give than to receive." -*ACTS 20:35

A little family lived way up in the mountains. There was the father, the mother, John, the older brother, Peter, a younger brother, and the little girl, Gretchen.

As Christmas came, this poor family went to the little village shop. The children pointed out the toys that they thought were particularly wonderful. Gretchen saw a little blue teapot with a creamer and a sugar and two cups and two saucers and said, "I want that for Christmas."

The day before Christmas, Peter thought he should get something for Gretchen. He took the one coin he had, he went to the store and said to the keeper, *"What can I buy with this coin?"*

The shopkeeper showed him a little candy heart. Peter thought, *"Gretchen will like that."* So he bought it, took it home and secretly slipped it into her stocking.

John, the big brother came home. He'd been doing some work and he saw that there was a bulge in Gretchen's stocking. He felt something in there and wondered what it was. He put his hand in and pulled it out. It was a chocolate. He smelled it and before he knew it, he had popped it into his mouth. He felt terrible! He had eaten Gretchen's Christmas present from Peter. What could he do?

He went to his room and he emptied his bank. He took the coins and he went to the store and said to the shopkeeper, "What can I buy with these coins?"

The shopkeeper looked at them and said, *"Well, all I have left is that blue teapot with the creamer, the sugar, the cups and the saucers."*

So, John came home with the teapot, the cups, the saucers, the creamer and the sugar and he put them in Gretchen's stocking. The next morning when they opened the gifts Peter could not figure out how that chocolate candy turned into a teapot.

The truth of the story is that if you give generously, your generousity will come back far larger, far more beautiful. The joy of giving, does it work? You bet. What makes it work? It works because it takes you away from yourself, your self-pity, your grief, your fear, your hurt, and your disappointment.

*Today receive the gift of
Jesus Christ and give Him your life.*

EXPECT MIRACLES!

"And the shepherds returned to their fields, glorifying and praising God for all the things they had heard and seen." -LUKE 2:20

It was Christmas morning, 1968. It was the first Christmas that the Tower of Hope was opened. We had our Christmas Eve candlelight service the night before. The church was filled with candles and twinkling lights, and the most glorious Christmas music you could ever hope to hear. The next morning, the children awakened early in anticipation of the presents piled under the tree.

When the gifts were opened, I decided to return to the church. My mind and pockets were filled with little notes that people had given me at the Christmas Eve service and I wanted to organize them. Sheila, my teenage daughter, the oldest of the family, agreed to ride with me so I wouldn't have to go alone.

The church was abandoned. There was only one lonely car parked in a corner of the parking lot. As Sheila and I approached the Tower, we noticed a petite young girl, huddled against the doors, virtually sleeping on her feet.

"I tapped her on the shoulder and said, *"Hello."*

Her eyes filled with tears. Her narrow shoulders trembled. She said, *"I spent the night in my car."*

It hurt to think of this poor young girl sleeping alone in her car on Christmas night. I asked her, *"Where are you sleeping tonight?"*

"I don't know."

So Sheila invited her to come and share a room at the house. She was our houseguest for quite some time, and during that time, she became exposed to our faith, and we encouraged her. *"You can go back to school, you can go to college, become anything you want to be, if you just let God take control of your life."*

Well, she began attending this church and made a confession of her faith in Jesus Christ and she found a new life filled with God's blessings. Now, thirty years later, she is a very successful and intelligent CPA.

Has this Christmas made a difference in your life? Are you returning to work glorifying and praising God as the shepherds did?

I praise God for His special touch this Christmas.

EXPECT MIRACLES!

"For this is God. Our God forever and ever; He will be our guide even to death." -PSALM 48:14

Some years ago, after I finished speaking at a conference in Sweden, Mrs. Schuller and I took a cruise through the Northern Cape. We were at sea for a day or two and had not met the captain. But as we were walking on the deck we suddenly stopped in our tracks when the intercom came on and we heard, *"This is your captain speaking."*

Everyone else stopped, also, when they heard this voice with its beautiful Scandinavian accent. As we listened, we did not know what he looked like, but we did know it was his voice.

All of us ride on a ship called planet earth. We are spinning at an incredible rate, flying through the universe. And I have news for you—there is a Captain, even though you haven't seen Him.

Believe in Him and sometime, somehow, someway He will speak to you through an event, an emotion, the Bible or a friend. You will hear the announcement, "This is your Captain speaking." At that moment of faith, miracles begin. For miracles cannot occur without faith. And faith only happens when you begin to step out on a great idea that is seemingly impossible. And the concept of God as the Captain of your soul is the beginning point!

God is my captain. I am trusting Him for today and tomorrow!

&xpect Miracles!

"My help comes from the Lord, who made heaven and earth."
-PSALM 121:1

Yesterday I described God as the captain of my life. David refers to his relationship with God as the shepherd. When you think of God, what symbol, or image describes your relationship?

The Lord is my _____

_____

_____

_____

_____

_____

_____

_____

The most accurate image any of us have of God is the person of Jesus Christ. Jesus is the heartbeat of God to the world. And He loves YOU and ME!

Think of it! The God of the universe loves me! How can I ever be afraid or perplexed?

*E*XPECT MIRACLES!

"Praise Him for His mighty acts. Praise Him according to His excellent greatness." -PSALM 150:2

Early one morning during a session of our Institute for Successful Church Leadership, a minister from Minnesota was suddenly called out for an emergency call. He was told that his three-and-a-half year old son had fallen into a swimming pool. His wife had lifted the little boy out of the pool and applied artificial respiration to his apparently lifeless body. When the ambulance arrived, the boy was beginning to respond.

The whole congregation of 400 ministers joined with me in praying for that little child. And what a great moment it was at the closing of the convocation, during the dedication service, to see the little lad and his parents come forward to kneel at the front of the church. I don't believe there was a dry eye anywhere.

After that service, the father told me that when they arrived at the hospital, x-rays showed that there was water in his son's lungs. Several hours after we had all joined in prayer, they x-rayed his lungs again and found no water present!

The doctor said, "It's a miracle!" And it was! For it only takes you and God to make a miracle!

Thank You, God, for the mountains in my life that You and I are turning into miracles!

EXPECT MIRACLES!

"Tomorrow I will stand at the top of the mountain with the rod of God in my hand." -EXODUS 17:9

Confidently and boldly, Moses spoke. The dynamic faith he had in tomorrow is the faith I want you to have.

I read about a lady who, realizing that the New Year was quickly coming, gloomily declared, *"Go away tomorrow."* That's sad isn't it? I say, *"Welcome tomorrow!"* I'm excited because every new day creates a new opportunity.

But you may be arguing, *"Dr. Schuller, I don't know about me. As I look into the next millennium, it looks to me like it's going to be controlled by computers. High technology is going to replace people. What's the next millennium going to be like? We will all be unwanted throwaways."* I disagree.

Really, the whole future of your life is not in God's hands but in **your** hands. You see, He gives you the freedom to choose to be a believer or not. What's going to happen will depend upon one person — the person who sets your goals. Who sets your sights for you? Who sets your goals? **You do.** The key to your future is within you.

The new millennium is filled with new goals, new hopes, new discoveries, new possibilities, new successes, new faith. Today make a commitment to welcome tomorrow walking with faith in God.

Welcome Tomorrow!

Expect Miracles!

"Tomorrow the Lord will work wonders among you." -JOSHUA 3:5

In 1991, I hit my head on a car roof in Amsterdam. I burst a vein which caused blood to seep into my brain. Twelve hours later, I was found on the balcony of my hotel room in a coma. The doctors opened my skull and vacuumed out the blood. It was a serious time. Those around me have explained that I almost died within minutes.

Five days later I tried to write a sentence that was consuming all of my concentration. But I failed. I could not coordinate my movements. Then more surgery was needed to stop the bleeding, and then I was able to write the sentence that I knew came from God:

**How sweet it is to stand
on the edge of tomorrow!**

Today you and I stand on the edge of tomorrow when a new millennium dawns. A new trip into the next century. A trip never taken before, to a place never visited before. It's a place called "tomorrow." What can we expect? I really don't know, but I do know one thing: everyone who takes the trip with me will find that God has gone ahead of us to meet us. "Tomorrow the Lord will work wonders among you."

And guess what? God will be waiting with a special gift in His hand for each one of us. It's a gift that He's never given before. It is the gift called "today." How exciting it is to stand on the edge of tomorrow!

*God knows more about
our tomorrows, than
we know about out
yesterdays!*